P9-APX-516

Thin Ice

Thin Ice

Money, Politics and the Demise of an NHL Franchise

Jim Silver

Jim Silver is a professor of political science at the University of Winnipeg. He was an active member of Thin Ice throughout its life and co-chair of the social justice group Cho!ces from 1992 to 1995. He is an editor at *Canadian Dimension* magazine, and has written extensively on the political economy of Manitoba.

Fernwood Publishing
Halifax

Copyright © 1996 Jim Silver

All rights reserved. No part of this book may be reproduced or transmitted in any form by any means without permission in writing from the publisher, except by a reviewer, who may quote brief passages in a review.

Editing: Robert Clarke
Design and production: Beverley Rach
Cover Design: Ian Lark
Printed and bound in Canada by: Hignell Printing Limited

A publication of:
Fernwood Publishing
Box 9409, Station A
Halifax, Nova Scotia
B3K 5S3

Fernwood Publishing Company Limited gratefully acknowledges the financial support of The Ministry of Canadian Heritage and the Nova Scotia Department of Education and Culture.

Canadian Cataloguing in Publication Data

Silver, Jim.

    Thin Ice

    Includes bibliographical references.
    ISBN 1-8956686-71-7

1. Winnipeg Jets (Hockey team). 2. Hockey -- Manitoba -- Winnipeg.
I. Title. II. Series

GV848.W56854 1996   796.962'64'091712743   96-950168-4

Contents

Foreword

In the spring of 1996, as most readers of this book will know, the Colorado Avalanche, recently relocated from Quebec City, won the Stanley Cup in their first year in Denver, defeating the expansion Florida Panthers. The Winnipeg Jets had bowed out in the first round, playing their final game in the Winnipeg Arena before becoming the Phoenix Coyotes. From the perspective of NHL headquarters in New York City these events were consistent with the league's strategy of building its presence in the prosperous and growing cities of the U.S. Sunbelt.

For many Canadians, though, the transfer of teams out of two Canadian cities in which hockey mattered and into U.S. cities where it was just one more product in the entertainment market signified a new and decisive stage in the Americanization of "our" game. The long-standing interests of Canadian fans, and indeed of Canada itself, were becoming increasingly marginal to the commercial future of a game that Canadians had popularized and that still occupies an important place in our popular culture.

Jim Silver has written a richly detailed account of the slow demise of the Winnipeg Jets and of the issues and personalities that dominated a series of campaigns, over many years, to keep the Jets in town. At one level this is a compelling drama, involving individuals, ambitions, interests and intrigues that will fascinate anyone with an interest in the exercise of power in local politics, as well as those whose interest is in hockey and the Jets in particular. And it is a reminder that top level professional hockey will in future be hard to hang on to not only in Winnipeg and Quebec, but also in Edmonton and perhaps Calgary too—cities of roughly 600,000 to 800,000 people where playing and watching hockey have long been an integral part of popular life. At one time teams in these places may have been able to compete with the vastly larger urban markets because enthusiasm for hockey meant bums in seats. The success of the Edmonton Oilers is a prime example: when total player budgets were still under $4 million, Edmonton could afford the best team in hockey. This is no longer the case. Now successful major league franchises need substantial corporate revenues, and most teams in the larger U.S. centres, as well as Montreal and Vancouver, have been building new arenas featuring state-of-the-art advertising space, upmarket restaurants and large numbers of luxury boxes.

The new importance of corporate revenues—as opposed to individual fans buying tickets with their own, non-tax-deductible, money—creates a league in which cities like Winnipeg and Quebec would have found it difficult to compete, even with new publicly funded arenas. It is also a league in which Edmonton, with its major employers in the public sector and in non-consumer businesses (eg. engineering firms, with less to gain from the marketing exposure) will find it increasingly difficult to survive, even with the NHL's very modest new revenue sharing plan. Successful major league cities today need to have a corporate sector that includes national brand name companies and head offices, and a business and professional class able to afford contemporary ticket prices on a regular basis. Calgary's somewhat better chances of survival, like Ottawa's, will depend upon the willingness of their major corporations (including Canadian Airlines and Corel, of course, but also others) to lease advertising space and luxury seating, and on the continued growth and affluence of their business and professional classes.

The problem of smaller centres points also to a deeper or more structural dimension to the saga of the Winnipeg Jets, namely the restructuring of the North American economy. In the 1990s, "restructuring" has meant the rationalization of many kinds of industrial production and the closure of many smaller or regionally oriented producers. This has led, in turn, to rationalizations in the transportation, distribution and retail industries. The net result is that many cities whose historic role was as a regional "hub" have found themselves facing decline, and Winnipeg and Edmonton are in this respect not unlike Minneapolis, Milwaukee and Kansas City, now also "small markets" in the new parlance of professional sports. In this context, some cities have sought to restructure their economies by promoting "postindustrial" advantages—lifestyle, leisure and tourist attractions—and most cities have become very sensitive about "civic image." This is why major league franchises have become much sought after commodities, and it sets up circumstances that franchise owners have sought to exploit. Barry Shenkarow in Winnipeg, Peter Pocklington in Edmonton and Marcel Aubut in Quebec all repeatedly used threats of departure to seek financial concessions from local governments desperate to hang onto their "big league" status. These pressures create very real dilemmas for local political leaders because, even when self-serving claims about the contribution of pro sports to the civic economy are revealed as inflated, the symbolic effects cannot be discounted so easily.

For better or worse, professional sports teams have become surrogates for, and mobilizers of, civic identity in an era when this is increasingly hard to find; and the loss of a major team does represent, for many people, a significant loss to the atmosphere and general "life" of a city. Though there is little hard evidence to support claims that the presence of major league sports is decisive in residential—let alone business—relocation decisions, sports teams contribute to a cumulative image of a city with "things to do". This is the context in which the Winnipeg business community's efforts to save the Jets need to be seen. Although there are numerous instances of self-interest described in the pages that follow, readers will also get a clear sense that the local business and political class resisted the departure of the Jets (and with it the loss of major league status) because it constituted one more sign, and a highly visible one, of Winnipeg's decline in importance. They thus saw their own resistance to this as a community-spirited action.

A final issue concerns whether, in these circumstances, the governments of cities like Winnipeg should commit large sums of public money to sustaining popular but money-losing civic institutions. Clearly boosters would say "yes," and there is probably a side of most Canadian hockey fans that would want to agree. Spending public funds to sustain our national heritage in the face of market forces has numerous precedents in other spheres of cultural activity. Yet there are important issues of social justice that also have to be taken into account, especially in times of hardship when governments are cutting back on many kinds of social spending. Keeping a major league franchise undoubtedly adds to a city's attractions, for all those who can afford to attend even sporadically. Yet there are growing numbers of people in Winnipeg and other Canadian cities who will never get to these events we routinely claim as part of "our" culture. Many fans, of course, follow sports almost entirely through the media, and they too regret the departure of their favourites. However, we have to stop and think about what we mean when we say that professional sports teams benefit the whole community, for they do so very unequally. We also have to recognize that our interests as fans, however powerfully felt, may not coincide with our interests as citizens. We may have to step back and put our lifelong "interests" in a truly social context—something that Jim Silver does in bringing this story to us, in all its dimensions.

David Whitson
Co-author of *Hockey Night in Canada*
Edmonton
September 1996

Preface

In addition to being the author of this book, I was actively involved in many of the events described in these pages. As a founding member of Thin Ice, the community-based group opposed to public funding for a new arena and for the Jets, I participated fully in the planning and implementation of the group's many activities and was frequently a spokesperson.

It follows that I bring a particular perspective to the writing of this book. It is appropriate that readers be aware of my involvement so that they can judge the book accordingly.

That having been said, every effort has been made to be accurate and truthful in the telling of the story. Thin Ice developed a well-deserved reputation for accuracy in its analysis of various proposals to save the Jets and for being determined to defend the principle of open and honest public debate no matter how heated the circumstances. In writing this book, I have striven to live up to that standard.

Acknowledgements

My first thanks go to the members of Thin Ice, the community-based group opposed to the use of public funds for a new arena for the Jets and for the subsidization of the Jets, of which I was proud to be an active member. The core members of this remarkable little group are Barry Hammond, Jeff Lowe, Valerie Price, Carl Ridd, Todd Scarth and our very able chairperson, Harold Shuster. More people—too many to name individually—were involved with and contributed to Thin Ice at various times. Our group also drew upon the economic analysis skills, provided free of charge, of Errol Black, Joe Dolecki, Van Hall and John Loxley, and the design and creative skills, also provided gratis, of Bill Kitson, Doug Smith and Randa Stewart. Rocky Kravetsky and Sandra Hoeppner provided outstanding legal advice, as did Yude Henteleff. The many members and friends of Cho!ces: A Social Justice Coalition, of which I was co-chair during the entire life of Thin Ice, were supportive in ways too many to mention.

Numerous friends read all or parts of this book at various stages. For their useful and in many cases very detailed and thoughtful advice, I am grateful to each of the core members of Thin Ice, plus Jean Altemeyer, Errol Black, Cy Gonick, Loa Henry, John Loxley, Pat Martin, Dave Plummer, Sid Rogers, Tim Sale, Don Sullivan, Judy Wasylecia-Leis and David Whitson.

Wayne Antony of Fernwood Publishing was helpful throughout the process. Robert Clarke did a fine job of final editing. Thanks also to Donna Davis for proofreading, Chauna James for typing revisions, Beverley Rach for design and production, Ian Lark for cover design and Errol Sharpe, the publisher. Lou Lépine typed the entire manuscript and made some useful editorial suggestions. I am also grateful to Dale Cummings for giving permission to use his cartoons.

I am grateful to the University of Winnipeg for providing financial assistance in the form of two small grants used to hire research assistants Carolyn Konopski, David Lawrence and Joe Strutt. I thank them for all their work.

Some of the people involved in the conflict over the Jets agreed to be interviewed, as did some Winnipeg media people. I am grateful to Donald Benham, Glen Cheater, Gary Doer, Paul Edwards, Riva Harrison, Sam Katz, Nick Martin, Barry Mullin, Cam Osler, Doug Smith, Robert Silver, Paul Sveinson, Diana Swain, and Alan Sweatman, as well as to those people who agreed to interviews but preferred to remain anonymous. Among those who did not agree to be interviewed are Izzy Asper, John Loewen and Barry Shenkarow.

I, of course, remain responsible for any errors of fact or interpretation that may remain in the book.

Finally, I particularly want to thank my wife and best friend, Loa Henry, and our wonderful ten-year-old daughter, Zoë, for their love and support throughout the sometimes raucous events described here.

1. Introduction

Dale Cummings

Thousands of Winnipeggers rallied on the streets while corporate businessmen fought each other behind closed doors. Information was manipulated. Arms were twisted. Politicians capitulated. Adults wept on open-line radio shows. Children broke open their piggy banks. This was the campaign to keep the National Hockey League's Jets from leaving Winnipeg. It was a campaign that many of us believed was truly skating on thin ice.

This book is about hockey, but it is not so much about the game as it is about the business of hockey and how changes in the business threaten the game's survival in Canada. And while the events take place mainly in Winnipeg, the story has repercussions beyond a single city. Given the new, corporate-driven, continental character of the business of NHL hockey, another version of this same story will almost certainly take place sooner rather than later in other small Canadian cities where NHL franchises are still located.

The story also involves money and politics, and how they are intertwined. Indeed, the long and often bitter conflict over the Winnipeg Jets affords the opportunity for a detailed look at the connection between money and politics. Again, what this look reveals may well be cause for concern for Winnipeggers, but the implications go well beyond a single locale.

In recent years the business side of pro hockey has shifted dramatically—perhaps best symbolized by the 1988 sale of Edmonton Oiler superstar Wayne Gretzky to Bruce McNall's Los Angeles Kings. That sale gave notice that in the corporate-driven, marketing-inspired drive for bigger profits the business of NHL hockey was headed south to the U.S. Sunbelt. Hockey, long a form of entertainment as much as a sport, has since become more intensely Americanized, commercialized and commodified. Hockey superstars, like key players in other professional sports, have become celebrities as much as athletes. The result is that the NHL has moved up-cost and down-south, and the relatively small Canadian cities of Winnipeg, Quebec City and Edmonton—and possibly Ottawa and Calgary—can no longer compete.

Introduction

****

Once considered the "gateway to the West"—a transportation and manufacturing centre located in the heart of Canada's vast east–west expanse—Winnipeg has long since seen its national star decline, its economic lustre diminish. Winnipeg had experienced a "meteoric rise" by the second decade of the twentieth century, with the opening of the West and massive European immigration doubling its population between 1901 and 1906. The third-largest city in Canada by 1911, Winnipeg served as the wholesale distribution centre for a vast hinterland stretching from Northwestern Ontario to the Rockies, and became a financial hub for the burgeoning grain trade.

At the core of this early economic boom was the great divide: an aggressive, Anglo-Saxon business class, most of its members living in stately homes in the city's genteel South end; and an ethnically mixed poor working class, most of whom lived, often in appalling conditions, in the North end. The two sides clashed frequently most notably in Winnipeg's historic 1919 General Strike. The harsh impact of this long strike and its "Bloody Saturday," when two men were killed and many other protestors injured, left its mark in many ways on the social and political fabric of the city.

Since the 1920s Winnipeg's history has been one of a gradual, economic decline relative to the rest of the country. Though still Canada's fourth-largest city in 1951, by 1991 Winnipeg had dropped to seventh-largest. In recent years the shift in the pattern of economic activity in Canada from an east–west to a north-south axis has accelerated, partly because of the free trade agreements. Key Winnipeg decision-makers have scrambled to find a new role for the city in an increasingly continentalized economy. One goal has been to refashion the historic gateway to the west as a new gateway to the south and the populous markets of the United States. The transition is playing havoc with the economic and social well-being of a large and growing proportion of Winnipeg's population of about 680,000—evidenced only too graphically by the city's consistently firm position either at or near the top of Canada's child poverty rankings.

****

Professional hockey in post-war Winnipeg has always been financially imperilled, and Winnipeg has been the site of a long and protracted conflict over the role to be played by the public sector in providing financial support for professional hockey. The problems were exemplified by the experience of the Winnipeg Warriors of the Western Professional Hockey League, a team that struggled to survive, then collapsed in 1961. The Winnipeg Jets lost money from the outset in 1972 and suffered several apparent deaths over the following decades. The team owners and their supporters in the media and in three levels of government took repeated steps to put in place great amounts of public funding to cover both the hockey club's operating losses and the construction costs of a new, larger arena complete with more expensive luxury seating. In the early 1990s Winnipeg's old business establishment and then a younger generation of wealth-holders tried to take charge, leaning heavily on governments to get their way. Study followed study and scheme followed scheme in an ultimately futile effort to raise money from the private sector.

The Jets were resurrected again and again—until the wild and frenzied days of May 1995 and the local Save Our Jets campaign, which was followed by corporate squabbling and then chaos and confusion in June. Sports fans, whose enthusiasm had resurrected the Jets—and whose pockets had contributed millions of dollars to the campaign—were left to wonder what was going on behind closed corporate doors and where all the money was going.

****

A group I was involved in called Thin Ice fought, along with many other people, to raise some questions about the proceedings and challenge the wild plans for expenditure of greater and greater amounts of public funds that would ultimately end up in private coffers. Thin Ice was established in October 1993 as a working group of Cho!ces, a Winnipeg-based social justice coalition formed in January 1991. By that year the Winnipeg Jets' repeated demands for public funds required a government decision. Cho!ces did some preliminary analytical work, motivated by the belief that the issue was consistent with the group's defining theme: public money was available but it was being used to subsidize the well-to-do, in this case Jets owner Barry Shenkarow and his partners. Cho!ces' position was that the city was better off if the Jets stayed in Winnipeg than if the team left, but keeping them in the city did not justify massive public expenditures, given competing needs.

By 1993 the question of public funding for the Jets and for a new arena had become a very contentious public issue. Cho!ces moved the matter up on its list of priorities, and the committee charged with doing the work decided to adopt a separate, identifiable name, one that symbolized the financial dangers posed by the Jets' incessant demands for more public money. We became Thin Ice, and threw ourselves into what would become an increasingly heated battle.

In the end, despite a huge effort put forth by thousands of people in the community and by the city's leading corporate powers, the private-sector money needed to save the Jets was simply not there. It never had been, despite the ever more far-fetched financial schemes concocted by contending business groups whose firm intent was to shift the bulk of the cost and the risk onto the public sector. The ill-constructed house of financial cards finally collapsed under the weight of its own inadequacies in August 1995. The Winnipeg Jets were finally dead. The Phoenix Coyotes were soon to be born.

The long, complex and increasingly acrimonious struggle over the Winnipeg Jets is, in its own terms, a fascinating and sometimes even dramatic story. The story is at the same time revealing and perhaps sobering for it lays bare—in a fashion more transparent than is the norm—the manner in which political power is exercised at the local level. It is a cautionary tale about who makes important decisions in our communities and how they make them, and it suggests that we would be wise to be more doubtful, and even more critical, of the claims being made by the most powerful people and organizations in our midst.

2. The Business of NHL Hockey

Globe and Mail

Hockey is Canada's national game. It is an integral part of Canadian culture, of what binds us together as Canadians. This has been so since at least the 1930s, when radio broadcasts of NHL games began to be heard coast to coast. By the end of the 1930s, two million listeners were tuning in each week to *Hockey Night in Canada*. As writers Richard Gruneau and David Whitson put it, "Never had so many Canadians in all corners of the country regularly engaged in the same cultural experience at the same time. Stories and characters from NHL games emerged as the stuff of Canadian folklore."[1] Heroes like Howe and Richard and Plante and Sawchuk became household names, their exploits discussed and debated in kitchens, school yards and workplaces in every corner of the country. Kids, wearing their treasured Boston Bruins or Chicago Black Hawks sweaters, trudged down to the local rink and picked up sides for a game, each player adopting a name. "Hull cuts in from the left wing, steps around the defence and *blasts* a slapshot!"—"Dryden—a great save!"

The joy of playing the game, and of imagining the glory of playing in the NHL, provides a common experience for millions of Canadian men and growing numbers of women. Canadians know about Paul Henderson's goal against the Russians in 1972, about Beliveau and Orr and Gretzky, about the Montreal Forum and Maple Leaf Gardens and the glamour of the NHL. Hockey *matters* to us. Former Canadiens goalie Ken Dryden, writing with Roy MacGregor, says, "It matters because communities matter. . . . Kids and parents and grandparents matter. . . . Dreams, hopes, passions . . . common imaginations; things that tell us about who we were, how we are, how we might be—they matter."[2] There is a mystique to hockey in Canada, and especially to the NHL, that has long been a part of the Canadian imagination.

But behind this beloved national institution—behind the mystique, the heroes and legends, the passion and the glory and the ties that bind us—lies another part of hockey's reality. It is much less attractive but every bit as real and, in some respects, more important. This reality behind the mystique is the business of hockey, and this reality, this business, would become the essence of the long and eventful struggle in Winnipeg over the future of the Jets.

Business NHL-Style

NHL hockey is a profitable business. It is profitable despite frequently having been badly managed; and despite a history of deception and dishonesty by some of the game's leading figures.

NHL hockey was dominated in the 1930s and long afterwards by the Norris family and their associates and successors. By the end of the 1930s Chicago-based Jim Norris, multimillionaire grain and shipping baron, was one of America's richest men, and at one time he owned or controlled four of the six NHL franchises.[3] While the league nominally forbade multiple ownership, franchises could be owned by companies and "conveniently," David Cruise and Alison Griffiths write, "the rules didn't require the disclosure of who was behind those company names."[4] Norris's hockey holdings were but a part of a larger entertainment empire. Norris "purchased or financed a dizzying array of events, including circuses, ice acts and musical revues, to fill up his arenas. He took over Sonja Henie's Hollywood Ice Revue and, in partnership with Hopalong Cassidy, bought the Cole Bros. Circus, then the second-largest in the world. Norris also had a stake in Ringling Brothers and sponsored a string of vaudeville troops. For added insurance, he bought into many of the major booking agencies, which handled everything from boxing to bicycle acts." In a way, Norris was establishing a persistent trend: the connection between the NHL and the entertainment industry would once again become a predominant feature of the game in the 1990s.

Clarence Campbell became league president in 1946, but despite his impressive credentials—Rhodes scholar, lawyer, prosecutor at the Nuremberg trials—he was largely a front man for the owners, especially the Norris interests. As *Sports Illustrated* put it in 1957:

> National Hockey League chief executives are chosen for their meekness in the face of authority. . . . Clarence S. Campbell . . . is a former referee who learned early in his career that if he wanted to get ahead in hockey he should never sass a magnate back. The Board of Governors, made up of a representative of each club, runs the league, usually according to the plans and specifications of the Norris interests; and Mr. Campbell, who besides being league president is also the secretary-treasurer, has to do little except look respectful and nod his head in the right direction at the proper time.

When someone complained to the Toronto Maple Leafs' Conn Smythe about a Campbell decision, Smythe's son Stafford replied, "Where would we find another Rhodes Scholar, graduate lawyer, decorated war hero and former prosecutor at Nuremberg who'll do what he's told?"[5] The distinguished Campbell provided the perfect veneer for the owners and the dominant Norris interests.

Jim Norris Jr., "Jimmy," came to dominate not only NHL hockey, but also professional boxing, and he surrounded himself with the boxing crowd which included "the grifters, touts and pimps that surrounded boxing like flies in a stable."[6] This inevitably brought him into close contact with the mob. By 1947, according to Barney Nagler, author of a book on Norris and boxing, Jimmy had "achieved widespread notoriety as the underworld's commissioner of boxing."[7] Members of the mob, Cruise and Griffiths say, "were his closest friends and business associates."[8] They included Sammy "Golfbag" Hunt, "a vicious hit man in the Al Capone era . . . who lurked in the corridors at NHL Board of Governors' meetings," and Frankie Carbo, "a member of the infamous Murder Inc." and "a gunman even more notorious than Hunt." Cruise and Griffiths point out, "In 1939, Carbo and Bugsy Siegel terminated Harry 'Big Greenie' Greenberg, a small-time enforcer who had been threatening to turn state's evidence. Carbo later gunned down Siegel for Meyer Lansky in one of the biggest gangland assassinations of all time."

Jimmy Norris, together with Arthur Wirtz and Joe Louis, formed the International Boxing Club in 1949, and by 1951 the IBC owned and managed a stable of the most important boxers as well as "the agencies that promoted them, the agencies that put together the rights and television packages and, of course, all the key arenas." The IBC ran the *Gillette Friday Night Fights*, along with a second weekly televised match, the two together grossing $10 million annually for Norris, "who also got "under-the-table cuts" from boxers whose rights he owned "and whose careers his agencies managed, both in flagrant contravention of boxing regulations stipulating that no promoter could own a boxer." His arenas and the IBC pulled in both the rich gate percentages and the gambling action, plus the shadier receipts from bribes and fight-fixing.

And always there was the mob. When Norris was promoting a big fight, according to Nagler, "His suite would be near Carbo's suite, and the occasion was marked almost always by a seeming convention of gangsters from all over the country. Carbo and Palermo were the hosts. Wherever one went in the vicinity of Norris' headquarters, he came upon a known gangster."[9] Eventually, after a long investigation, Norris and Arthur Wirtz were found guilty in 1957 of operating a boxing monopoly and conspiring to restrict trade.

Norris's interests in boxing and related activities—in 1957 he was chairman of the board of the Norris Grain Company, senior partner in the

Chicago brokerage house Norris & Kenly, director of numerous corporations and owner of a Kentucky horse-breeding ranch—resulted in Norris's hockey interests being sorely neglected. The on-ice record of his Chicago Black Hawks plummeted in the 1950s. From Norris's point of view the Black Hawks were low on the long list of priorities, little more than a captive tenant for his building, the Chicago Stadium. The same fate befell the similarly Norris-owned and Norris-neglected New York Rangers. According to sports writer Bruce Dowbiggin: "The Rangers filled the calendar dates at Madison Square Gardens when boxing or the circus left the building dark." Indeed, in the spring when the circus came to New York the Rangers would have their playoff games bumped to another city.[10] Meanwhile, Jimmy Norris's fun-loving brother Bruce managed to squander most of his share of his father's fortune over a twenty-five-year period while driving his inherited Detroit Red Wings, who had won the Stanley Cup four times between 1950 and 1955, into near-permanent ineptitude. According to sports writers William Houston and David Shoalts, "Bruce was a weak man and heavy drinker who presided over the downfall of a once-great franchise."[11]

Future NHL President John Ziegler would emerge out of this same Bruce Norris-run Red Wings organization. An ambitious young lawyer, Ziegler bought a condo next to Norris's place in North Miami, Florida, partied relentlessly with the team owner and "became Norris's top corporate caddy, holding his coat until the wee small hours of the morning."[12] By 1966 he had been appointed to the team's board of directors, had become the Red Wings' alternate NHL governor and was the brains behind a club whose on-ice performance had slid rapidly downwards.

When Ziegler emerged from the Detroit branch of the Norris empire to become president of the NHL in 1977, he joined hands with Bill Wirtz who had been appointed president of the Chicago Black Hawks in 1965 by his father Arthur. The Wirtz family fortune was estimated in the billions, and members regularly appeared on *Fortune*'s list of the wealthiest families in the United States. Thus the Norris legacy carried on. Ziegler and Wirtz, who both owed their rise to power to the Norris family, became the two most important powerbrokers in the NHL of the 1970s and 1980s.[13] They would also both become close personal friends and business associates of Alan Eagleson, executive director of the National Hockey League Players' Association (NHLPA).

With this carrying on of the Norris family tradition, the NHL remained, in business terms, backward, almost feudal, compared to other major professional team sports. NHL franchises were profitable, no doubt—but not as profitable as possible. Major league baseball, the National Football League and the National Basketball Association exploded in the 1970s and 1980s into a new business era characterized by network television deals, rapidly rising salaries and relentless marketing of "products." The entry of the NHL into this new business world was delayed: the tight, closely held world created by the Norris family was sustained long past its time by the efforts of Wirtz and Ziegler, with the close collaboration of Eagleson.

The Players, the Unions and the Eagle

NHL players had tried to unionize, most recently in 1956–57, and failed, crushed by the owners. The need.or a union was great. Players had long been poorly paid—most had to find summer jobs to supplement their hockey salaries—and completely controlled by the owners. As Houston and Shoalts put it, "They were ruled by autocrats—greedy, hypocritical businessmen, some of whom associated with criminals or were themselves felons."[14] If a player felt he was underpaid, he could not seek work with another team. The "reserve clause" tied him to the team that "owned" him unless and until management decided to "trade" him. He could be traded or demoted at any time for any reason. If he suffered an injury that prevented him from working in the off-season he would not be compensated. If he got in trouble he appeared, without representation or rights of due process, before NHL President Clarence Campbell who was paid by the owners. If he tried to moonlight by charging for public appearances or for endorsing products he needed the written consent of the club owner. The players were chattel.

In the summer of 1956, Detroit Red Wings captain and perennial all-star Ted Lindsay met with New York lawyers Norman J. Lewis and Milton Mound, who had helped major league baseball players negotiate a contract with baseball owners. The lawyers' assessment, according to Dowbiggin, was that NHL hockey was "locked in the Dark Ages. Owners controlled the revenue, the players, and the facts about both." It was "plain and simple indentured servitude," Lewis said. Mound described hockey in the 1950s as "Outrageously corrupt, outrageously wrong—far worse than baseball." He added, "Hockey was so medieval—as if it were a dynasty. When you are born, you are already indentured to the lord and master . . . and he could tell them what they had to and what they shouldn't do. The fellow who was the president of the team was God to them."[15]

In the first half of the 1956–57 season Lindsay secretly signed up all but one NHL player, and he announced the formation of the Players' Association on February 12, 1957. The owners instantly retaliated. Toronto Maple Leaf owner Conn Smythe and Detroit's "Jolly" Jack Adams spread the notion that Mound was an interloper who knew nothing about hockey and sought to impose a form of socialism on the NHL. In November 1957 Smythe, in a tirade in the Leafs' locker room, "harangued the players about the intrusion of New York lawyers and 'Jews' into the purity of the hockey business."[16] He traded his captain, Jimmy Thomson, secretary of the Players' Association, to Chicago, after calling him into his office and denouncing him "as a traitor and a communist."[17] Adams turned on Lindsay, calling him a "cancer," a "dupe," who was "only out for himself," and traded him to Chicago. Throughout the league, union leaders were purged in what was "a brutal but effective exile." By November 1957 his own former teammates had turned against Lindsay—partly the result of an obsequious Detroit press parroting the owners' line—and the Detroit Red Wings players withdrew from the Players' Association. Dowbiggin sums it up: "Sabotaged from without and within, the Players' Association lasted only six more months. It was replaced by an Owner/Player Council, a punchless platform given to the players as a reward for dropping their anti-trust and unfair-labor demands."[18]

The owners were safe for another ten years, from the players if not from themselves. Conn Smythe sold his interests in the Leafs to his son Stafford Smythe and Harold Ballard, and Ballard in particular would carry on the NHL owners' tradition—he was later charged with defrauding Maple Leaf Gardens of $475,000, convicted on forty-seven of forty-nine charges and sentenced to three years in prison. Ballard served eighteen months of the sentence and, when released in 1972, he was firmly in control of the franchise, and hockey in Toronto entered its own version of "the Dark Ages."[19] When asked later, in 1985, about the Leafs' poor on-ice performance Ballard replied, "Our stocks are all right and we're making money, so what the hell do we care?"[20]

But, unlike the Red Wings, the Maple Leaf players had not totally capitulated to their owners. At the conclusion of his November 1957 locker-room tirade, Conn Smythe had insisted upon an immediate player vote to reject the Association, but "his beloved Maple Leafs failed to give in to his demands."[21] They voted in favour of the Association, planting the seed for the next union attempt ten years later.

It was with these same Maple Leafs that Alan Eagleson came into the picture, making his first NHL contacts "doing legal work for them or just helping them dodge speeding tickets." By 1964 Eagleson was representing Bobby Orr, hockey's newest superstar, who took the NHL by storm in 1966–67. The next step was a players' association. According to Dowbiggin, "Using Orr and his Maple Leaf contacts as a springboard, Eagleson flew everywhere around North America, enlisting virtually every hockey player in the NHL and the minor leagues for the NHL Players' Association within a six-month period in 1966–67."[22]

The owners, so hostile to Lindsay's efforts in 1957, raised few objections to the Eagleson-led Players' Association. The owners, Houston and Shoalts write, "did not want a union and would have jumped at the chance to crush it. But with Eagleson, they felt they could do business. He wasn't a labour lawyer, had no experience in labour negotiations and showed no sign of militancy." Conn Smythe gave his stamp of approval: "I don't like unions but I'm glad it's Eagleson at the head of the players' association rather than somebody else." Clarence Campbell added: "Eagleson hasn't been a tooth fairy. But when chips are down he has acted like one."[23]

No formal collective agreement was negotiated with the NHL until 1975, and that agreement was extended by NHL President Ziegler and "my friend Alan Eagleson" well into the 1980s, "with few significant changes—no small feat considering the revolutionary changes occurring in other sports." The 1975 collective agreement and its successors through to 1992 did not conform to labour codes: "No secret ballots were held, printed copies of the agreement were often unavailable at the time of acceptance, election of the officers of the NHLPA was never ratified by the full membership."[24] Official minutes of meetings were not kept. Annual meetings at the palatial Breakers Hotel in Palm Beach, Florida, were perfunctory affairs deliberately kept short so they wouldn't impinge upon the player reps' customary one o'clock tee-off time.

Ziegler, paid by and accountable to the owners, continued as sole arbitrator in contract disputes, an arrangement, outrageous though it was, that Eagleson agreed to and that was embodied in successive collective agreements. Eagleson operated the NHLPA with a skeleton staff, so that, Dowbiggin says, "Research and preparation were almost unheard of in advance of collective bargaining. Eagleson bragged to the NHL player representatives that this thrift saved millions, but it never made up for what was lost in the way of salaries and benefits."[25] Hockey players fell further and further behind other sports professionals.

In 1989, when disgruntled players hired Ed Garvey, former head of the National Football League Players' Association, to investigate Eagleson's activities as union head, Garvey delivered a scathing report. He described Eagleson's close personal friendship with Zeigler and Wirtz and concluded: "Alan Eagleson has been a vital part of the NHL establishment. He has contributed greatly to keeping salaries down, profits up."[26]

Eagleson's relations with key owners and NHL executives were remarkable for a union leader. Although Arthur Wirtz was the NHL's chief negotiator, players "remember seeing Eagleson arrive at a players-owners meeting in the 1970s aboard the Wirtz yacht." Former player Mark Johnson began to wonder, "Is he working for us? Or is he working for them?" Ziegler was one of Eagleson's best friends. According to Dowbiggin: "The two holidayed together in Florida, the Caribbean and in Europe. They were found golfing together or yachting together with Bill Wirtz, or in London on business at the same time. . . . The League's owners laughed all the way to the bank every time they witnessed the alliance of Ziegler and Eagleson, or 'Ziggy and Iggy' as they were dubbed." The result, inevitably, was that "the lines between labour and management became blurred."[27]

Also blurred were the lines between Eagleson's job as executive director of the Players' Association and his many and varied personal financial interests. Conflict of interest was frequent. A central part of the Eagleson network of business interests was his player agency. By the early 1970s Eagleson represented more than 150 players in the NHL, about half the league total. As well as being lucrative, this arrangement constituted a conflict of interest—half the players were represented by other agents who were in effect Eagleson's competitors. Players complained that Eagleson would frequently not return their calls if they were not his clients, even though he was their union representative, and when he did call back he was often less than supportive. An example, one of many, is the case of Murray Wilson, former centre with Montreal and Los Angeles, who called Eagleson regarding problems with a disability claim. Wilson says that Eagleson told him, "You're not a client of mine. You're a client of Art Kaminsky. Tell him to take care of your problems."[28] Another example was third-round St. Louis draft pick Gord Buynak. In 1974 Eagleson delivered Buynak to the Blues for less than the salary the Blues had budgeted. In return the Blues paid Eagleson $50,000. Lou Angotti, acting general manager for St. Louis, hand-delivered the first $10,000 instalment to Eagleson. Angotti said that Eagleson "made it clear that he could sign this player for 'X' dollars. He could save St. Louis some money and everybody would be happy. . . . The player's contract was more or less downgraded in terms of money, and the difference was paid to Alan Eagleson. It was a helluva deal for St. Louis, and a helluva deal for Eagleson, but not so good for the player."[29]

The conflicts of interest did not end there. In addition to his player agency Eagleson developed a network of companies offering such services as financial management for players, endorsements and public relations work for players and real estate work. Eagleson made a fortune in real estate, but according to Houston and Shoalts, "Often his real estate dealings have involved close friends and clients of his law firm . . . and were financed by money from the players' association and players he represented as an agent."[30]

At the same time Eagleson was charging the NHLPA for a variety of expenses. The NHLPA paid almost $1.1 million in fees and expenses to Eagleson or firms tied to him from 1987 to 1989, for example. This was in addition to Eagleson's salary which, for the period July 1, 1987 to June 30, 1991, totalled $768,000 U.S., though he was contracted to work for the NHLPA as executive director only 60–65 percent of this time.[31] This very favourable contract was negotiated in 1986 when Eagleson informed the NHLPA executive members, just hours before the beginning of negotiations with the owners, that if he did not get a new contract immediately he would resign. The players panicked and caved in. Eagleson had proved far more demanding in negotiating his own contract than in negotiating on behalf of the NHLPA. "It made him one of the best-paid, if not *the* best-paid, union leader [sic] in North America."[32]

Ed Garvey's full forty-four page report, presented at the NHLPA annual meeting in Palm Beach, Florida, in June 1989, was a "stunning indictment of Eagleson's twenty-two-year reign," including details of conflicts of interest, unauthorized loans of NHLPA funds to Eagleson companies and cronies, questionable expenses, inadequate preparation for collective bargaining and the extent to which NHL players had fallen behind players in other big league sports.[33] Immediate attempts to oust Eagleson failed, but the process by which he would be brought down had been set in motion. In 1991 the FBI began an investigation into the affairs of Eagleson and the NHLPA, finding enough evidence for the U.S. Justice Department to convene a grand jury hearing into Eagleson's running of the NHLPA.[34] As of March 1996, the United States was still awaiting Eagleson's extradition on thirty-four charges of fraud, racketeering and embezzlement.

The case moved more slowly in Canada. Senator Louis Robichaud, former premier of New Brunswick and former federal Liberal cabinet minister, told journalist Russ Conway in 1991 that he expected Eagleson would never be fully investigated: "He has too many connections in high places." Robichaud added, "He's one of the most powerful people in Canada. He's close friends with the prime minister, cabinet ministers, judges, many people in parliament. Alan gets anything he wants. And he takes pretty good care of them too."[35] By March 1996 the RCMP had still not charged Eagleson and continued to remain silent about the case.[36]

Alan Eagleson was a worthy successor to the Norris tradition; his actions as NHLPA executive director and as part of a ruling triumvirate are, in more ways than one, part of a direct line of succession. Like too many of the NHL owners, he was brash, arrogant, manipulative and prone to secrecy and back-room deals. He got away with his abuse of power for almost twenty years in part because "he was, without question, the best-connected man in Canada."[37] And he got away with his abuse of power because of the mystique of "the game," of NHL hockey. Like the owners, he was trusted—by the media, the fans and many of the players. NHL players have been, "for the most part, small-town Canadian boys who were raised not to question authority. In time, the unquestioned authority became Eagleson."[38]

These same themes—links between the NHL and those with power; the abuse of power by these people; and the willingness of so many, including the media, to suspend disbelief because of the mystique of the game—would also be central features of the conflict in Winnipeg over the Jets and their demands for a new arena.

The Changing Economics of Professional Sport

The cosy arrangements engineered by the likes of the Norris and Wirtz families and their faithful servants Campbell, Ziegler and Eagleson, isolated

NHL hockey from the changes taking place in big league football, basketball and baseball. David Cruise, for example, argues that the NHL stagnated after the owners smashed the Lindsay-led union drive of 1957:

> Because without an aggressive union driving up salaries, the NHL owners did not need to bother hustling an American television contract. They were content to depress players' salaries and rake in healthy profits from the live gate along with some television, as well as concessions and parking revenue, since most of them owned the arenas as well. With American networks discovering just how profitable sports programming was in the 1960s, hockey missed out on the boom and has been playing catch-up ever since. When Eagleson came along, his tame union just helped perpetuate the status quo.[39]

The NHL clung to the "status quo" far longer than other big league sports did. Ziegler's oft-repeated refrain was, "If it ain't broke, why fix it?" Other leagues were aggressively marketing their "products," but as hockey writer Stan Fischler puts it, marketing "was never a part of Ziegler's lexicon, or his persona. . . . 'Think small' was Ziggy's philosophy."[40] Bill Wirtz, like the other old-line owners, was satisfied with this approach. His Chicago Black Hawks were hugely profitable and his formula was simple: cater to the loyal and dedicated Chicago-area fans who attended Black Hawk games. There was no need to seek the big television deals and related advertising revenue that other professional sports leagues had been tapping into since the 1960s. Arenas in established NHL centres were full; Eagleson was cooperating in holding player salary levels far below those of other sports; profits were strong; and thus the aggressive and multifaceted marketing that drove the economics of the other big league sports was, until very recently, conspicuously absent in the NHL. It just wasn't needed. The result was that small-city NHL franchises like the Winnipeg Jets were able to hang on much longer than would otherwise have been the case.

It was television that, since the 1960s, had revolutionized the economics of big league team sports in North America. Network television's broadcasting of baseball, football and basketball games generated huge direct revenues for franchises in those leagues, while also setting in motion a process that made it both necessary and possible, by means of aggressive marketing, to generate a variety of lucrative ancillary sources of revenue. Hockey and baseball had been broadcast on radio in the 1930s, but it was the 1939 World Series that made it apparent to corporate America how very valuable sports advertising could be. In that year, Gillette paid the then huge sum of $100,000 for the rights to advertise during the World Series. The results were remarkable, as related by Gillette's general manager: "We couldn't believe our eyes. Sales were up 350 percent for the Series. It wasn't even a new product and here were these fantastic records coming in. We didn't wait, we went running all over the country to buy every major event we could find."[41] Radio broadcasting of sports events was producing large audiences—far larger than those who physically attended the games. Advertisers were anxious to reach these audiences, and professional teams were therefore able to sell the rights to broadcast their games for rapidly growing sums.

Television merely picked up from radio. In 1946 the New York Yankees sold the rights to televise their games locally for $75,000. By 1953 fifteen of major league baseball's sixteen teams were selling local television rights. The sale of TV and radio rights, which had generated 3 percent of major league baseball's total revenue in 1946, grew to 16.8 percent in 1956 and exploded throughout the 1980s to constitute, by 1990, more than 50 percent of major league baseball's total revenue.[42] The same happened with NFL football. Overshadowed by college football and confined largely to the U.S. snowbelt, the NFL was transformed in 1960 when Pete Rozelle, a marketing man, became league commissioner. Rozelle revamped the NFL's relationship with television by selling the rights to televise not just the games of individual teams, but of the league as a whole. By 1964 CBS had agreed to pay $28.2 million, ten times the pre-Rozelle television revenue, to televise NFL games for two years.[43]

The race was on. The televising of sport established large audiences to which commodities could be sold; more importantly, it produced "a specific audience for which networks can match specific advertisers." Beer has been a particularly good example of this tendency. The demographics of beer consumption are virtually identical to the demographics of sports interest—both peak in the same age range. Indeed, while young males aged eighteen to thirty-four make up 20 percent of the U.S. population, they drink 70 percent of the beer consumed. They are most efficiently reached through sports events, and brewers have thus been prepared to spend vast sums on sports-related advertising and not infrequently have even purchased teams in order to gain exclusive access to their fans, with exceptionally positive results for sales of their product.[44]

As NBA Commissioner David Stern put it, sports can be seen "as a highway broad and strong enough to carry thousands of saleable things."[45] The greater the demand by advertisers to place their "saleable things" on this highway, the more the networks could charge them and thus the more the professional sports leagues could charge the networks. By the early 1990s television revenue constituted more than one-half the total revenue of big league baseball and basketball, and almost two-thirds the revenue of NFL football.

But hockey was left lagging far behind.[46] Not that it hadn't tried to get in on the network television gravy train. Knowing that to do so required a more widespread U.S. presence, the NHL located all six of its first postwar expansion franchises, in 1967, in U.S. cities. This approach appeared to work: a year later the league secured a network contract with CBS. From 1968 to 1972 NHL games were broadcast nationally in the United States by CBS, and then from 1973 to 1975 by NBC. Still, NHL hockey never did catch on in much of the United States, and in 1975 NBC dropped the NHL because there just wasn't enough interest among U.S. viewers, especially those in the South. Business reporter Brenton Welling found that, "To their dismay, the owners discovered it's tough to interest people in a game where it has never been played before—in the Sunbelt, for example. Television stations in the South and Southwest just wouldn't carry hockey."[47]

After that the NHL, as a matter of policy, abandoned the attempt to secure a national U.S. television contract. Throughout the rest of the 1970s and all through the 1980s, "We principally emphasized that our teams develop their local market," Ziegler said in 1991. As a result, Jerry Gorman and Kirk Calhoun point out, "While the major networks were negotiating multimillion-dollar, multi-year contracts with football, baseball and even basketball in the 1980s, hockey stumbled along with low-paying agreements." It was not that NHL franchises were unprofitable; rather, they were not yet earning the huge profits that might be made by following the lead of big league baseball, basketball and football. Starting in 1985–86, Ziegler signed television deals with cable companies, first ESPN and then Sports Channel, which produced annual revenues for the league ranging from $5.5 million to $17 million—minuscule sums compared to earnings of other big league sports. Four-year television deals signed in 1992 paid the NFL $3.6 billion or $900 million per year—more than fifty times what the NHL was getting. Major league baseball got $1.46 billion or $365 million per year.[48]

The failure to secure a national U.S. network television contract reflects the NHL's failure to penetrate the U.S. South with its new franchises. Although the six new teams added in 1967 were all based in the United States, only two of them reached beyond the U.S. Northwest and Midwest, and one of those two, the California Seals, relocated to Cleveland in 1976 before merging with the Minnesota North Stars in 1978. Atlanta, a deep South franchise, was added in 1972, but relocated to Calgary in 1980.

In the meantime, to hold down salaries, the NHL was forced to effect a merger with the World Hockey Association, but the price paid was the unwanted addition of yet another four Northern franchises—Hartford, Quebec, Winnipeg and Edmonton. By 1980 the NHL had still not secured a presence in the U.S. Sunbelt—the fastest growing region in the United States, the heart of the booming new information and communications industries—with the single, shaky exception of the Los Angeles Kings, and this situation remained the case throughout the 1980s.

In other big league sports, once network television revenues began to grow, players formed unions to ensure that they would get their fair share. In late 1965, pitching great Robin Roberts of the Philadelphia Phillies, referring to the increased revenue he foresaw being available from network television deals, told fellow players: "There's going to be a lot of money involved, and without a negotiator we won't get our share." The next year Marvin Miller, former research economist with the United Steelworkers of America, was appointed executive director of the Major League Baseball Players' Association (MLBPA). Miller proved to be an exceptionally able negotiator and baseball players' average salaries, which had inched up slowly from $13,000 in 1951 to $19,000 in 1967, exploded. By 1975 they had almost doubled to $35,000. Two years later they had more than doubled again to $74,000, and by 1980 they had doubled yet again to $143,750. Throughout the 1980s and early 1990s, fuelled by the huge growth in network television revenues, average major league baseball salaries continued their precipitous climb: 1985—$369,000; 1989—$489,000; 1991—$880,000; 1992—$1 million.[49]

NHL salaries also climbed during this period, but far more slowly. In 1967, the year that Alan Eagleson formed and became executive director of the NHLPA, average salaries in the four professional team sports were roughly on a par, in the $19,000 to $25,000 range. By 1972, five years later, the average NBA salary had soared to $90,000, "more than twice any of the others." The average salary in the NHL went from 77 percent of that in the NBA in 1977 to 38 percent in 1988. In 1986 average salaries in the NBA and major league baseball were roughly two and one-half times the $170,000 average in the NHL.[50] The dynamic process by which higher network television revenues make possible higher salaries—and higher salaries necessitate still more marketing-induced revenues—had not yet taken off in the NHL, so that hockey franchises could still exist on gate receipts and the relatively small revenues generated by cable deals and Canadian television. NHL owners were making money; they just weren't making *as much* money as possible. The "Dark Ages" were not yet over.

Gretzky, McNall and the Challenge of Tractor Pulls

All of this was to change dramatically with the 1988 Gretzky sale. Los Angeles Kings owner Bruce McNall paid a huge sum for Gretzky: some $15 million in cash, plus an initial eight-year contract at $2 million per year. The sale symbolically represented the beginning of a new, marketing-driven era in the NHL, an era that would fully take flight with the exit of Eagleson in 1990 and Ziegler and Wirtz in 1992, and an era that would see the dramatically rapid corporatization and Americanization of the NHL, its further absorption into the media-entertainment industry and the decline and fall of at least two smaller Canadian franchises. It is perhaps symbolically significant that the 1988 Gretzky sale, which sparked this process, occurred in the same year that Prime Minister Brian Mulroney's Conservatives won re-election in Canada on a promise to implement the Canada–U.S. Free Trade Agreement. More money would be made from hockey—indeed, much more. But Canada would not necessarily benefit; smaller Canadian cities would lose.

McNall quickly demonstrated that paying a seemingly vast sum to bring Gretzky to Los Angeles made financial sense, at least to him and his franchise. The Los Angeles Forum began to sell out, ticket prices were raised and the number of radio stations broadcasting Kings' games jumped from one to fifteen. Advertising revenue took off. According to Roy MacGregor, "In Gretzky's first year the franchise took in an additional $5 million at the gate, $1 million in increased advertising revenue, another $1 million in television rights, $500,000 in increased jersey sales alone. Gretzky's salary was covered, McNall was able to pay off the $4 million loss from the previous year, and there was more than enough to handle the financial and interest payments on the $15 million that had gone into Pocklington's coffers."[51] McNall had given the other NHL owners a glimpse of what marketing could do. He had shown them that NHL hockey was really about celebrity and entertainment and marketing a "product." If the NHL could secure a network television deal, he insisted, even more could be earned.

At the same time, Gretzky's huge contract put enormous pressure on other NHL salaries. Two years later, in 1990, Bob Goodenow, a hard-nosed negotiator, replaced Eagleson as head of the NHLPA. By 1992, NHL players were on strike. The Gretzky example plus Goodenow's arrival resulted in a great leap in player salaries. In 1989 three NHL players had earned $1 million or more per year; in 1995, 147 did. Average player salaries over that period almost quadrupled.[52]

Now a U.S. network television deal became essential, as did a new emphasis on marketing. More revenue was needed to pay rapidly rising player salaries. The NHL was forced to abandon the comfortable old era and replicate what the other big league sports had already done. But the NHL, conservative and provincial and for so long "dominated by a backward-looking handful of eccentric entrepreneurs," had a long way to go. One survey had ranked the league "40th in popularity among American viewers, behind tractor pulls and bowling."[53] The task was to market pro hockey throughout the United States and especially in the Sunbelt, where hockey was relatively unknown but where support had to be created if the league was to secure a national U.S. network television deal with its huge revenue potential.

McNall, the key player, led the drive to unseat Wirtz and Ziegler. In 1992 McNall himself replaced Wirtz as chairman of the NHL Board of Governors and then actively pursued Gary Bettman, third in command at the financially lucrative and marketing-driven NBA, to take Ziegler's place. "We want to get out of the Dark Ages," as McNall put it. Ziegler, in keeping with long NHL tradition and despite heated conflicts over the inadequacy of NHL veterans' pensions, was awarded a "$2 million golden handshake and a pension of $250,000 a year"—about thirty times Bobby Orr's annual pension. Bettman took over as NHL commissioner in 1992, his selection a function of the emergent view, pushed most aggressively by McNall, "that television was a priority and that hockey had much to learn from the NBA." With Ziegler, Wirtz and Eagleson gone, replaced by Bettman, McNall and Goodenow, almost all of the pieces were in place for a shift in strategy. The NHL had finally, according to MacGregor, "dropped its conservative attitude and embraced McNall's stated assumption that sports are 'in their infancy of exploitation.' The other owners now had a dreamspinner in charge, one who understood, as Wirtz did not, that there is much more to the hockey business than filling seats."[54] The final piece was to bring in more professional "dreamspinners."

Again McNall was the catalyst, luring the Walt Disney Company and Blockbuster Video in as owners of two new franchises awarded in December 1992. To reach the Sunbelt, hockey's image had to be improved, the league had to be marketed and the Walt Disney Company was the proven master of image-making, of marketing. While Ziegler had told *Sports Illustrated* in 1988 that "our last priority is image building," McNall set about "to move image building from last priority to first."[55] With Disney and Blockbuster on board the shift in the economics and philosophy of the NHL was firmly in place.

That move was accompanied by a massive geographic shift. The NHL added new franchises in San Jose, California, in the 1991–92 season; Tampa Bay, Florida (plus Ottawa) in 1992–93; and Miami, Florida and Anaheim, California, owned by entertainment giants Blockbuster Video and Disney, for the 1993-94 season. The Minnesota North Stars moved to Dallas, Texas in 1993. The Quebec Nordiques were sold to Denver, Colorado in 1995. The team was talented enough to win the Stanley Cup in 1996 as the Colorado Avalanche—in a Stanley Cup final in which their opponents were the Florida Panthers. The Winnipeg Jets were relocated to Phoenix, Arizona in 1996. And in Edmonton the Oilers were barely hanging on—likely candidates for yet another move south, thus bringing full circle a process that began with the Gretzky sale. What the NHL had tried and failed to do in the late 1960s and 1970s, it had now accomplished: it had established a presence in the U.S. South and Southwest. Smaller Canadian cities, where the NHL has deep roots, were being abandoned, replaced by cities in the booming U.S. Sunbelt.

The NHL has become Americanized in other ways. For example, before McNall's resignation, according to Stan Fischler, "The 'Big Three' among hockey's power brokers—board Chairman Bruce McNall, Bettman and NHL Players' Association boss Bob Goodenow— were all U.S.-born. At 650 Fifth Avenue [in New York City], the NHL's fortress, Bettman, with precious few exceptions, filled almost every available league command post with non-Canadians." The Americanization was primarily a byproduct of the pursuit—now made necessary by skyrocketing player salaries—of the big money being made in other professional team sports. The corporate and marketing-driven NBA was the model. "The NBA'ing of the NHL put the accent on bigness and a more corporate feel than ever before. . . . The roots of today's game are in the board rooms. Decisions are made not because they have a good or bad impact on hockey, but because of the manner in which they will be received by large corporations—and all those corporations are American."[56]

What is more, many of these corporations are media-entertainment giants. Disney, owner of the Anaheim Mighty Ducks, is the most obvious example. Blockbuster Video, owner of the 1996 Stanley Cup finalist Florida Panthers when they entered the NHL in 1992–93, has since merged with Viacom Inc. to become "part of one of the biggest entertainment companies in the world."[57] Paramount Pictures owned the New York Rangers—as well as the NBA Knickerbockers and Madison Square Gardens—when the Rangers won the Stanley Cup in 1993–94. And the New Jersey Devils recently considered moving to Nashville—a city with no hockey tradition whatever, but a major entertainment centre, the home of country music. As New York hockey reporter Fischler put it: "Nashville's bid to steal the Devils from New Jersey was symbolic of hockey in the 1990s." Added McNall: "What you're hearing and seeing are the various entertainment companies taking a serious look at sports. I know all the people at Sony and Warner Brothers are watching what Paramount did. . . . It's pretty evident that in the future more and more electronic giants like this are going to get involved in professional sports. It just makes too much sense not to."[58]

Wayne Huizenga, founder of Blockbuster Video, was included in *Entertainment Weekly*'s 1990 list of the ten most powerful people in entertainment. Michael Eisner, CEO of Disney, topped the list.[59] Two years later, each was the head of a new NHL franchise. The era of hockey as entertainment, as glitter and glitz and celebrity, had arrived. How else could the sport be marketed in the Sunbelt? And what was the new NHL about, if not marketing?

The New Era: Commodification, Celebrity and Luxury Suites

The process by which sport becomes commodified, or its elements turned into things to be marketed, was about to begin in earnest in the NHL. Everything related to sports is now marketed. In the NBA, for example, the "endless season is now overwhelmingly commercial," writer David Guterson points out. "Arenas and the vast perimeters of stadiums are thoroughly festooned with advertisements and big-screen graphics that fans can neither ignore nor turn away from: the scoreboard, the game clock, the scorer's bench, the chair where NBA players rest, the shirts and sweatpants worn by ball boys, the cups players drink from and the towels around their necks—even the shoes they wear on their feet—are chockablock with sales messages." The game itself is sliced up into identifiable parts, each of them separately marketed: "A power play, fast break, or steal; a report on rebounds, assists, or blocks; an instant replay or twenty-second time-out—all have become occasions for celebrating the name [and selling the products] of a paint manufacturer, telephone company, or overnight courier service."[60]

Also marketed, in addition to the game itself, is licensed merchandise related to the game. The NBA and NFL have been particularly aggressive in marketing licensed merchandise festooned with team and league logos. Under Commissioner David Stern, whose view was that "marketing was the key to the health of a modern professional sport," the number of full-time marketing specialists employed by the NBA to sell league merchandise jumped from one in 1984 to sixty in 1992. By 1991 the NBA had become the first big league sport in which sales of licensed merchandise exceeded ticket sales. The NFL has been similarly aggressive. NFL Properties, the league's licensing and marketing arm, created in 1963 by the same Pete Rozelle who pioneered the NFL's sale of league television rights, employs 130 marketing people and sells some $2.1 billion worth of NFL-related commodities annually. Gorman and Calhoun write:

> You can buy bowling balls with the logo of your favourite team, and golf umbrellas and pool cues and even bags of potato chips. You can buy pewter belt buckles decorated with team symbols. You can buy Christmas tree ornaments and rhinestone jewellery, watches and inflatable helmets, briefcases and mugs and card tables, floor mats for your car and collars for your dog, pacifiers and teething rings for your kid and birdhouses for passing robins, all in designs that celebrate your favorite NFL team. And yes, they even sell bumper stickers and pennants; and clothes, all manner of clothes.[61]

The NHL was slow, as usual, in aggressively pursuing this source of revenue, but in the five years following Gretzky's move to Los Angeles the sale of licensed NHL apparel grew tenfold, from $100 million to $1 billion. The addition of a Disney-owned franchise was intended to promote further dramatic increases in such sales. After all, Disney has long been a pioneer in such cross-marketing—"the strategic use of the various entertainment products in a corporate empire to promote and give visibility to one another"—linking food and souvenirs to its films and theme parks. Disney even employs fifty people in its "Synergy Department" to identify ways of using one part of the company to promote and make money for another part. This was a central element in Disney's thinking in acquiring an NHL franchise. It could create a merchandising tie-in with its movie *The Mighty Ducks* and the team.[62] Disney's expertise would help the NHL catch up to other big league sports in generating revenue through the sale of league merchandise.

Pro sports have come a long way in marketing their licensed merchandise since George Weiss, general manager of the New York Yankees, rejected a request to have a "Cap Day" at Yankee Stadium by asking, "Do you think I want every kid in this city walking around with a Yankee cap?" By 1992 retail sales of all licensed sports merchandise reached an estimated $12.2 billion, and some 150 U.S. MBA programs and law schools "offered extensive sports-marketing courses as degrees." The author of a U.S. sports-marketing textbook estimates that by the year 2000 some $30 billion will be spent annually on global sports advertising.[63]

In this marketing maelstrom star athletes play a central role. Their celebrity, their fame and the imagery and emotions that their skills inspire are tapped by corporations—indeed, are often deliberately manufactured by corporations—so that the athletes can be used to endorse particular products, for which they are handsomely rewarded. *Forbes* magazine estimates that in 1994 the Chicago Bulls' Michael Jordan earned an endorsement income of $40 million—in addition to his $3.9 million salary. The basketball star has earned around $170 million since 1990, exclusive of the $25 million per year player contract he signed in 1996, and his soaring, slam-dunking image is an international icon. Reporter Stephen Brunt says, "The image—his image—has become part of some graphic Esperanto. . . . Walk down the street in Paris or Nairobi or Tokyo, and that same silhouette of the soaring Jordan will pop up somewhere."[64] The NBA's deliberate promotion of a "culture of celebrity" has been so successful that even before playing his first NBA game, Shaquille O'Neal of the Orlando Magic—who in 1996 would sign a multiyear playing contract for $120 million—was able to secure endorsement contracts with Reebok and Spalding worth $40 million over seven years. Star players have become walking billboards. Indeed, at the 1992 Barcelona Olympics, the great British decathlon champion Daley Thompson sported a T-shirt that read "This space for rent."[65]

Running-shoe manufacturer Nike, a pioneer in manufacturing the culture of celebrity as the means of marketing its products, has been so hugely successful that the company's founder and chairman, Phil Knight, has ridden the celebrity and sales power of Jordan and other athletes to become one of the richest men in the world. Marketing has become so important to professional sports and its stars that in 1993 Knight was named "the most powerful man in sports" by *The Sporting News*.[66] It is easy to forget that the women in Asia, the Caribbean and Central America who make most of Nike's shoes can earn as little as fifteen cents an hour, are often subject to mandatory overtime and live in company barracks. Their lives are most assuredly not part of the marketing of celebrity that has become such a central feature of the business of professional sports.[67] On the contrary, their exploitation is the flip side of the huge sums earned by the corporations and their stables of celebrity athletes.

The NHL was, as always, slow in entering the process of commodification, but the 1988 Gretzky sale opened the floodgates. Gretzky earned almost $12 million in fees and royalties for the 1993–94 season which, when added to his renegotiated salary of $11.6 million, pushed his annual income to almost $24 million. Corporations pay him because his name and image sell products. His first endorsement income was earned from Finnish-owned Titan hockey sticks. Gretzky's name pushed Titan from number fifteen in the hockey stick world in 1979 to number one by 1989. But the $125,000 per season earned from Titan was small potatoes compared to what could be earned in the vast U.S. market. While with the Edmonton Oilers he had been almost unknown in the United States, despite his astonishing on-ice achievements. "That attitude changed when he moved south," journalist James Deacon writes. "Overnight, hockey became cool in California, and Gretzky became a hot commercial property." His image, his celebrity, sells products. "He is no longer a mere athlete, he is a full-blown celebrity."[68]

Other NHL stars quickly caught on. Mark Messier, who had played with Gretzky on the Oilers' five championship teams in Edmonton, had to win a Stanley Cup in New York before he could become "the object of marketing desire." It was the knowledge of precisely this phenomenon—that "it is not so much what you do as where you do it"[69]—that drove Eric Lindros to refuse to play for the Quebec Nordiques and to hold out for a contract with a franchise in a large U.S. city with a significant corporate presence. The difference in the amount of money to be made by a star of Lindros's calibre is so large that great hockey players will continue to move south, in the way that Canadian resources have done for so long. As *The New York Times* noted in 1991, "A hockey player would give his front teeth—if he hadn't surrendered them already—rather than play in Winnipeg or Quebec."[70] This only serves to add to the pressure pushing Canadian franchises south of the border.

To be able to stay in Canada, NHL franchises need, at a minimum, to be able to generate more revenue than that available from general ticket sales. In the last thirty years luxury suites have become a crucial source of revenue for franchises in other sports. Their use, now common in the NHL, began in earnest with the 1965 construction of Houston's Astrodome, where every single "Skybox" was "snapped up" before the first game was even played.

The luxury suites are usually leased by corporations for whom the annual costs are a tax-deductible business expense because they are used to entertain clients. Spokeswoman Marie Archambault explained why Hydro-Québec was spending $125,000 on a box at Montreal's new Molson Centre: "A corporate box is a tool, like many others, to generate and increase business." These corporate-oriented luxury suites generate significant direct cash flows: $43,500 per year per box at the New Orleans Superdome; $215,000 at Madison Square Garden; as much as $250,000 at Toronto's Skydome. Bill Wirtz's United Centre in Chicago, opened in 1994, has 216 suites leased for between $55,000 and $175,000 each per year, generating in excess of $20 million annually in direct revenue. In addition, the considerably more affluent crowd in attendance in the corporate luxury suites means that in-arena advertising can be sold for more, and that the building itself—or the building's name—can be sold as well. The U.S. brewer Coors, for example, paid $15 million to have the new baseball stadium in Denver called Coors Field.[71] New arenas in Montreal and Vancouver got the names Molson Centre and General Motors Place. The Calgary Saddledome is now called the Canadian Airlines Saddledome. Luxury suites and the revenues they can generate, both directly and indirectly, have been the driving force behind the push for the construction of new arenas in the 1980s and 1990s.

Franchises have increasingly demanded that local governments construct new facilities with luxury suites, wholly or partially at government expense, and have threatened to leave if governments fail to comply. Cities desperate for the big league image, the "world-class" image which the presence of a professional sport franchise is thought to convey, are often prepared to accede to the demands of franchise owners because of the very real threat of relocation.

The shift in population and economic activity from the U.S. Northeast to the booming South and Southwest—coincident with the shift from smokestack industries to the new information technologies and communications industries, which are linked to the media-entertainment industries—coupled with cheaper air travel and the increased prominence of professional sports on television, has made the relocation of professional sport franchises desirable, possible and profitable.

Big league franchises, once considered civic institutions, began to move in earnest in the late 1950s. After seeing the huge economic success of major league baseball's Braves after they moved from Boston to a new stadium and sweetheart lease in Milwaukee in 1953, the Brooklyn Dodgers broke the hearts of their loyal and long-suffering fans by relocating to California, and taking the New York Giants with them in 1958. Nowadays communities with existing franchises are repeatedly held to ransom, forced by profit-seeking owners to contribute more public amenities and money or risk losing what in many cases has become an institutional source of local pride.

A similar process had happened decades earlier in hockey. Prairie and West Coast leagues that had competed with the NHL in the 1920s were forced to fold, as Whitson points out:

> As the culture of mass entertainment developed in North America, and arenas seating over fifteen thousand people were constructed in New York, Boston, Chicago and Detroit, it was soon obvious that the future of hockey as a business lay in these big-city markets. Canadian-based teams playing in smaller cities and markedly smaller arenas could not hope to compete for the best players. Entrepreneurs in Montreal and Toronto built the Forum and Maple Leaf Gardens, while owners in the smaller western cities seized the chance to sell their players to the new American clubs before the players themselves simply jumped.[72]

The dynamic that forced the relocation of professional hockey franchises from Western Canada to Central Canada and the U.S. Northeast in the 1920s is strikingly similar to the dynamic that is now forcing the relocation of NHL franchises from Canada—and especially Western Canada—to the U.S. Sunbelt. The first shift, in the 1920s, led to the tight control of the NHL by the Norris family and their descendants and allies. The second shift, in the post-1988 era, has led to the remaking of the NHL as a business and the relocation of its centre of gravity to the Sunbelt.

The response to the second shift has been similar to the first. A 1927 *Maclean's* article bemoaned the loss of the Pacific Coast League and its replacement with franchises in the U.S. Northeast, saying: "Millionaires back the organizations. Fine ladies in evening gowns with polite gloved palms, applaud the efforts of the skating roughnecks. Hockey has put on a high hat."[73] Then, as now, hockey followed the money, in terms both of geographic location and of the socio-economic status of the targeted audience.

NHL franchises must now take full advantage of the revenue potential that can be spun from the "circuits of promotion" created by the alliance of professional sport with corporate marketing and the media-entertainment industry. Network television, sports stars as celebrities, cross-marketing, endorsements, luxury suites, in-arena advertising, corporate sponsorship, corporate advertising—these integrated circuits of promotion constitute a money-machine for the new business of hockey, the business of hockey as entertainment. The logic of these circuits of promotion forces NHL hockey to follow the money—to the U.S. Sunbelt, to the well-heeled fan, to the corporate centres. It is the size and the demographics of team and league markets, and the myriad of ways in which commodities can be sold to and money can be made from those markets, that matter. It is not just that the more franchises are located in the United States, the more likely is a U.S. network deal, with all the massive revenue possibilities that would generate. It is also that individual franchises located in large cities with a significant corporate presence will be able to generate a great deal more money—from luxury suites, in-arena advertising and concessions, the sale of a wide array of sports merchandise and richer local media contracts. The increased revenue makes possible the purchase of better players who can be marketed as celebrities, thus adding more loops to the circuits of promotion and still more revenues for the franchise and for the players.

Competitive pressures force NHL franchises to plunge into the new Disney-fied world of the NHL. The Vancouver Canucks, now playing in General Motors Place, are an example. "What we're trying to create is a Disney-style atmosphere," said part-owner Arthur Griffiths. Griffiths is now only part-owner because the cost of big league sports is such that he was compelled to bring in Seattle communications billionaire John McGaw—who sold his McGaw Cellular Inc. to AT & T in 1994 for $11 billion—as 65 percent owner of Orca Bay Sport and Entertainment, the corporation that owns the NHL Canucks, the NBA Grizzlies and General Motors Place. The direction they are taking is American, corporate and entertainment-oriented. "Three of the four most important men in Orca Bay . . . are from the United States. They know that sport in the 1990s sells best when it is turned into a show," reporter Neil Campbell writes. These men have moved quickly to a "corporate way of doing business, a stark contrast to the mom-and-pop ways of the pre-Orca Canucks."[74] This is a big-money operation with private ownership of two big league franchises, private ownership of a new arena with luxury suites and a corporate name and a determination to market sport as part of the entertainment business.

This can be done in Vancouver, a large and growing city with a significant corporate presence on the economically booming Pacific Rim. It probably cannot be done in Canadian cities far removed from the new and improved sources of money. Franchises in smaller Canadian cities are left with few alternatives other than to demand more public support, especially but not only for publicly built facilities with expensive luxury suites. Even then, as Whitson argues, "Without both a salary cap and far-reaching revenue-sharing, it is clear that player costs will continue to rise, while the ancillary revenue sources that make hockey an attractive marketing vehicle in populous American regions will be of much less value to the small-market Canadian teams."[75] The tendency has clear consequences for teams such as the Winnipeg Jets.

The consequences for the NHL as a whole are less clear. It may be that NHL hockey is set to become the "hip" sport of the next century, as an April 10, 1994, *New York Times* feature argued. The league could be on the verge of "unprecedented visibility and prosperity" as it increasingly moves into the populous and prosperous cities of the U.S. South and West. Yet this new strategy is fraught with danger. Already the ghosts of NHL owners past have re-emerged, this time in the key figure of LA Kings owner Bruce McNall. After paying Gretzky $15 million to move south and establishing a presence among NHL owners such that they made him chairman of the Board of Governors in 1992—an act that "marked a profound shift in philosophy for the League"—McNall convinced Disney's Eisner and Blockbuster Entertainment Chief Huizenga "to bankroll the glitziest expansion teams in League history, the Anaheim Mighty Ducks and the Florida Panthers."[76] The result is the new, marketing-driven, entertainment-inspired, Southern-based future of the NHL—"the greatest thing that's ever happened to hockey," said Gretzky, himself a relentless promoter of NHL hockey in the United States. As McNall put it: "This is huge. The magnitude—I don't think most people in sports realize how big this is. Even me, I'm not sure I understand. Disney and Blockbuster have made a commitment to hockey. You have two of the greatest companies in American history involved in hockey. We have their clout, their marketing abilities and their creativity. It's huge."[77]

The multimillionaire owner of the aptly named McNall Sports and Entertainment, composed of sixty-seven companies, owned the LA Kings, a share of the Toronto Argonauts, a stable of racehorses, seven homes, nine cars and a fortune in rare coins. He was "widely hailed as the smartest, most glamorous mogul in sports." Hollywood stars were his friends and his fans. "He was proof of the American dream."[78]

But the whole thing was a façade, a lie. In December 1994—after resigning as chairman of the NHL Board of Governors in April 1994, when it was revealed that a federal grand jury was investigating his finances, and after two of his McNall Sports and Entertainment associates had been charged with related criminal offences—McNall pleaded guilty to bank fraud, wire fraud and conspiracy and admitted to tricking investors out of almost $250 million. By that time a total of six of his associates had entered similar guilty pleas. In the end, McNall's wealth was a sham—all glitter and glitz, no substance.

"None of us knew exactly what was real," admitted McNall Sports and Entertainment vice-president Joanna Orehek, who might just as easily have been talking about the Norris interests or Alan Eagleson. On the day after McNall's guilty plea, *Los Angeles Times* hockey columnist Helene Elliott wrote: "We got taken in. Played for suckers. Hoodwinked. All of us. NHL executives, fans and reporters, too. Bruce McNall fooled us, but we were willing accomplices. . . . We thought he was the best thing to happen to hockey since frozen pucks."[79]

The rise and fall of Bruce McNall may be a metaphor for the new marketing-driven, image-oriented world of the NHL. The sleek new corporate-controlled, big-money world of the NHL may well be, like McNall, an over-inflated bubble that will burst. In the meantime, the NHL is rapidly moving away from its roots. When a fan in Los Angeles complained to McNall that the average person could no longer afford a ticket to see a game, McNall replied, "Basically, you're right. It is a business and the people who can't afford it aren't going to go to games. Unfortunately, that's the nature of the business."[80]

The business of professional sport has been dramatically transformed by the wealth generated from television. The role of the fans, the role of the average working people who attend games and support their teams for the sheer joy of the sport, is rapidly becoming a thing of the past. As Tom Fennell and D'Arcy Jennish put it, "The sports fan, who was once the foundation of every successful franchise, has been pushed aside by corporate interests and television, becoming a bit player on a large stage."[81]

Similarly, the future of NHL hockey in smaller Canadian cities where the game has long-established roots and meaning and is part of a national tradition is also being pushed aside. Al Morgani, writing in *The Hockey News*, put it like this: "Hey Canada, this is going to hurt, but you might as well admit the obvious: you've lost control of your game.... The fact of the matter is the sport has gotten too big for you. Small markets, thin wallets and lack of vision don't cut it anymore. The new order is marketing, marketing, marketing—and it doesn't make much sense to sell the game in the mini-markets north of the border. .... The rules of hockey expansion have become like the three rules of real estate: location, location, location. And Canada just is the wrong location."[82]

Bigger profits are waiting to be made in the larger markets south of the Canada–U.S. border; the business of NHL hockey is about bigger profits. Smaller Canadian cities, no matter how dedicated their fans, are therefore at risk, and the struggle over the future of the Winnipeg Jets provides a prime example of this dilemma.

3. On the Margins: Pro Hockey in Winnipeg

Dale Cummings

The great Jets/arena private-sector/public-sector battle of the 1990s had been in the making for decades. When the Winnipeg Stadium was built in the early 1950s the project involved the creation of a non-profit company, the Winnipeg Enterprises Corporation (Enterprises), to construct and manage a stadium of just over 10,000 seats, plus government assistance in the form of a city guarantee of a $500,000 loan made by the Winnipeg-based insurance company Great-West Life, plus the donation by the city of the land and an exemption by the city from property taxes.[1]

Then, as later, the symbolism of the new stadium was especially significant. A newspaper editorial lamented the loss in recent years of "the faith and vision of the pioneers" who "thought big, talked big and did big things," and offered up the hope that with the construction of the new stadium "the city and its people are again on the march, that they are determined to be progressive, that they are intent on catching a vision of what the future can bring." The association of the stadium with "vision" and "progress," and with the desire to be "big time," was an expression of the boosterist mentality that was, and still is, a part of professional sport.[2]

In December 1953 Enterprises announced plans to build a new arena that would be "second to none in Canada." The arena was financed with a $2 million loan from the city, with that loan later converted to an outright grant. Talk of admission to the NHL accompanied the plans for the arena.[3]

Even then the building of the stadium and the arena did not come without opposition. A money bylaw to secure stadium financing by the city was twice defeated, and at least two other stadium proposals proved unable to secure financing. In 1954 a group of ten members of the Winnipeg Chamber of Commerce argued that risky undertakings such as the arena should be undertaken only by the private sector, not by government. "It is not in the public interest to provide privileged groups with services by the city and other governments at the expense of the taxpayers." This meant no government loans or loan guarantees, and no exemptions from property taxes. Their principal concern was the impact of such measures on property taxes and the city's credit rating, but they also expressed the case that would become the dominant grounds for opposition in the 1970s and again in the 1990s: "There are other and much more essential projects badly needed in the city."[4]

For their part, the businessmen who spearheaded the effort to build the stadium and arena were expressing a new optimism about Winnipeg's future and breaking out of the conservative orthodoxy that had held the province in its grip for three decades. The enthusiasm they inspired was expressed in press accounts of the day. "Winnipeg now has one of the finest, if not the finest, winter sports auditorium on the continent," one said. Winnipeg can now "feel big league. . . . Our town is verily on the sports map." And "the arena is almost too good to be true."[5] Such hyperbole would be used again in the 1990s in an attempt to get a new arena built, but in the 1950s it reflected the more positive mood of the times, a mood underpinned by the beginnings of the long, postwar economic boom.

From the Warriors to the Jets: Pro Hockey in Town

In 1955–56 the Winnipeg Warriors played their first season in the newly constructed Winnipeg Arena. The franchise, part of the high-calibre Western Professional Hockey League, was owned by mining entrepreneur J.D. Perrin Sr. and his son John Jr., the general manager. The league was anxious to have a Winnipeg entry because the Winnipeg Arena was, until the late 1960s, "the best facility in any Canadian city west of Toronto," according to sports historian Morris Mott.[6]

The Warriors were exceptionally successful in their inaugural season, winning the league championship, drawing close to six thousand fans per game, and earning a profit "of perhaps as much as $80,000." Mott argues, "It is hard to imagine a more profitable minor pro franchise than the Winnipeg Warriors in 1955–56."

It didn't last. The Warriors lost money almost every season thereafter, including their disastrous last campaign in 1960–61. According to Mott, "The last four home games attracted hardly anyone . . . and average attendance for the season was about 2000, less than half the number required to break even." Total losses for the Warriors' six seasons were about $200,000.

Some of the same problems that contributed to the Warriors' financial decline would later plague the Winnipeg Jets. For one thing, the Warriors were never able to work out a satisfactory arrangement with an NHL club for good-quality players, and the resulting deterioration in play hurt attendance. Their rental arrangement with Winnipeg Enterprises was the worst of any club in the league, and the subject of frequent complaints by John Perrin. The Warriors paid 20 percent of gross revenues from ticket sales, and Enterprises took *all* the revenue from parking and concessions. The directors of Enterprises insisted this was the best deal they could offer because they were still paying down the $2 million debt incurred to build the arena.

Most importantly, the emergence of televised NHL games cut deeply into attendance. Starting in the Warriors' second year, 1956–57, Winnipeggers got access to CBC-Television's broadcast of live NHL games on *Hockey Night in Canada*, and now "you couldn't run a game on Saturday night." The opportunity to see the fabled stars of the NHL, live on TV, wreaked havoc with Warriors' attendance.

Television had a similar impact on other minor pro hockey franchises. Many Canadian minor league teams relocated to U.S. cities to gain access to a fan base not yet exposed to televised NHL games. This was a major contributor to the folding of the Eastern Professional Hockey League which had teams in Kingston, Ottawa–Hull, Sudbury and Sault-Ste. Marie, and its re-emergence in the United States in the mid-1960s as the Central Pro League with teams in St. Louis, Omaha, St. Paul, Kansas City and Memphis. Television had the same Americanizing impact on the Western Professional Hockey League. The New Westminster franchise moved to Portland in 1960, the Victoria franchise went to Los Angeles in 1961 and the Calgary and Edmonton teams folded in 1963. "In short, television was a major cause of the transformation of the Western League of the mid-50s, which was a Canadian league with one U.S. city (Seattle), into the Western League of the mid-1960s, which was a U.S. league with two Canadian cities (Vancouver and Victoria)." This relocation of minor pro franchises to U.S. cities was a forerunner of what would happen to Canadian-based NHL franchises in the early 1990s.

As early as 1958 Enterprises was incurring losses, and that year it had to ask city council for an additional $500,000 loan.[7] After the Warriors folded in the summer of 1961, Enterprises had increasing difficulty paying its bills for an arena with no primary tenant. Continued losses led to a 1966 agreement by which the city turned the remaining $2.4 million that Enterprises owed to it into an outright grant. By the 1960s then, both the arena and pro hockey in Winnipeg had shown themselves to be financial losers.

A decade later, in 1972, the Winnipeg Jets began play in the newly formed World Hockey Association (WHA). The team's founder Ben Hatskin had owned the Junior A Winnipeg Jets of the Western Canadian Hockey League. He had played for the Winnipeg Blue Bombers from 1936 to 1942, helping them to two Grey Cup victories, and prior to that had played football at the University of Oklahoma where he was one of the first Canadians offered a U.S. football scholarship.

His subsequent business career was varied. He had been a nightclub operator, a racehorse owner, a jukebox distributor, a manufacturer, and in 1972 he listed himself as president of eight different companies. As *Free Press* reporter Reyn Davis put it at the time of Hatskin's death, "He had a past, and business escapades and associates he would prefer to forget."[8] But he was a risk-taker and he was prepared to take a risk on establishing a new franchise in a new league.

Gary Davidson, founder of the new WHA, believed that the NHL had grown fat. The league, Davidson said, "had not faced any competition and was spoiled. It had only scratched the surface of potential television. . . . It had only begun to . . . put franchises in major population areas. . . . NHL players were the lowest paid in sports, averaging only about $25,000 a season. Some superstars were making less than $50,000. The players were getting only about a fifth of the operating monies. Obviously, they were ripe for the picking."[9] Hatskin proved a key man in getting the new league off the ground. Not only did he have money and drive, but in June 1972 he was also able to sign Bobby Hull, the great Chicago Black Hawk left-winger, for a $1 million bonus—paid for by the league and the other WHA teams—plus more than $1 million in future annual salaries and benefits. The signing of Hull was the single most important step in securing the WHA as a viable competitor to the NHL.

Thousands of Winnipeg fans cheered wildly on June 22, 1972 as Hull held aloft a giant reproduction of the $1 million cheque at Winnipeg's famous Portage and Main intersection. The story has it that even as the crowd was cheering, Hull sent his agent, Harvey Wineberg, to the main branch of the Toronto-Dominion Bank at Portage and Main to confirm that Hatskin had enough money in the bank to cover the huge cheque. Minutes later Wineberg emerged and signalled to Hull "from the top steps of the bank and Hull proceeded to sign the Winnipeg portion of the contract."[10]

Hull's debut as a Winnipeg Jet was delayed for fifteen games while the WHA and the NHL fought in court about whether NHL players were bound to their clubs by the reserve clause. At one point Hatskin was fighting thirteen separate legal suits. "They sue me and I sue them. Then I sue them and they sue me back. Someone's up one suit but I'm not sure who it is." In the end Hatskin and the WHA won in the courts, and Hull took to the ice as a Winnipeg Jet. His impact was dramatic: 51 goals scored; winner of the League's first Most Valuable Player award. Fans flocked to WHA rinks to see the Golden Jet. "Wherever Hull went, the gate soared. 'I figure Bobby meant at least 1,500 tickets for each game,' said Hatskin."[11]

This great start notwithstanding, Hatskin was one of the WHA owners who, as early as April 1973—the end of the Jets' first season—was already meeting with NHL representatives to discuss a merger between the two leagues. Hatskin had always had his eye on the NHL. Establishing a franchise in a rival league was a potential way in the NHL door that would otherwise be closed to Winnipeg. But the NHL was not interested in a new Winnipeg franchise. Indeed, NHL owners made it clear in 1973 that they were opposed to a merger because they did not want Winnipeg, Edmonton or Quebec City in their league.

Even the WHA wasn't overly excited about Winnipeg's place in the new league. As Davidson put it in 1974, "Bobby Hull may be wasted in Winnipeg," which is "not a big or a rich city." Hatskin, Davidson noted, was unhappy with the lease for the old building. As a result the WHA founder thought the Winnipeg owner "could succumb to the offers he's had for his franchise." Davidson speculated wistfully on the dramatic impact Hull would have if he were playing in one of the large U.S. cities.[12]

Thus, from the beginning the continued presence of the Jets in Winnipeg was questionable. The original merger talks had collapsed but the stage was set. How long would it be before the WHA and the NHL would merge? Would the merger, when it happened, include the Jets? Would the Jets still be a Winnipeg-based franchise by that time? As would soon become apparent, the Jets would have a struggle from the start just to stay afloat financially.

The First "Save the Jets" Campaign

The Jets under Hatskin and co-owner Saul Simkin, a lawyer who founded a contracting company that became a major Winnipeg development firm, lost money in each of their first two years. By the second year rumours abounded that the Jets would be sold away from Winnipeg. A local group spearheaded by Lieutenant-Governor Jack McKeag, Inter-City Gas president Bob Graham and Great-West Life vice-president Jim Burns emerged to try to keep the team in the city. They devised a community ownership scheme similar to that of the Winnipeg Blue Bombers.

The community ownership route was taken because of a reluctance by Winnipeg's business elite to risk money on professional sports franchises. Pointing out that the business community had been less than enthusiastic supporters of the Jets, Hatskin observed, "For a city the size of Winnipeg the private way is tough. Private business can't stand quarter million dollar losses very long."[13] In early 1974 the new community owners agreed to purchase the team for $2.3 million with a $500,000 down payment. The deal required that $900,000 be raised immediately—the down payment plus $400,000 for operating expenses to start the 1974–75 season.

A task force recommended that the city and province be asked for interest-free loans of $300,000 each, with the remaining $300,000 to be raised in the business community. The city agreed to lend $300,000, but the province said no. Premier Ed Schreyer had initially indicated support but balked when the deal required the province and city each to pick up one-third of the Jets' losses. The media lambasted Schreyer and his NDP government, using words like "fraud," "jackasses" and "idiot" and condemning the "socialists."[14] The irony was not lost on business columnist Harry Mardon who noted: "What stuns me is that some of the businessmen associated with the proposed purchase of the Jets team take the position they do in asking for government financial assistance. . . . several of them have been very vehement in speeches as well as in private conversation about the need for government at all levels to cut back on spending programs."[15] The same irony would re-emerge two decades later.

In the wake of the province's rejection and a tepid response from business, the task force hesitantly recommended making a pitch to the public. Newspaper ads elicited over 3200 responses, all but nine supportive, and a "Save the Jets" Campaign was duly launched. Led by radio station CJOB's open-line host Peter Warren and assisted by Jets' players and local celebrities, the campaign took pledges from the public while the Winnipeg Jets Booster Club "swarmed over the city knocking on doors."[16] The response was dramatic—over $600,000 was raised. The community, ordinary Winnipeggers, had risen to the occasion.

The Jets were saved, for the moment. But the club's financial problems had not changed and a year later, in spring 1975, a campaign to expand the Winnipeg Arena by 5000 seats was launched. The "edifice without equal in the nation" was now deemed too small for a struggling WHA franchise. The Jets had lost money again in 1974–75 while fans were being turned away at the door. Without a costly arena expansion the team could not last. *Tribune* columnist Vic Grant was emphatic: "Neither the League nor the Jets can survive in Winnipeg with 10,000 seats. We need—must have—5000 more seats minimum."[17]

Community opposition emerged. Public funds, the opponents argued, should not be spent on a $7.8 million arena expansion when there were more pressing needs in the community. Led by city councillor Bob Bockstael and university professor Carl Ridd, the opponents argued that "housing and living conditions" should be improved first and that rather than build ever bigger arenas to meet the needs of the increasingly "unreal world of professional sport," governments should be spending more money on "smaller local sports facilities," swimming pools and community centres, municipal services and sewer lines.[18]

The supporters of an arena expansion insisted that without it the Jets would be gone and the city's future imperilled. The Jets attract business and tourists, Mayor Stephen Juba insisted. An NHL franchise was coming, the supporters argued: "The extra seats are needed to put Winnipeg in the big time." The symbolic importance of professional sport, the belief that it put a city "in the big leagues" and "on the map" played as important a role in the 1970s as it had in the 1950s, and would again in the 1990s. Nevertheless, at a city council meeting on March 24, 1976, with the gallery nearly filled, councillors voted to reject the arena expansion proposal.[19]

But the deal was far from dead. The March 24, 1976 vote was but one battle in what would become a protracted war of attrition that would grind on for another two and one-half years. At a luncheon reception two months later for the championship Jets—winners of the WHA's Avco Cup in 1975–76—Mayor Juba talked to the press about "hush-hush negotiations" for a new arena. It was soon confirmed by Jim Burns, president of Great-West Life (GWL) and vice-president of the Jets, that his company was considering the construction of a new arena as part of a massive housing-commercial-office redevelopment of the CNR's East Yards in downtown Winnipeg—part of what is now called "the Forks," an area north of the confluence of the Red and Assiniboine Rivers, and just east of the corner of Portage and Main. The 1976 GWL-Forks proposal would cost about $15 million. GWL would put up $3 million with the remaining 80 percent to be borrowed by the city. The city would also have to make up, presumably on the property tax, an annual shortfall in the arena's operations which GWL estimated at just under $1 million.

The Great-West Life proposal was primarily a property development deal. The company would lease the land for $1 per year and build the arena, "providing a development agreement is reached on the rest of the redevelopment project involving, as a minimum, land use, zoning, street and road systems, and parkland areas."[20] Again, the proposal was a harbinger of future schemes: the ideas of arenas to be built at the Forks, and arenas as fronts for property development plans, would come to the fore again in the 1990s.

A second arena proposal emerged in late 1976, this one promoted by Winnipeg businessman Al Golden, who later became a city councillor. His 20,000 seat arena would be located next to the Assiniboia Downs race track just beyond the city's western limits and would cost $20 million, with almost all of the money to be raised by selling "life memberships" to individual members of the public. Each membership would sell for between $400 and $2500. Those with life memberships would get first chance to buy a ticket for their reserved seat for any event; if they did not exercise the right, a ticket for the seat would be sold to the public. The arena would cost the public sector nothing.[21] This deal, too, met with considerable opposition. Enterprises expressed concern that cost overruns and operating losses would be borne by the city. "It's going to end up in the City's lap, you can bet your sweet life, if it loses money," said councillor and Enterprises' chairman Jim Ernst. Council was also concerned about the "private club" character of Golden's financing scheme. Those able to afford "life memberships" would get preferential treatment for all events, in perpetuity, at the expense of the broad public.[22]

Meanwhile the Jets, despite doing exceptionally well on the ice, continued to struggle financially. In January 1976 their community-based owners announced they were eight months behind in payments to Hatskin and Simkin. In 1976–77 the Jets again incurred a loss.[23] And the league, too, was struggling. In November 1976, Jets' superstar Bobby Hull said publicly that the WHA was unable to attract high-quality young players, had become a second-rate league and was on its death bed, about to fold in the absence of a merger with the NHL. Hatskin, now president of the WHA, acknowledged, "everyone's concerned, damn good and concerned."[24] A year later *Sports Illustrated* reported: "In the past twelve months four WHA teams have folded, and the League has lost some $10 million."[25]

The dismal financial situation of the Jets and the WHA created a quandary for city council. The Jets continued to insist that to improve their revenues they needed an expanded arena. Yet this alone would not necessarily solve the problem—the league and/or the Jets could collapse even *with* an expanded arena. Council responded with a decision that offered both some hope for the Jets and some protection against the outside forces beyond city council's control. By a razor-thin 23-22 vote on January 21, 1977, the council committed itself in principle to a major league arena—so long as Winnipeg was guaranteed a franchise in a financially sound major hockey league. The intent was twofold: to protect council against the possibility of the WHA and the Jets folding after the city had incurred the capital cost of expanding the arena or building a new one; and to improve the city's chances of winning an NHL franchise.

On August 9, 1977, the NHL rejected the desperately needed NHL-WHA merger, leaving the Jets to play at least one more season in the struggling WHA. By the start of the 1977–78 season the money made available to the Jets in 1974 had been exhausted by accumulated losses. Council's January 21 decision to do nothing about the arena until the city got an NHL franchise was not good enough for the Jets' owners who argued that they needed more revenue now. In late November Jets' president Jack McKeag warned councillors that a new arena had to be built or the Jets would be gone.

The Opposition and the Hockey Lobby: "Blowing into a Windmill"

When the matter returned to city council on December 21, again the opponents were vocal. Indeed, for the first time opponents of a new or expanded arena outnumbered proponents in the packed gallery of city hall.[26] Nevertheless, city council committed itself to a 16,000 seat arena for the Jets by September 1980, conditional only upon the Jets being able to refinance their operations by January 15, 1978. Opposition at the December 21 council meeting was led again by Councillor Bob Bockstael and Carl Ridd, who had become familiar fixtures in what was by then a lengthy battle over the arena issue. Although there seems to have been considerable public support for their position, they were being worn down by the much greater political power of those who demanded a bigger arena. Bockstael acknowledged that fighting this issue for such a long time—arena expansion had been first rejected by council two and one-half years earlier—was "like trying to blow into a windmill. . . . I'm being worn down, I don't mind telling you. I know that this attempt is going to come and keep coming until we finally give in to it."[27]

Ridd and Bockstael were unlikely leaders of the opposition to a new or expanded arena. Ridd, a professor of religious studies at the University of Winnipeg, had in the 1950s been known as "King Carl"—"the undisputed monarch of Manitoba basketball" as he is described in the Manitoba Sports Hall of Fame. He led the Winnipeg Senior Mens league in scoring six times, was offered a contract with the NBA's Milwaukee Bucks in 1952 and won "every honour the game has to offer" during a brilliant fourteen-year career in Winnipeg. Subsequently elected to the Canadian Basketball Hall of Fame as well as the Manitoba Sports Hall of Fame, he remained an enthusiastic supporter of local sports. Bockstael, a future Liberal MP, was a small contractor, a councillor for Tache ward in St. Boniface and a member of the powerful Independent Citizens Election Committee. The ICEC, the local business establishment's civic electoral vehicle, had its origins in the Citizens Committee of 1000 which opposed the 1919 Winnipeg General Strike. Ridd operated from outside city council, Bockstael from within.

From the beginning Ridd emphasized that his concerns were linked to the rapidly changing character of professional sport. He referred to "million-aire owners and overpaid athletes" ruining sports. It was a form of "madness," a "bubble about to burst," he said.[28] A November 1976 *Sports Illustrated* article on the NHL reported that in the past ten years NHL player salaries had risen by about 533 percent and ticket prices had more than doubled. At least three expansion teams were not making payments on their expansion fees and attendance was falling. "This season the decline is alarming," NHL President Clarence Campbell was reported as saying.[29]

Ridd linked these changes in professional sport to broader economic forces. The long, postwar economic boom was over, he emphasized. There was no longer enough money to finance everything. People had to learn to live more simply and he himself "would choose smaller, local sports facilities and the hiring of coaches and coordinators, over the building of these giant showpiece additions." It was a matter of priorities, he said. "With one-third of our city at the poverty line or below it," there were many more pressing needs to be met.[30]

In the early going the media, especially reporters on the sports beat, ridiculed Ridd. Expressing his contempt for "small-time thinkers," sports columnist Jack Matheson intoned, "The last thing we need here is a village mentality."[31] In a column written in a sneering and condescending fashion— it referred to the Hall of Famer as a man who "used to be a fair to middling dribbler on a basketball court"—Vic Grant depicted Ridd's reasoned objections as consisting of his "trotting" down to City Hall "with his soapbox" and being "a bit of a bore" on the whole issue. Grant also misrepresented Ridd's position on the issue. When Ridd lodged an official complaint the *Tribune*'s ombudsman ruled that Grant "was not fair to the Professor," adding: "Mr. Grant would have done well to have read Professor Ridd's brief before writing his column. . . . The incident points up anew how essential it is for columnists to get their facts straight before publishing."[32]

The Ridd-Bockstael opposition came from the middle of the ideological spectrum. Ridd, who would later move to the left as a result of his involvement in Central American issues, was at the time an ideological liberal. He had many personal friends who were members of the Winnipeg establishment; he admitted to having voted Liberal, Conservative and NDP in recent elections; and in a letter to Mayor Bob Steen he acknowledged that "its knee-jerk developmentalist bias apart, I am probably philosophically close to an 'ICEC' position myself." Ridd's position on the issue was moderate and became more so as the struggle progressed. From the beginning he had argued that public funds for a new or expanded arena would be acceptable so long as the amounts were not excessive. By 1977–78 he was acknowledging that a new arena might well be appropriate, but only if the Jets were ensured an NHL franchise.[33] He was particularly opposed to a new or expanded arena so long as the Jets remained part of the financially collapsing WHA. The risk of being stuck with a large debt-load and no big league franchise was too great, he argued.

Ridd and Bockstael also insisted that the whole matter of public funding for professional sport was of sufficient importance that it deserved to be debated, openly and publicly, in a rational rather than a purely emotional manner. The issue, Ridd insisted, should not simply be "steamrollered."[34]

The Ridd–Bockstael side, though vocal and visible, was not well organized. They operated largely as individuals, primarily by means of presentations at council meetings, letters to the editor and, in Ridd's case, via a constant barrage of letters and phone calls to politicians. As time passed and the issue became more and more frustrating Ridd's letters took on an ever-angrier tone. A letter to Councillor Gary Filmon in January 1978 was bitter and scathing, referring to councillor and Enterprises' chairman Jim Ernst as an "incompetent hustler." In notes for a September 1978 meeting with Councillor Bill Norrie Ridd again attacked Ernst and said that his letters to the editor a week earlier "have brought a ton of response—all positive. I could run against you on this issue and beat you."[35]

If Bockstael spent two and a half years "trying to blow into a windmill," the pro-arena forces propelling that machinery were relentless. On the public level their approach was to make a "powerful appeal to our patriotism and civic pride," facilitated by "clamorous promotion through the sports media." At city hall, "blatant manoeuvring" and "eleventh hour tactics" were organized by the ICEC caucus, at the heart of which was a "vigorous hockey lobby."[36] The ICEC, with its city council majority, dominated civic appointments. All six councillors on Enterprises' board and both councillors on the Jets board were ICEC members. Ridd came to refer to the whole issue as the ICE(C) Folly.

But the ICEC took its instructions from outside caucus. Describing the simple mechanics of "the interlocking relationships," Ridd pointed out: "The 'pro' forces chose, in general, to be silent. But their movements declared everything. Councillors Ernst, Filmon, Ducharme (on the Jets' board), Angus and O'Shaugnessey kept running over to Messrs. McKeag [past-president of the Jets and former lieutenant-governor of Manitoba] and Graham [president of the Jets] in the civic gallery for instructions. The real centre of the Chamber was not the Mayor's Chair, but Mr. McKeag's."[37] McKeag, former president of McKeag-Harris Realty, one of the city's largest landowners, was also a former chairman of the ICEC. Graham was president of Inter-City Gas, which was owned by Montreal's Power Corporation, which also owned Great-West Life and Investors. Winnipeg's finance-dominated business establishment was a closely knit and powerful group.[38] In the 1990s the interlocking relationships of the 1970s would re-emerge in familiar form. Filmon and Ernst would again be major players in the Jets/arena conflict as provincial premier and cabinet minister respectively, while Angus and O'Shaugnessey would be leading pro-Jets/arena voices on city council.

Despite the power of the local establishment and its control of the ICEC caucus, and despite the booster mentality of the media in the early going of the conflict, some media, especially the *Winnipeg Tribune*, gradually began to shift. On October 21, 1976, the *Tribune* ran an editorial headlined "City Hall Needs Sense of Priorities," saying council was characterized by "lack of foresight, impaired hindsight, and perhaps most of all, no leadership." Reporter Grant, chastised by the *Tribune*'s ombudsman in January 1976 for not getting his facts straight, and referred to shortly after in a letter to the editor as "one more of the parasitic journalistic barnacles which habitually attach themselves to the bottom of sport," wrote a column two months later extolling Bockstael's courage and convictions because "the man took a lot of flak. . . . He was berated, hissed and booed." Bockstael, Grant said, "used his head at a time when most of us backing expansion were using our hearts . . . . I realize now how simple my argument was. Bockstael was right when he kept saying there are more important things to spend money on."[39] Two years later Grant again wrote, "Yes, a new arena would be nice. . . . But how does one rationalize a $20 million arena when there are other, more important day to day necessities that the city has to go without because of a general lack of finances?"[40] Unfortunately, later on in the 1990s Grant would revert to his original "simple argument," advanced aggressively and derisively in his role as CJOB radio sports-line host.

From Creative Financing to 8 Hockey Ventures

In response to the council's December 21, 1977 condition about the Jets successfully refinancing the club's operations, the team's owners floated a creative financing scheme. The plan was to establish a limited company, to which player contracts would be sold and which would then serve as a tax shelter for investors. "One of our hidden assets is our tax loss," said Jets' chairman Bob Graham, who estimated that $3 million could be raised "from individuals and companies interested in the Jets as an instant tax-shelter and a future profit-maker." The deal was to involve two "levels" of investor— one for the general public, to be called General Partners; the other for "those who can afford to invest a bundle, whether they be corporate investors or individuals who have the ways and means." The intention was to raise as much as $2.8 million by April 1, 1978. Hatskin and Simkin agreed to leave in the $1.2 million still owed them by the Jets' owners, turning it into equity, in return for 50 percent control. This left $1.6 million to be raised by selling partnership shares to Winnipeg businesses.[41]

City council approved the scheme on January 18, 1978 despite strenuous objections from some councillors who complained that "the proposal was . . . poorly drafted and 'loop-infested.'" These councillors "pointed to at least three errors and omissions in the proposal . . . including a $350,000 difference in the amount of money needed from the public to make the plan operative."[42] The plan had not yet received tax approval from Revenue Canada or approval from the Manitoba Securities Commission. The sloppiness of this 1978 refinancing proposal and the absence of the necessary approvals—which did not stop council from supporting the plan—would become regular features of the various business proposals advanced during the struggle over the Jets/arena issue in the 1990s. So too would the reluctance of most Winnipeg businesspeople to risk their own money on the Jets.

The 1978 refinancing scheme failed. The private-sector money was not there. When the Securities Commission held up approval pending further information on the state of the Jets' finances, the application was withdrawn. The Jets' players were paid in mid-February 1978 and an arrangement was made with Enterprises to defer rent payments until season's end, but the club's bank account was empty. According to a *Free Press* report that month, the Jets "faced the prospect of asking the players to perform without pay for the remainder of the season or fold."[43] The Jets were effectively bankrupt.

In February 1978 a group of eight businessmen came to the rescue, purchasing the contracts of the Jets' players. The group, called 8 Hockey Ventures Inc., was headed by Michael Gobuty, owner of Victoria Leather which manufactured leather outerwear. The other seven were: Barry and Marvin Shenkarow of Sterling Cloak, also a clothing manufacturer; Harvey

Secter, owner of Ricki's, a retail clothing chain; Bob Graham, president of Inter-City Gas; John Shanski of Sprague Distributors, a lumber products firm; Dr. Gerry Wilson, who was largely responsible for bringing to Winnipeg the Jets' great Swedish players; and Jets' superstar Bobby Hull. 8 Hockey Ventures purchased the Jets' player contracts for $600,000 to $700,000, with each of the eight contributing financially and apparently equally to the purchase of the team.[44] Graham stayed on as chairman; Gobuty served as president. Barry Shenkarow was initially assistant secretary and legal counsel.

The 8 Hockey Ventures group purchased the Jets only when it had become apparent that businesspeople who were part of the old Winnipeg establishment would not step in. Graham had invited eighty of Winnipeg's "most successful and influential businessmen" to a meeting February 16, 1978 at Great-West Life to ask them to purchase forty tax-sheltered limited partnerships in the Jets costing $10,000 each in order to raise the $400,000 needed to get the team through the balance of the season. The money was not forthcoming. "Four offers came forward while the Jets executive came up with five. But $90,000 wouldn't even meet the first payroll, due tomorrow," the *Free Press* noted on February 27.[45]

Gobuty and Shenkarow, present at the meeting and seeing that the refinancing scheme would not fly, met the next morning in Gobuty's office; later that week they submitted their offer which was accepted. The Jets were once again a privately owned team, and 8 Hockey Ventures now owned a franchise that was effectively bankrupt and a proven money-loser in a league on the verge of collapse. Prospects of Winnipeg getting an NHL franchise were dim. In March New York sports writer Stan Fischler assessed the possibilities: "Its rink isn't big enough; it hasn't got the money to fill it if it was; and it's a pass-the-hat town populated by nickle-and-dimers."[46] Two months later, in April 1978, a proposed NHL-WHA merger was rejected a second time and the Jets continued to play in an arena with a 10,077 seating capacity—too small to generate the revenue needed even to reach the break-even point.

To make matters worse, it was announced in March that the Jets would lose their brilliant Swedish stars, Anders Hedberg and Ulf Nilsson, both huge fan favourites, to the New York Rangers for the 1978–79 season. The Rangers could afford to pay their exorbitant salaries. As Gobuty remarked: "Most of the teams are owned by large corporations which can use the hockey team as a tax loss and for advertising purposes."[47] Even the *Free Press* saw the forces that lurked behind the loss of Hedberg and Nilsson, and the dangers that these forces posed for small cities like Winnipeg. Sports editor Hal Sigurdson remarked: "The Rangers are merely one small tentacle in the corporate structure of an international conglomerate known as Gulf and Western Industries. By the time Gulf and Western's tax accountants are through, any losses sustained by the Rangers aren't going to make a particle of difference to the corporate bottom line. . . . The disease is corporate ownership—ownership which because of tax write-offs and juggling of assets permits payment of salaries beyond the means of teams owned by private groups or individuals."[48] Still, despite the obstacles, Gobuty and his group set about immediately to secure a franchise in the NHL and to get an arena with expanded seating capacity.

In April 1978, an ad hoc Committee of Council recommended that the city build a new $20 million arena at the CNR East Yards, the Forks site, on condition that the Jets secure an NHL franchise and that the federal and provincial governments contribute $5 million and $2 million respectively to the new arena. Gobuty and Shenkarow were less than pleased with this proposal. They told council they preferred an immediate, 5000 seat arena expansion: "We want more seats. We want them cheap and we want them now." Gobuty added, "If you sell us the arena for a dollar, we will do the expansion."[49]

On August 18, city council decided by a 12 to 11 vote to add 5000 more seats to the existing arena, but only on condition that the Jets' owners give personal guarantees of at least $650,000 in the event the team defaulted on lease payments. The owners resisted and were supported by Councillor Ernst who remarked, "I find it abhorrent. . . . These people have bailed out a bankrupt hockey team. . . . This rider is a slap in the face to them."[50]

Council was badly split on the issue but in the end gave in. The Jets would fold at season's end otherwise, the owners insisted. At a September 20 meeting city council voted 23–6 in favour of a $3.5 million, 5000 seat expansion of the existing arena, with no conditions attached. Said the *Tribune*, optimistically and as it turned out profoundly mistakenly: "Wednesday's vote to proceed with the expansion appears likely to put to rest an issue which has raged at city hall for the past three years."[51]

In January 1979 the Jets agreed to an eight-year lease based on the proposed expansion to the existing arena. Gobuty remarked that the club "has no complaints whatsoever" with the terms of the lease and is "looking forward to many, many more years in the Winnipeg Arena."[52] Their delight would not last.

The Conflict with Winnipeg Enterprises

In March 1979 the NHL finally agreed to a merger with the WHA, largely to hold down soaring player salaries, but it refused entry to Winnipeg, Edmonton and Quebec City. The NHL did not want new franchises in small Northern cities. Fans in all three centres, following Winnipeg's lead, immediately protested. A boycott was launched against Molson, owners of the Montreal Canadiens, which had voted against expansion. Bullet holes were found in the glass doors of Molson's Winnipeg brewery; a bomb threat was issued in Quebec City. A huge banner was hung in the Winnipeg Arena: "Molsons Don't Want Us: We Don't Want Molsons."

The NHL backed down. The vote was reversed and finally Winnipeg, Edmonton and Quebec City were admitted to the NHL. Once again, Winnipeg fans had come to the rescue of their Jets. Winnipeg's acceptance as an NHL franchise had not come a moment too soon. Attendance had been way down in 1978–79, partly because of the deteriorating quality of the team's play with the loss of Hedberg and Nilsson and partly because, as *Tribune* sports editor Matheson put it, "They're playing in a house league now."[53]

Gobuty had worked tirelessly to secure an NHL franchise for the city but success brought new costs, including a $6 million NHL entry fee. The result was an attempt by 8 Hockey Ventures to renegotiate the terms of its lease to increase revenue—a mere eighteen months after Gobuty had said the lease left them with "no complaints whatever." The Jets wanted full control of concessions and the right to all advertising revenue in the building, rather than the 50 percent set out in the lease. If such changes were not forthcoming, 8 Hockey Ventures threatened to sue Enterprises for $424,000 to cover losses incurred when the arena upper decks had to be closed from October to mid-December 1979. If the lease could be successfully renegotiated, the lawsuit would be dropped. Enterprises was outraged, insisting that 8 Hockey Ventures had agreed to pay reduced rent until the construction was completed.

The conflict between 8 Hockey Ventures and Enterprises would become an ongoing and ever more bitter feature of the Jets' presence in Winnipeg. The Jets would constantly be in need of more revenue; Enterprises would always be constrained by its need to cover costs for both the arena and the stadium—the corporation still carried a large debt on the arena and the stadium on which it had to pay debt service charges.

Such conflict is a structurally inevitable part of the reality of NHL hockey in a small Canadian city, as the long conflict between Edmonton Oilers' owner Peter Pocklington and the Northlands Coliseum, or the similar struggle between team and arena owners in Calgary, shows. In Edmonton Pocklington has repeatedly demanded a greater share of the revenue-generating capacity of, and a greater degree of control over, the Northlands Coliseum, while simultaneously insisting that someone else pay for expensive renovations. In Calgary the Flames owners have made similar demands with respect to the Saddledome.

From the perspective of 8 Hockey Ventures, the group had gone out on a limb in buying a bankrupt franchise in a shaky league in February 1978. They also put in the considerable effort required to secure an NHL franchise for the Jets. Said Gobuty: "We spent a year of our lives bringing the NHL to Winnipeg. We put our necks in a ringer. Now I wish the city would give us a break." As Winnipeg sports writer John Robertson put it in 1982, Winnipeg had NHL hockey because Gobuty and his associates were prepared to take a risk "while the cold, calculating old money people in this town sat on their collective assets, afraid to take a chance on Winnipeg, for Winnipeg."[54]

Certainly, revenue sources available to other NHL franchises were not available to the Jets: 8 Hockey Ventures got no part of concession or parking revenue and only half of the in-arena advertising revenue, and was annoyed by relatively minor things such as free admission for Enterprises' officials. Worse, TV and radio revenues were severely limited by the size of Winnipeg's market. In 1982–83 the Jets got $600,000 in TV revenue; the Montreal Canadiens got $3 million. The problem was described succinctly by the Jets' director of marketing: "An NHL franchise cannot survive on gate receipts alone. It's what you can sell on the outside that makes the difference."[55] The severe restrictions on what the Jets could "sell on the outside," especially compared to NHL franchises in bigger cities and with newer arenas, made it very difficult for the club to turn a profit and necessitated its constant battles with a debt-burdened and equally squeezed Enterprises for more revenues. This was the hard economic reality that drove the perpetual Jets–Enterprises conflict.

In three of the four years after buying the team in 1979, according to the Jets' owners, the team lost money—a total loss since 1980 of $10 million, said Shenkarow, who had replaced Gobuty as president in late 1982. The owners had fought hard to have a new arena included in the North Portage mall complex and had failed. In 1983 Shenkarow declared that he was tired of fighting Enterprises. "The new building was one solution to the problem," he said. "There is not to be a new building so now we'll see if there's another solution to the problem."[56] The other solution would be to ask for government assistance.

To increase the pressure on government, Shenkarow threatened in October 1983 to sell the team in thirty days unless a more favourable lease arrangement could be worked out. Rumours abounded of potential buyers, and Shenkarow let it be known that the NHL would not oppose a move away from Winnipeg. "The NHL didn't want Winnipeg to begin with. They would be just as happy not to have Winnipeg. It isn't like St. Louis, which represents a big market to the NHL." Rumours had it that a group in Phoenix was prepared to offer $8 million (U.S.) for the Jets' franchise. Bill Hunter was reportedly prepared to make an offer to move the Jets to Saskatoon in the wake of the NHL's refusal to approve the sale of the St. Louis Blues to Saskatoon. And sports reporter Sigurdson noted, "A new modern arena is under construction in Hamilton and a 20,000 seat arena has been recently completed in Seattle-Tacoma. It's hardly shocking news that the operators of both buildings would like an NHL team as a tenant."[57]

These rumours and threats were an integral part of Shenkarow's negotiating strategy, as they would continue to be into the 1990s. The pattern was always the same: we're losing money; if we don't get additional revenue we'll sell the team. Deadlines were set; pressure was ratcheted higher and higher. As Sigurdson commented as early as 1983, Shenkarow had already threatened to sell the team out of Winnipeg "so often to so many people, you almost expect to hear 'this is a recording' at the end of his statement."[58]

Shenkarow is a skilled negotiator—clever, tough and rarely burdened, it seems, by overly rigid conventions. He knows how to do a deal. He has had to—the Jets were, from the begininng of his tenure, a marginal under-taking. Shenkarow's family made its money in a marginal industry—the highly competitive garment manufacturing business, where profit margins have historically been narrow and an entrepreneur's skills could mean the difference between success and bankruptcy. Coming out of this industry Shenkarow, like Hatskin before him, was not part of Winnipeg's comfort-able, finance-based corporate establishment. But he was more than the establishment's equal in the rough and tumble world of negotiating a deal. Indeed, he made money, lots of money, from an NHL franchise that regularly posted losses—a feat that despite their best efforts, corporate leaders would later prove unable to replicate.

In January, 1984 Shenkarow submitted new demands to Enterprises. The group's proposed new lease agreement would give the club an addi-tional $1.2 million annually.[59] City council was reluctant. Shenkarow *claimed* the Jets were incurring losses. But were they really? The losses appeared to be coming after large personal expenses charged by the owners to the club. Councillor Jim Ragsdill, for example, expressed concern about the excess of "highball expenses" incurred by the Jets. According to Ragsdill, as president of the club Shankarow was getting a salary of more than $100,000 annually, plus a house, cars and a gasoline account of $30,000. "They've got to trim a lot of fat before coming to the taxpayer for help," Ragsdill stated. With the owners apparently doing so well out of the club—whether the Jets were technically incurring losses or not—how could the investment of public dollars in the team be justified? More than one city councillor argued that "there's no way you can justify any significant tax dollars to a private group." Provincial sport minister Larry Desjardins concurred: "There is no way the province can make a direct grant to a professional hockey team."[60] But the Jets continued to play hardball: we get a better arrangement, or we leave.

Meanwhile, the problem had moved onto a different plane. The press, referring to "personal battles" between members of the Jets' and Enter-prises' boards, reported, "Shenkarow refused to meet any further with the committee." There was even a refusal to recognize that public funds were at issue. "Shenkarow has conceded that the philosophical difference of opinion that the City is dealing in public funds while the hockey club believes it is merely renegotiating its lease on the arena, is still a major stumbling block." Yet Enterprises still did not have full access to the Jets' books and did not know the full extent of the club's debt. "The Jets' debt is confidential," said co-owner Harvey Secter.[61] The net result was that to make it possible to improve the Jets' lease arrangements, public money was being used to write down Enterprises' debt and improve the team's financial position, but the Jets would not acknowledge this involvement of public money, would not reveal the amount of the club's own debt and would not agree to share profits above an agreed-upon amount—even though the owners still said they were incurring losses. The conflict between Enterprises and Shenkarow, rooted in the hard economic realities of each party, in turn a function of Winnipeg's small market, descended even further into personal recriminations, animosity and mistrust.

A deal was finally struck, though only after the intervention of Mayor Bill Norrie and provincial sport minister Desjardins and a tough fight at city council. It involved rent-free use of the arena plus a share of concession revenue for ten years, made possible by the city and province agreeing to take over the $3.7 million debt remaining from the 1979 arena expansion. They had done the same kind of thing in 1966 by writing off the original $2 million loan incurred in 1953 to build the Winnipeg Arena. Total cost in public money over the ten-year period was some $10 million, and the Jets agreed to stay in Winnipeg for at least the first three years of the deal.[62]

Yet only three months later a Jets' financial statement projected a net profit of $891,690 for the season. Councillors immediately objected—they had approved the $10 million Jets' support package believing the Jets were incurring losses. Shenkarow insisted the projections were flawed and that in fact no profit would be earned. The confusion over whether or not the Jets were losing money and what relationship such losses might have to the earnings of the owners would be a lingering part of the Jets story. In the meantime the parties agreed to a new and, for the public sector, less expensive lease agreement in January 1985. The Jets would pay an annual rent of $300,000—more than the rent-free agreement of March 1984 but still half the original $600,000 annual charge.[63]

Securing the Winnipeg Future: Public Equity and an Arena

Any thought that the saga was over just because fifteen months of bitter and rancorous negotiations had finally secured a new lease would be sadly premature. The Michael Gobuty story would now intervene, enabling Shenkarow to wrest still further concessions from the city.

Gobuty, president of 8 Hockey Ventures from its inception in February 1978 until September 1982, had played a crucial role in securing an NHL franchise for the Jets. But by the early 1980s, with his other business interests unravelling, Gobuty was pushed out as Jets' president and Shenkarow took over. Shenkarow had been devoting full-time attention to the Jets since leaving his law practice at Thompson Dorfman Sweatman—a departure that apparently caused considerable animosity between Shenkarow and Alan Sweatman who would later chair The Spirit of Manitoba Inc., the organization which would seek to purchase the Jets from Shenkarow in 1995.

Gobuty's business practices are a story in themselves—one consistent with the "colourful" tradition of NHL owners. In 1982 Victoria Leather, the family business owned by his father, went out of business, as did the Assiniboia Downs racetrack, acquired by the Gobuty family in 1981. Gobuty has since been involved in a variety of controversial business deals. In the early 1980s and again in 1990 he sold proposals for big property development deals to the small resort town of Winnipeg Beach, north of the city on the southern end of Lake Winnipeg. The first deal promised eight hundred luxury condos and a "recreation paradise." The project left twenty-six condos and "acres of weeds." The second venture promised a $7 million luxury hotel financed with overseas dollars, but its financial prospectus made no mention of the difficulties of Victoria Leather and Assiniboia Downs. It did include a testimonial from Gary Filmon, now premier, who said he had not given permission for his name to be used. The deal collapsed, leaving a substantial sum in unpaid back taxes.

Gobuty subsequently used federal government money ostensibly to set up a clothing manufacturing company in Winnipeg. He soon pulled up stakes in the middle of the night, leaving behind unpaid bills, and moved the equipment to the small town of Quincy, Florida, located in one of that state's poorest counties. The town paid for relocation and related expenses. Gobuty never put in his promised share of the capital investment and soon departed without warning, again leaving a trail of unpaid bills. He was, as a CBC documentary described him—using words eerily reminiscent of Bruce McNall—"the dreamweaver," searching for "the one big deal to get back on top."[64] In 1994 he was arrested in France, the allegation being that he had attached phoney Christian Dior labels to a shipment of clothing that he intended to sell in Ukraine.

In 1984 Gobuty had relocated to Toronto after being bought out of the Jets and a year later he made a bid to regain control of the Jets. It was rumoured that he was acting as front man for Leafs' owner Harold Ballard who intended, it was said, to move the Jets to Hamilton. Gobuty managed to secure 45 percent of the Jets' shares, and as Shenkarow described the ensuing conflict, the Shenkarow-Secter-Randy Moffat faction emerged victorious—the "saviours" of the Jets.

That Gobuty would be a front man for Ballard seemed plausible. In Toronto in 1984 Gobuty had struck up a friendship with and borrowed money from Ballard. Gobuty later described himself in court documents as "a close personal friend and constant companion of Ballard," and said their friendship was "equivalent to a close bond between father and son."[65]

It is not clear whether the threatened relocation of the Jets to Hamilton was real. Although Gobuty had refused to sign a letter of intent with Enterprises saying he would keep the Jets in Winnipeg, he insisted he had no intention of moving the franchise. "My offer to buy the club was to keep the club in Winnipeg. . . . Why would I, of all people, one of the people who was instrumental in getting NHL hockey in Winnipeg, want to move it?" Still, a reporter with the *Hamilton Spectator* wrote that he had overheard Ballard and Gobuty on the phone discussing the Jets' relocation to Hamilton.[66] Whichever was the case, Gobuty's intervention served Shenkarow's interests by kick-starting Enterprises into action to secure the franchise's future in Winnipeg.

In May 1985, in response to the Gobuty relocation rumours and after being approached in April by Jets' co-owner Harvey Secter about the threatened takeover and relocation, Enterprises called an emergency meeting.[67] The result was an offer to inject another $2.8 million into 8 Hockey Ventures in return for a 36 percent interest in the team. Shenkarow improved significantly upon the lease arrangement agreed to only four months earlier, and he improved his public standing by being perceived—as in fairness he probably was—as the saviour of the Jets.

Yet some onlookers saw the new situation of a public body, Enterprises, owning a minority position in the privately owned Jets as dangerous. Mayor Norrie, for one, expressed his concern that an equity position in the Jets could result in either Enterprises or the city having to pour more and more funds into the team if the Jets continued to lose money.[68] His concern would turn out to be well-founded.

The details of Enterprises' acquisition of 36 percent of the Jets' shares and of a new fifteen-year lease that gave Enterprises a potential veto on any attempt by the Jets to leave the city were kept confidential. However, the lease appeared to involve an exemption on the 10 percent amusement tax and a reduction in annual rental payments to $200,000—"pretty close to zero," as Shenkarow put it. What is more, the deal denied Enterprises access to the Jets' finances: "Shenkarow refuses to divulge details but admits that the restrictions effectively prevent Winnipeg Enterprises from exercising strong influence over the Jets."[69]

Shenkarow maintained full control over the franchise and over information about the franchise's finances. And he had, once again, improved the terms of the club's lease arrangements with Enterprises. But he did not yet have a new arena, with the additional revenue sources it would bring, and there would be no peace until a new arena was built.

By the end of the decade new arenas, most of them at least partly paid for by the public, were being erected or contemplated in most NHL cities. As the *Winnipeg Sun* put it in early 1990: "There's an epidemic sweeping the NHL as owners, already trembling at the prospect of increased player salaries and operating costs in the next few years, are scrambling to boost their revenue. And the first area they are looking at is their facilities."[70]

The Jets' owners, who had long sought a new arena, savoured the possibilities. "Costs in professional sports are going up [so] quickly people have to find other sources of revenue," Shenkarow said. "Things like sky boxes started in football and have evolved down into arenas. So buildings that don't have them want them." And when owners in other cities have new arenas built for them, "They tell us about all the things they're going to put in their new building and we stand there saying 'Holy mackerel.'" If somebody else has it, and it generates more revenue, then we should have it too is the reasoning. The construction of new arenas was undertaken to generate more revenue in the face of rising costs. Once some cities built new arenas, a competitive dynamic was set in motion creating not only the desire but also the necessity—if a competitive team was to be afforded—for a new, revenue-generating arena.

That necessity was keenly felt in Winnipeg. The existing arena was old and relatively small, without adequate space for luxury boxes. A new arena in Winnipeg could use about thirty luxury boxes, Shenkarow believed, each costing about $50,000 per year, plus about 1500 special seats. "In some cities you'd have a lot more boxes, but we don't have enough corporations to have a lot of boxes. But I do think we have enough small companies that you could sell specialty seating." New arenas were the means to accommodate a larger number of more expensive seats but how many seats, and how expensive, depended on the city. Shenkarow explained Winnipeg's competitive disadvantage: "In our top price category we have 3,000 seats. Calgary has 9,500. If you want to charge $25 for your top seat, well . . . we're selling more $14 tickets and they're selling more $25 tickets." But an arena needs more than expensive seats. "You need state of the art studios," Shenkarow said. You need restaurants; you need good acoustics. Everything has to be done just right. "You can't skimp anywhere because you'll fall behind too fast." The competitive race goes to the swiftest, the biggest, the most elaborate and the most expensive. This is particularly the case, Shenkarow observed, in Winnipeg. "In this city, the market's too fragile to make any mistakes."

By early 1991 Shenkarow was again exerting pressure for a new arena, with rumours abounding of potential U.S. buyers for the team. Seattle was reportedly interested, leading Shenkarow to issue yet another warning in March. "It's now one minute to midnight. If something doesn't happen soon, midnight could strike a lot sooner than some people think." Three months later Shenkarow was reportedly contemplating a $32 million offer made by San Diego business interests, who intended to move the team to California.[71]

Two related problems now arose, each having to do with Enterprises' 36 percent interest in the Jets. The first was the fear that the Shenkarow interests might sell their 64 percent share of the team to a U.S. buyer, leaving the city, through Enterprises, holding a 36 percent interest in a U.S.-based franchise. The $2.8 million spent to purchase the 36 percent interest would then be effectively lost. The second problem was that the 1985 deal gave Enterprises right of first refusal with respect to any offer to purchase the Jets, in return for which Enterprises agreed to cover all Jets' losses exceeding $400,000 in a two-year period. If the corporation did not cover the losses it forfeited the right of first refusal. In July 1991, the Jets announced projected losses for the 1991–92 season of $2 to 3 million. The city would soon either be paying for Jets' losses or running the risk of the franchise being sold away from Winnipeg. Shenkarow insisted that "the crunch is here," and that the Jets' owners "are through waiting."[72]

What was apparent, however, was that many councillors remained adamantly opposed to public funding for a new arena. "Any new arena should be financed by the private sector; there should be no public money," said Councillor Peter Diamant. "Barry Shenkarow should put his own money into the arena. . . . It's key actually," added Councillor Joseph Yuen. Councillor and Enterprises board member Chris Lorenc, seemingly unaware of the irony of his comments, tried to allay their fears by observing, "I don't think that Barry Shenkarow, in his wildest dreams, expects someone to build an arena and turn it over to him for a dollar."[73] Shenkarow's dreams would get much wilder, as would the great arena debate, over the next four years, and Councillor Yuen's observation that "It's become a soap opera" might have led an observer with the capacity to see into the future to think, "You ain't seen nothin' yet!"

Conflicting Interests and Appetites

By the first years of the 1990s—on the eve of the "modern history" of the great Jets/arena battle—there already exist a long and complex history of conflict over the team. Many of the elements that would become central features of the conflict in the 1990s were already in place: proposed arenas as fronts for property development schemes; corporate/city council alliances aggressively promoting the building of such arenas; flawed financial deals advanced by arena promoters; public opposition to the spending of public funds on such ventures; and threats of various kinds, particularly the threat of team relocation, should such public expenditures not be undertaken. A long history of conflict between the Shenkarow interests and Winnipeg Enterprises Corporation was also part of the mix. That conflict had become deeply personal and bitter, but the root of the problem was really structural—big league hockey in Winnipeg was and always had been, at best, a marginal undertaking. The Jets were financially squeezed because they had access only to a small market lacking a large and vibrant corporate sector, and they played in a small arena from which they got relatively low ticket revenue and few ancillary revenues. This was bad enough in the old NHL; it became impossible with the changed economics of the NHL from the mid to late 1980s.

The Shenkarow interests, who seemingly alone among Winnipeg's business leaders were concerned about keeping the franchise in Winnipeg, had no choice but to bargain hard for additional revenues from their facility. At the same time their landlord, Winnipeg Enterprises, was extremely limited in the extent to which it could free up revenue flows for the Jets because Enterprises itself always carried a substantial debt burden, repayment of which necessarily had first claim on the arena's revenue flows. The result, inevitably, was conflict.

Yet this inevitable structural conflict was worsened by the dominant mode of negotiations. Shenkarow never let Enterprises know the full details of the Jets' finances. He always ensured that his personal needs were well taken care of out of the Jets' revenues, insisted on full control of all aspects of the Jets' operations and repeatedly moved the goal posts when bargaining with Enterprises—no sooner would agreement appear to have been reached than Shenkarow would ask for more. More importantly, Shenkarow repeatedly used the threat of relocation as a lever to pry concessions out of the public sector. The most important of these was the 1985 deal by which Enterprises took a minority position in the Jets and agreed to pick up Jets' losses beyond a minimal amount. By the late 1980s–early 1990s the obligation to pay Jets' losses beyond a minimal amount was on the verge of becoming a major problem, and the pressure to construct a new arena with the luxury suites and club seats needed to maximize revenue flows was mounting. But in the new decade the stakes for the public sector were about to be raised dramatically.

4. To Build or Not to Build . . .

Dale Cummings

By the late 1980s and early 1990s—with the Jets' already precarious financial situation deteriorating rapidly—the city and provincial governments and the corporate sector had once again begun to ponder several arena proposals, with a resulting array of questions asked. Should a new arena be built? Could a new arena be built? If so where? Who would pay? The issues were complex. Yet Shenkarow was insistent on the need for more seats and greater income.

The first two proposals for a new arena were advanced in November 1989. One plan called for a location adjacent to the downtown Convention Centre and the other was to be at the North Forks site. Suspicions were soon aroused that the North Forks proposal was part of a property development scheme. The chairman of the Forks Renewal Corporation announced that a vacant building on the site was to be converted to a hotel. Sources indicated that the CNR and the wealthy Richardson family, who owned property at Portage and Main adjacent to the North Forks, were discussing joint development projects associated with the arena.[1] The Richardsons denied any such intentions, yet the model was similar to the 1976 Great-West Life proposal which had included the construction of an arena at the Forks as part of a massive CNR/GWL Forks commercial redevelopment scheme. The Forks was an exceptionally attractive site for profit-seeking property developers, and a government-supported arena built to ensure that the Jets stayed in the city could be a useful front for just such an undertaking.

Public opposition to the North Forks proposal was not long in coming. Kent Gerecke, University of Manitoba city planning professor and editor of *City Magazine*, was spokesperson for a small community-based group, Greening the Forks, which wanted to ensure that the historic Forks site was not seized by developers. Gerecke reacted angrily to the arena announcement. "All they want to do is develop, develop, develop and to hell with what the people want or what makes sense. Where does an arena fit in there with the history and archaeology of the site?" Gerecke was insistent: "Let's stop this development and instead create a wonderful historic and cultural park at the Forks."[2]

Public consultations organized to determine how the Forks might best be used resulted in the publication of *Future Directions for the Forks*, in which Winnipeggers made it clear that their vision was much closer to that expressed by Greening the Forks than to the latest arena-as-part-of-the-commercial-development-of-the-Forks scheme. By September 1990, Mayor Norrie was acknowledging public opposition to an arena at the Forks and the North Forks site was placed on the back burner.

In the next four years the location most actively considered for a new arena was the Convention Centre site. It was favoured by Shenkarow who said he doubted that the Jets' board would agree to move the club into a facility owned or managed by Enterprises, as was intended at the Forks.[3] It was also the choice of the city's business establishment. As Shenkarow told the press in July 1991, referring to a new Convention Centre proposal, "There is a group of the city's finest international businessmen prepared to get the hockey club on the right track. . . . They have given Mayor Norrie a proposal that could mean the difference in the team being in Winnipeg or not."[4]

Others pointed out that the new proposal was seriously flawed. Councillor Peter Diamant called it a "public relations scam," adding, "I was surprised that such well-respected businessmen hadn't done their homework." Councillor Don Mitchelson said, "This was not a viable solution to the problem. I expected more substance." Mayor Norrie summed up by saying, "We were unanimous in concluding it was a rotten deal."[5] The "rotten deal" would have had the city bear all the risk with the private investors, the cream of the city's business establishment, earning a guaranteed return. Although the plan was rejected, it was nevertheless in every respect a model for what was to come.

Other arena proposals did emerge. In May 1991, the Winnipeg Convention Centre announced its Manitoba Gardens option—an 18,400-seat arena intended to cost $65 million and including a 250-room luxury hotel. The driving force was Convention Centre General Manager Scott Walker, a "dynamic" young man hired in March 1990 and described by a local concert promoter as "hard-nosed and a little brash, but . . . honest to a fault." Walker would be fired in January 1993, "amid allegations of misappropriation of funds."[6]

Over the next year the Manitoba Gardens proposal evolved into a massive, $300 million arena and twin office-tower deal brokered by Edgecombe Properties, the real estate arm of North American Life which owned part of the proposed site.[7] This deal, too, was a property development scheme in disguise. As our organization Thin Ice later described it, "The arena is really just a vehicle for a massive speculative land grab. One cannot even discern the outlines of the arena facility in the drawing, so freighted down is it with high rise office towers."

Business supported this proposal. A Winnipeg *Sun* poll in April 1992 found, "Nearly two-thirds of Winnipeg business leaders who were surveyed gave their thumbs up to North American Life's proposal to build a new arena adjacent to the Winnipeg Convention Centre downtown." What is more: "Not one respondent indicated a preference for building an arena at the Forks."[8]

Apparently, then, in 1992 neither the public nor the business community supported using the Forks for the construction of a new arena. Nevertheless there were two proposals for the Forks, both for multiplexes—buildings designed not only for hockey but also for football, basketball and baseball.

One proposal, for a "Superplex," was promoted by Rick Koswin, former Winnipeg Blue Bomber and investment dealer. Koswin began his "crusade" to build a superplex at the Forks following the November 1990 release of the Lavalin Report, a study on the future of NHL hockey in Winnipeg commissioned by the city, the Jets and Winnipeg Enterprises. Montreal-based Lavalin's report was exceptionally shoddy and threadbare—at a cost of $80,000. It concluded that a new arena at a downtown location was the best option and rejected the multiplex facility preferred by the Bombers and Enterprises. Enterprises was "extremely disappointed" with the quality of the report, calling it "a document substantially lacking in hard, objective fact."[9]

Shenkarow, however, approved of the report. He wanted a single-purpose facility built specifically to accommodate the Jets, not a multiplex as preferred by the Bombers and Enterprises. Shenkarow didn't want a multiplex because then he wouldn't control the building—and he felt he needed to control the building because he knew by then that the Jets' losses would soon be skyrocketing. The Lavelin Report supported his preference for a single-purpose facility. Koswin then picked up the multiplex idea.

Consistently marginalized by the establishment, Koswin would become a near-tragic figure, a man virtually obsessed with his quest, to no avail and at great personal cost. As *Free Press* reporter Hal Sigurdson described it in late 1995: "During his campaign Koswin lost his car and was obliged to move his wife Arlene and four children to a smaller rented house. His phone was disconnected when he couldn't pay the bill. It was not re-connected until . . . John Loewen [Chairman of Manitoba Entertainment Complex] quietly handed him $1000 to cover it. Until then he used an outdoor phone booth around the corner."[10]

A second multiplex proposal, Snowcap Sportsplex Inc., was a sophisticated proposal with backing from individuals associated with investment dealer Wood Gundy and the support of several other local businesses. Paul Sveinson, president of Snowcap, worked full-time in 1990 on the plan for the $235 million soft-topped facility modelled on the Florida Sun Coast Dome. The Snowcap multiplex was to have been located on the western edge of the Forks. But the project was eventually shut down because of a tangled web of corporate connections. Wood Gundy was owned by the Canadian Imperial Bank of Commerce, which also owned Comcheq Services whose CEO was the main spokesperson for the Manitoba Entertainment Complex (MEC), another major arena proponent in the 1990s. CIBC, in short, owned companies behind competing projects. But CIBC's links with one of those projects, MEC, were particularly close by virtue of the long-standing connection between CIBC and the powerful Richardson family. The Richardson building houses CIBC's regional headquarters, and Richardsons had long served on the CIBC board of directors. The Richardsons backed MEC; indeed, Hartley Richardson was a member of MEC's executive committee. These connections came into play when, some months after the formation of MEC, Bob Vandewater, a Snowcap backer associated with Wood Gundy, was called out of a meeting to take a phone call from Toronto. When he came back to the meeting, Vandewater was "ashen-faced." The call had been from CIBC headquarters, instructing him that neither he nor Wood Gundy were any longer to be involved with Snowcap. The Snowcap people are convinced that this was the result of Loewen and MEC leaning on CIBC headquarters. It was, in short, an example of MEC using heavy-handed tactics to knock an opponent out of the running. When the MEC and Spirit of Manitoba proposals failed in mid-1995, Sveinson reactivated the Snowcap proposal and began working once again to advance the project.

There were, in addition, at least two proposals to establish multifaceted entertainment complexes with the centrepiece and cash cow of each being a casino. Top Gun Sports Inc. proposed building "The Ice Hangar" at the Convention Centre site and investing $215 million subject to Winnipeg's Crystal Casino being relocated to the proposed new "entertainment, exhibition and convention centre complex." The Top Gun consortium included Ogden Entertainment Services which would manage the new arena; Miller & Schroeder Financial Inc., a privately held, Minneapolis-based investment banking firm which would underwrite a bond issue; Grand Casino and Resorts of Canada Inc., a U.S.-based casino management company which would manage the relocated Crystal Casino on a fee-for-service basis; Sunset Development Corporation, a Manitoba First Nations Company which would own the Complex's "Family Entertainment Centre" including a "Mall of Americas"; and Mr. Canada Touring Network which would operate tour packages to the casino–entertainment–sports complex.

A second, conceptually similar proposal was advanced by the Four Winds group, headed by David H. Brant, whose idea was to establish an "International Destination Resort Complex" at an urban Native reserve to be located at the Canadian Armed Forces' Fort Osborne Barracks site in southwest Winnipeg. To be called "Meg-A-Plex," it was to be owned by the proposed Four Winds Tribal Council and financed by U.S.-based and primarily Aboriginal "gaming enterpreneurs." It was to include not only an arena and stadium, but also a new convention centre, a world class resort hotel and the Four Winds Casino and Bingo.

Both proposals—Top Gun and Four Winds—contemplated financing the arena and the Jets with the massive profits to be made from legalized gambling. The arena in each case was, in short, a cover behind which to gain access to gambling profits. The province, however, was not prepared to give up its gambling revenues on which it had become increasingly reliant.

The final, substantive arena proposal—first made public in September 1991—was advanced by the Winnipeg Forum Group, headed by Michael Rattray of MMP Architects. The Forum Group proposed to build a new arena on the foundation of the existing arena at a cost of $60 million, and to do so entirely with private money. The proposal thus minimized the cost of a new arena to the public, but it was never given serious consideration by the business establishment. Shenkarow himself opposed the plan because Enterprises would still have been running the arena and he was determined to escape from Enterprises. Just as importantly, the Forum Group project was not part of a property development scheme like the North Forks and Convention Centre proposals, and thus the people with big money had no incentive to get behind the deal. There were no quick and easy profits to be made from appreciation in property values. All Rattray's group stood to gain was the architectural fees involved in designing the project. With the support of neither the establishment nor Shenkarow and the Jets, the Forum Group proposal, sensible though it was, never got off the ground. The only arena projects ever given serious consideration were those at the North Forks site and the Convention Centre site—both of them as much about property development as about hockey.

The Interim Operating Agreement and Report after Report

By 1991 Enterprises was balking at paying Jets' losses which, it was suggested, could be as high as $2 million that year. Shenkarow was threatening to leave Winnipeg, and the press was reporting that "the great arena debate is heading to a climax."[11] An interim solution was needed—short of building a new arena—that would respond to the immediate needs of the Jets while allowing time to lay the basis for a long-term solution. The result, in November 1991, was "The Preservation of NHL Hockey in Winnipeg," a seven-page document setting out the rudiments of what would soon become the complex legal contract between the city, province and Jets' owners known as the Interim Operating Agreement (IOA). The IOA would be a crucial feature of the 1990s version of the Jets/arena debate.

Seen as a response to the 1985 deal by which Enterprises invested $2.8 million for 36 percent of the Jets' shares, bore most of the risk for Jets' losses, yet had no say in the club's financial operations, the IOA offered distinct advantages to the City of Winnipeg. It removed the pressure to build an arena immediately, allowing more time to investigate the alternatives. It brought the province in to share with the city the burden of paying the Jets' losses—the city and province agreed to share equally the cost of paying all Jets' losses from July 1, 1991 to June 30, 1997. It included a "take-along" clause specifying that if Shenkarow were to sell his 64 percent of the Jets' shares, the 36 percent held by Enterprises had to be sold at the same price and on the same terms; no such prior agreement was in place. It specified that any NHL expansion revenues had to be used to cover Jets' losses; no such prior agreement was in place. It set up a monitoring mechanism, in the form of an Interim Steering Committee with representation from both public and private sectors, to which the Jets' owners had to report their financial operations and that had the authority to approve expenditures. This provision placed a ceiling on such expenditures—in the normal course of events they could be no higher than the top team in the bottom one-third in the NHL in operational expenses. The IOA also afforded to the city and province—and this was its main attraction—an option to purchase the 64 percent of the Jets' shares that were privately owned at a price of $32 million up to June 30, 1994, and it committed the Jets to staying in Winnipeg until June 30, 1997. From the city's point of view, and without taking advantage of the benefit of hindsight, this may have been a defensible deal. It addressed several of the flaws of the 1985 Enterprises–Jets agreement, afforded the city and province the opportunity to purchase the Jets at a relatively attractive price, promised to keep the Jets in the city for at least another five years and bought time before making a final decision on a new arena.

In hindsight, the cost of the deal turned out to be far too high. The Jets' losses would skyrocket, eventually exceeding $40 million. That the losses might climb so high was not known by councillors in November 1991 when they approved the IOA, although a document prepared by the provincial auditor and made available to the premier and his cabinet, but not to councillors or the public, accurately predicted that losses would reach $43.5 million by June 30, 1997.[12] Had city council known about these figures, the IOA might not have been approved. That, presumably, is why Premier Filmon kept it secret. In doing so he set a precedent of secrecy and of withholding crucial information from the public and the public's representatives—practices that would become characteristic of the Jets/arena debate in the 1990s.

The IOA also set up a Capital Fund out of which certain payments were to be made. The Capital Fund was raised privately, but repayment of the principle and interest was jointly guaranteed by the city and province. Derek Riley served as chief fundraiser, raising $7.8 million of a $10 million target. The contributors were some of the city's biggest firms: Great-West Life, Investors, Richardsons, Cargill, North American Life, Gendis, the Northwest Company and Comcheq.[13] It appeared as if Winnipeg's corporate sector had finally committed itself financially to saving the Jets.

But, as Riley explained, the corporate contributions to the Capital Fund cost the donors virtually nothing and were completely risk-free. Donors were paid interest at the prime rate less 3 percent. So if they borrowed the money that they contributed to the Capital Fund at the prime rate, their real cost was only 3 percent of the size of their contribution. Said Riley: "When you are talking about $10 million, what we are really talking about is a donation from the private sector of $300,000 a year."[14] Since only $7.8 million was raised, the real contribution from the private sector was $234,000. As had been the case in the past, and would continue to be the case during the coming years, the Winnipeg business establishment was not prepared to risk significant amounts of money on the Jets.

The Jets' owners did well out of the deal. In addition to having all the Jets' losses paid by the public, they received an annual "management fee" that amounted to anywhere from $1 million to $2 million per year depending upon interest rates. It was a guaranteed profit. For Shenkarow and his partners, the Jets were now a risk-free, profit-making undertaking. Since repayment of the $7.8 million Capital Fund was guaranteed by the city and province, the Interim Operating Agreement was risk-free for Winnipeg's corporate sector too. All the risk was borne by the public sector. The city and province not only had to guarantee repayment of the $7.8 million Capital Fund, but also had to pay the full amount of the Jets' losses. Attempts as late as October 1991 to cap the public liability for Jets' losses at $5 million were removed in the final version of the deal, at Shenkarow's insistence.[15] The public was responsible for *all* the Jets' losses.

The IOA generated considerable opposition from city councillors, though it was finally approved by a 22–7 council vote on November 18, 1991 after "a debate that rivalled the harangue over the failed Meech Lake Accord." Councillor Glen Murray complained, "We didn't have an independent legal opinion in six months" on the deal, describing it as "welfare for the rich." Councillor Harry Lazarenko added, "Barry Shenkarow and Harvey Secter are laughing all the way to their banks."[16] Don Mitchelson was one of seven councillors to vote against the IOA. His wife, Bonnie Mitchelson, was a provincial cabinet minister and so presumably would have known that the provincial auditor believed that the Jets' losses could climb as high as $43.5 million.

The character of the deal was perhaps symbolically represented by two factors. First, it was unveiled to the public in October 1991 at a "by invitation only" session at the exclusive, establishment-oriented Manitoba Club. Second, Premier Filmon attempted to avoid signing the deal by sending Finance Minister Clayton Manness in his place and agreed to sign only when Mayor Norrie refused to sign unless Filmon did.[17]

Filmon was painting himself into a difficult corner. He had agreed to the Interim Operating Agreement even though by October 1991 he knew the statistics on the Jets' potential losses. He was on record, repeatedly, as being against any significant public contribution to cover Jets' losses or build a new arena. In November 1989, after the North Forks and Convention Centre proposals were announced, Filmon said a new arena "certainly is not a priority that ought to be paid for by taxpayers' money." During the 1990 provincial election he described a large provincial contribution for a new arena as "an absolute last resort." And in 1993, talking about a new arena, he acknowledged, "I have always said I don't think it's feasible for the government of Manitoba to be in for big amounts of money."[18] Given these views it is not surprising that Filmon tried to hide his involvement in a legal agreement that he knew could lead to large provincial contributions for Jets' losses.

Filmon was clever enough to at least partially obscure his involvement by making it appear that city council was the final decision-maker on Jets-related matters. And council would repeatedly be forced to make important decisions on such matters without sufficient information and time. In the case of the IOA, council had less than a week to approve a particularly complicated deal. This artificially induced time pressure, justified by the existence of arbitrary "deadlines," would also become a recurring feature of the ongoing Jets/arena debate. Prudence and rational analysis were being squeezed out, and a very dangerous form of public decision-making was evolving. Part of this involved making use of the sometimes dubious findings of various studies produced by Coopers and Lybrand, a large accounting/consulting firm.

In early November 1991—just prior to city council's voting on the Interim Operating Agreement—industry Minister Eric Stefanson released a copy of a 1990 Coopers and Lybrand report to the *Free Press*. The report led the councillors to believe that keeping the Jets in Winnipeg would generate $48 million per year in economic activity and create, directly and indirectly, between 960 and 1,440 full-time jobs. The report had been commissioned by the Jets, and like the Lavalin Report it was seriously flawed. For example, Coopers and Lybrand used a multiplier of 2.5 to determine the indirect benefits flowing from the presence of the Jets, when according to other researchers a multiplier of half that magnitude would have been more accurate. Therefore, the results seriously overestimated the hockey team's economic benefits to Winnipeg. More importantly, the consulting firm used a "gross benefits" rather than a "net benefits" form of analysis. The net benefits method, generally acknowledged to be the more accurate, takes into account the likelihood that most of the money spent on something like Jets' tickets will be spent on some other form of entertainment if the Jets are not there. Thus it will still ripple through the economy, creating very similar levels of economic activity, jobs and taxes. Thus the net economic benefit of the Jets' presence in the city would be smaller than it might otherwise seem. The *Free Press*, however, merely parroted the results of the Coopers and Lybrand study as if they were "facts," without any analysis of the method employed in the study, leading many to believe, mistakenly, that the Jets were a boon to the city's economy.

In July 1992, consistent with the terms of the Interim Operating Agreement, an Interim Steering Committee (ISC) began its work. Chaired by Investors Group Chairman Arthur Mauro, the ISC had the responsibility of overseeing the Jets' expenditures to ensure that they did not exceed those of the top team in the NHL's bottom one-third in team expenditures.

The ISC was ineffective in fulfilling its mandate. Indeed, it was mired in confusion. Mauro appears to have resigned as chair in December 1993. Almost a year later Carl Ridd, by then a member of Thin Ice, called the ISC's executive director to ask who had become the new chairperson. "There is no chair," Ridd was told. The executive director said that Mauro had resigned when the Implementation Committee, chaired by James Burns, was struck, and that no replacement had yet been appointed. Curious that an important committee, the public's watchdog, had no chair and had been in that situation for some nine months, Ridd faxed the Mayor, Susan Thompson, and asked, "Who is the chair of the Interim Steering Committee?" The mayor's secretary telephoned later in the day with Thompson's answer: Arthur Mauro is the chair. Ridd then double-checked with the ISC's executive director: no, she reiterated, Arthur Mauro resigned late last year.

When our group Thin Ice invited Mauro to participate in a February 1994 conference on the Jets/arena issue, Mauro declined, saying he considered his responsibilities with the ISC to be finished. Yet the city and province were still liable for any losses incurred by the Jets and still relied on the ISC to monitor the Jets' finances. Thus it appears that the Jets' expenditures and finances were not being adequately monitored. No one was home at the public watchdog's office, particularly after Mauro completed what he considered to be his real job, which was to oversee the preparation of a study called for by Article 5 of the IOA.

That study, *The Report on the Preservation of NHL Hockey in Winnipeg*, more commonly known as the Mauro Report, was released in late July 1993. Its purposes were to confirm the economic contribution of the Jets to the city; to determine the capacity of the city and province to support an NHL franchise; and to set out the financial arrangements by which a new arena could be constructed and the Jets made viable.

The Mauro Report, at a cost $200,000, was also seriously flawed—a pattern that was now well established by the Lavalin and Coopers and Lybrand reports. To begin with, in "confirming" the economic contribution of the Jets to the city the report merely reiterated, uncritically, the inflated figures derived from the Coopers and Lybrand "gross benefits" analysis.

Indeed, for Jets' supporters these figures—a $48 million annual contribution to the local economy and the equivalent of from 960 to 1,440 full-time jobs—became a mantra repeated on every conceivable occasion, and by virtue of this repetition they came to be widely believed.

The Mauro Report also appears to have made no attempt to consult the existing literature on the economic benefits to host cities of professional sport franchises. It did not mention the work of U.S. economist Robert Baade, perhaps the leading authority on the economics of professional sport. Baade has demonstrated repeatedly that a city gains negligible economic benefits from the presence of a professional sport franchise. In a 1990 study, for example, Baade and Richard F. Dye concluded: "The presence of a new or renovated stadium has an uncertain impact on the levels of economic activity and possibly a negative impact on local development relative to the region. This result is consistent with the possibility that stadium subsidies might bias local development toward low wage jobs."[19] Numerous other independent economic impact studies had confirmed this finding. The Mauro Report avoided this type of economic analysis and instead "confirmed" the economic contribution of the Jets by relying on unsophisticated reports commissioned by the Jets for the express purpose of bolstering Shenkarow's case for a new arena.

As well the report did not adequately consider the viability of NHL hockey in Winnipeg and said virtually nothing about the changing economics of the NHL. Some of the data in the Mauro Report were revealing in this regard: Manitoba has the lowest population of any province or state with an NHL franchise; average attendance at Jets' games, 12,787 in 1992–93, "is not an acceptable level" and was the lowest among Canadian franchises; and average ticket prices, $21.52 in 1992–93, were the lowest in the NHL. Mauro recommended that average ticket prices be increased by 50 percent, from $21.52 to $32.25, yet projected that despite the higher ticket prices, attendance would then rise, by approximately 15 percent, to 14,600 per game. Most importantly, the report expressed grave concerns about rising salaries, saying: "The problem of player costs must be resolved, whether through salary 'caps,' revenue sharing or some combination. Without such resolution, new facilities alone may not sustain teams in smaller markets."[20]

The Ogden Report of April 1994, commissioned by the ISC, echoed the Mauro Report, saying: "Unless the salary cap and/or revenue sharing issues are resolved by the NHL, the likelihood of a financially viable Jets' franchise would be extremely remote." And still another, the Burns Report of June 1994, said the same, that there "must be resolve or material progress" on salary caps/revenue-sharing "before any public sector commitment of major capital or new financial assistance is made."[21]

Nevertheless, despite its legitimate expression of concern about rising salaries and the need for salary caps and/or revenue-sharing, and despite there being no prospect of either in the foreseeable future, the Mauro Report concluded, "The City and Province have the capacity to support an NHL franchise in a new, state-of-the-art facility."[22] All of these reports shared an extremely truncated analysis of the changing economics of the NHL, and they largely ignored the ramifications of the one aspect of the economics that they did seem to grasp—that salaries were exploding and salary caps/revenue-sharing would be needed to enable smaller cities to survive. A system of revenue-sharing—the transfer of funds from financially stronger to financially weaker franchises—has the potential to enable franchises in medium-sized cities to survive. However, in the new economics of the NHL, with more and more franchises owned by huge corporate infotainment giants seeking to maximize their profits, the prospects of a revenue-sharing plan that would keep smaller cities in the NHL were minimal. Yet the reports ignored this reality. The Mauro Report recommended that a new arena be constructed at the Convention Centre site, at a total cost of $111 million; that the public sector increase its ownership share in the Jets so that both the arena and the franchise will be owned 51 percent by the public sector and 49 percent by the private sector; and that the three levels of government share equally a $30 million contribution of public funds.

Despite its many weaknesses, the $200,000 Mauro Report was well received by governments. Both Filmon and Thompson said they had no choice but to go ahead "because the Winnipeg Jets, which generate $48 million in direct and indirect business in the city, are too important to the city's economy."[23] The bogus $48 million contribution to the local economy had become "a fact," whereas the *fact* that revenue-sharing was necessary but extremely unlikely was ignored.

It is clear that the Mauro Report was not a serious investigation of whether a small city like Winnipeg could support a franchise in the dramatically changed NHL. To the extent that the issue of rising salaries was addressed, the conclusions did not follow from the evidence. Indeed, Arthur Mauro told Thin Ice that a new arena ranked very low on his list of the city's real priorities. When we asked him why he had not said this in the Mauro Report, Mauro told us: "That wasn't my mandate."

On December 15, 1993, Mayor Thompson, elected in 1992, and Premier Filmon appointed an "Implementation Committee" chaired by Jim Burns, who was executive vice-president of Power Corporation, former president of Great-West Life and former vice-president of the Winnipeg Jets. The committee's task was to implement the recommendations of the Mauro Report and to find the private-sector money needed to build a new arena. It was an impressive group. As Scott Taylor, sports writer for the *Free Press* and leading media booster for a new arena, put it, "The nine people named yesterday to the committee that has been charged with finding enough private sector funding to build a $100 million arena in Winnipeg are among the biggest names in the money game in this community."

And money was the issue because the arena and the Jets, according to the Mauro Report, were to be a unique, public-private-sector partnership, and that meant raising private capital. If private capital could be found, the Burns Committee members were the ones to find it. Said Taylor, more prophetically than he could realize, they "know where the corporate treasure is buried. And frankly, if those folks can't get an arena built, it can't be done."[24] Taylor would soon forget these words—selective memory being another feature of the inexorably unfolding decision-making process.

When Burns finally reported on June 24, 1994, the news was not good. His report concluded that a new downtown arena at the Convention Centre site—deemed by, the Burns Committee as the best location by far—would lose money every year. It would be unable to cover its debt-service charges. It would barely be able to cover even its operating expenses—by "razor-thin" margins under optimum circumstances. The Jets, too, would continue to lose money: on June 8 the provincial auditor had finally released the 1991 report showing that Jets' losses could total $43.5 million by June 30, 1997. There had to be "resolve or material progress" on salary caps and revenue-sharing "before construction proceeds."[25] The public-sector contribution would have to be considerably more than the $30 million called for in the Mauro Report.

Most importantly, the Burns Committee found not a nickel of private equity. Its mandate was to determine how much the private sector was prepared to invest, and the committee found that the business community was not prepared to invest at all in a risky, money-losing venture. "No private sector investors have expressed interest in purchasing the hockey club because of the existence of excessive losses and the potential for continued losses in the future."[26] The Burns Committee—those nine people who were among Winnipeg's "biggest names in the money game" and who were supposed to "know where the corporate treasure is buried"—found no corporate treasure for the Jets. Despite all the efforts to make the deal happen, one thing remained completely unchanged: Winnipeg's corporate sector would simply not invest its own money in the Jets. The risks were too great.

The Thin Ice Challenge

Cho!ces was founded by a group of community activists concerned that their efforts to deal with the social and economic problems of Winnipeg's inner city were being thwarted by the relentless slashing of public spending by all levels of government. Most inner-city organizations were in one way or another reliant on public money and thus constrained from speaking or acting politically for fear of having their own funding cut back. A new organization was needed to deal with the problem at its source—by taking a political stand against public spending cuts.

In January 1991 more than 150 people crowded into a rented hall in downtown Winnipeg in response to the organizers' call. John Loxley, chair of the University of Manitoba Economics Department and long-time community activist, was elected the group's first chairperson, soon to be joined by inner-city activist Jean Altemeyer as co-chair. Cho!ces' theme was that cuts to public spending were politically driven—they were the result not of economic necessity, as the public was being told, but of the ideological preferences of those holding political office. They were the result, in short, of political choices. Different choices were needed, and possible.

One of the new group's projects was to examine the proposals for a new arena for the Jets. Loxley prepared an early version of what would later become known as the Black and Dolecki Report, and he and Jeff Lowe began to analyze the financial viability of the Forum Group proposal, which called for a new arena to be built on the foundation of the existing Winnipeg Arena at minimal public cost. Cho!ces preferred this option, but those with money and power did not. Cho!ces argued that although it would be preferable to keep the team in Winnipeg if at all possible, this goal did not justify massive public expenditures, given the city's competing needs.

Cho!ces began to make its case in a variety of ways. For example, the Filmon government was cutting funding to public education while increasing funding to elite private schools. Funding to desperately needed inner-city programs was being cut while bank profits, which continued to be virtually untaxed, were soaring. On these and many other public funding issues Cho!ces did the analytical work to show what was happening and to set out alternatives, and it designed various kinds of innovative political actions, often relying upon humour and various forms of political theatre to draw public attention to the issues. Perhaps most significantly, Cho!ces began to prepare alternative provincial and civic budgets—technically sophisticated comprehensive budgets prepared in cooperation with broad sectors of the community. The group quickly established itself as one of the most vibrant and effective social justice organizations in the country. By 1995 Cho!ces, working with the Ottawa-based Canadian Centre for Policy Alternatives, had prepared its first alternative federal budget. Cho!ces was able to demonstrate in each of its alternative budgets that governments' massive spending cuts were not financially necessary and that choices more in keeping with what the majority of Canadians needed and wanted were possible, and indeed preferable.

In November 1991 a Cho!ces delegation addressed city council. Acknowledging the problems of the 1985 Enterprises–Jets deal, Harold Shuster warned about the dangers of the Interim Operating Agreement and urged the council to "not exchange one bad deal for another." In June 1992 Cho!ces again addressed council, articulating several themes later elaborated by Thin Ice: large sums should not be spent on a new Jets arena when other social necessities were being cut; the Convention Centre arena proposal was a property deal in disguise; the luxury boxes in the proposed new arena would constitute a huge public subsidy because the cost of renting them can be written off as a business expense on a company's tax returns; and the public was being excluded from the decision-making process, which was taking place exclusively behind closed doors even though the public was covering the Jets' losses.[27]

The first meeting of the Cho!ces' committee that was to become Thin Ice—the name was coined by Jeff Lowe—took place on October 5, 1993. After recruiting a few non-Cho!ces members, the group numbered about ten people and began meeting every Tuesday morning at 8 a.m., initially to consider how best to approach the issue. Most of us in the Thin Ice group were not especially knowledgeable about the political economy of professional sport. We got involved because we saw a social justice issue in the expenditure of large sums of public money on the business of professional hockey while libraries and recreational facilities and health, education and social services were being cut. Thin Ice determined that our first task was to educate ourselves—and then the public—about the Jets and the arena and the economics of the NHL, an approach that set the tone for our work over the next two years.

As a first step in its education campaign, Thin Ice planned a conference for mid-November 1993. In preparation the group contacted Professors Robert Baade, Bruce Kidd, and David Whitson, all specialists in the academic study of professional and amateur sport, and through them came in contact with the growing literature on the political economy of professional sport. The group members learned about recent dramatic changes in the economics of the NHL, about how franchises in smaller Canadian cities simply couldn't survive without large public subsidies, and about how most of the new large arenas built in North America in recent years were unable to break even. The new sports palaces could cover their operating costs but not their debt-services charges, and therefore they too required public subsidies. Indeed, in 1989 the subsidy to publicly owned arenas and stadiums in the United States was estimated to be $500 million.[28] It quickly became clear to us that the cost of keeping the Jets in Winnipeg would mean a huge expenditure of public funds, and that Winnipeg was not alone in this; given NHL economics, the same would be the case in all medium-sized Canadian cities.

After analyzing the Mauro Report, the Interim Operating Agreement, and related public documents, we also began to see that the politicians and their well-paid consultants were largely unaware of these realities and thus of the sheer magnitude of the public subsidy that would be required to save the Jets. In January 1993 we concluded that the Jets' losses, payable by the public, would accumulate to at least $40 million by June 30, 1997. Although the media and other Jets/arena boosters either ridiculed or ignored this figure, it proved to be an underestimate. Thin Ice, concerned that large public subsidies to the Jets would erode public spending on more essential services, adopted the position "no public funds for a new arena or for continued subsidization of the Jets." The conference on November 20, 1993 elaborated upon these themes and upon the failings of the Mauro Report and the Interim Operating Agreement.

At a second public conference in February 1993, David Whitson, co-author of the book *Hockey Night in Canada*, elaborated upon the changing economics of the NHL. He particularly emphasized the extent to which NHL hockey, like all professional sport, had become a commodity, an "entertainment product" integrated into a "continental entertainment market," and that young people in particular increasingly constructed their identities in this continental consumer context. This tendency was, of course, precisely what the post-1988, "Disney-fied" NHL was building on.

Thin Ice had prompted a debate on the issue at the rational rather than the emotional level, and by spring 1994 the group's name and message were widely known in Winnipeg. Two conferences had been staged and the keynote address of the first one, filmed by community access television, had been repeatedly broadcast. We had made presentations to city council and committees of council at every opportunity. Members had published articles in the local press. At a news conference held on February 1, 1994, the group linked the Jets' demands for public funds for a new arena to the city's proposed closure of eleven outdoor skating rinks. Thin Ice had also published and distributed a tabloid-size newspaper, *Arena Chronicles*, which included analyses of the Mauro Report and the Interim Operating Agreement and of "who benefits and who loses" from public spending on a new arena and on the Jets as well as the details on changing economics of the NHL. All these initiatives added significantly to the growing public debate by raising questions about whether, and how much, public money should be spent to keep the Jets in Winnipeg.

Thin Ice frequently argued that large expenditures of public funds for a new arena and for the Jets' losses were adding to the city's financial squeeze and contributing to the closure or reduction in services of sports and recreational facilities. Ironically, kids would have reduced opportunities to *play* hockey in order that adults—and, given rising ticket prices, well-to-do adults—could continue to *watch* hockey. Thin Ice argued that the Jets' arena boosters were in this way missing the very purpose of sport. Indeed, Shenkarow, Hartley Richardson and other business leaders who supported public funds for a new arena and for the Jets had written an open letter to the mayor in February 1993, and in a particularly blatant expression of irony called for a property tax freeze, in the full knowledge that a freeze could only be achieved by making even deeper cuts to such recreational facilities.[29]

It also became apparent that in its campaign Thin Ice was expressing the view held by the majority of Winnipeggers and Manitobans. In February 1994 we commissioned Viewpoints Research, a Winnipeg-based professional polling firm, to survey six hundred Manitobans on their support for public funding for a new arena and for continued subsidization of the Jets. The results revealed that 74 percent of Manitobans were opposed on both fronts.[30]

Who Benefits? Who Loses?

An Excerpt from the Thin Ice Publication, *Arena Chronicles*, 1994

Who will benefit and who will lose if we cave in to demands for a new arena?

First to benefit will be the private sector owners of the Jets—Barry and Marvin Shenkarow, Harvey Secter and Randy Moffat. The public—that's us—will be subsidizing them.

Real estate owners and developers will benefit—downtown property values will rise. Architect firms, contractors, lawyers will benefit, as usual, from such a large development.

Corporate executives will benefit. They will purchase luxury boxes. Executives, clients and cronies will watch hockey games in plush surroundings. The rest of us will subsidize these affluent people when they deduct the costs from their tax bills as entertainment expenses.

Some politicians might benefit. They could point to something tangible as evidence of their concern for Winnipeg. They could claim to be "builders," even though what they build hurts the city more than it helps.

Sports writers would benefit. Some of them are the biggest boosters of a new arena, and their views carry considerable influence among hockey fans. It is in their self-interest to have an NHL team to report on. They get to attend big league games and rub shoulders with the "stars."

And, of course, the fans benefit. We will be able to attend NHL games in our own home town—a considerable attraction.

But, who loses?

The average ticket price in a new arena will increase by 50% to over $32. For a parent to take one child to a game will be $75 or more including parking and refreshments. Most Winnipeggers cannot afford this. Hockey will become even more elite.

The large subsidies will result in more cuts to or user fees for community recreation services like pools, rinks, playing fields and other services like libraries.

We all—rich and poor—lose in the long run if scarce resources going to an arena and the Jets result in further cuts to health, education and social services. These cuts will create more poverty, more violence, more despair and more frustration.

Working people and the poor, in this "child poverty capital of Canada," will suffer, further widening the gap between the rich and the poor.

Loaded with these polling results and with a detailed knowledge of the NHL and the local Jets/arena issue, Thin Ice arranged to lobby politicians. In March and April 1994, members of the group met with members of the provincial NDP and Liberal caucuses, Finance Minister Eric Stefanson, the city councillors who were members of the Winnipeg in the Nineties (WIN) caucus and councillor and Winnipeg Enterprises board member Bill Clement. With the exception of Clement and WIN councillor Glen Murray, the politicians tended to be unaware of the changed economics of the NHL and its relevance to Winnipeg. They were generally prepared to accept, uncritically, the conclusions of the Coopers and Lybrand and Mauro reports and were unwilling to do or say much of anything until the release of the then long-delayed Burns Report. The issue, we feared, was unfolding along the same lines as the 1988 debate about the Canada-U.S. Free Trade Agreement—the more people knew about it, the more they were opposed, yet the business community and its political supporters wanted it and would use their positions and power to get their way.

Thin Ice's capacity to fight the local business establishment was limited. A financial statement prepared May 31, 1994 by Harold Shuster, who had become the Thin Ice chairperson, showed that we had raised a total of $1,214 (conference registration, donations and sales of Thin Ice T-shirts) and had liabilities (conference costs, the Viewpoints survey, the cost of printing and T-shirts) totalling $1,280. Our members were not "among the biggest names in the money game in this community." Indeed, the core members—seven people who would stay involved to the end in August 1995—included a community health organizer, a part-time sales clerk, a full-time student, a retired teacher, two professors, and one unemployed city planner. The number of people actively and directly involved with Thin Ice at any given time was relatively small, ranging between six and twelve.

Still, most of these people were experienced activists who had developed their political and analytical skills in a variety of previous social justice campaigns. The group was not made up of political novices. In addition, although by early 1994 the group had, for public relations purposes, taken on an identity separate from Cho!ces, it continued to be very much a part of the broad Cho!ces network and was able to draw upon the skilled people in the community who regularly provided Cho!ces with various forms of technical and creative support. Thus the small size of the core group was deceiving—the group had a broad reach in the community and by early 1994 had succeeded in making its name and message well known and putting forth some convincing figures. With limited financial resources the group was effectively giving voice to concerns felt by a majority of Winnipeggers.

This opposition had to contend not only with the business establishment and the gung-ho politicians but also with the media who were, with occasional exceptions, unabashed Jets/arena boosters. For the most part the media had been completely uncritical in their treatment of the Coopers and Lybrand and Mauro reports. They accepted these analyses as truth and made no attempt to solicit independent evaluations. They demonstrated only a limited understanding of the changed economics of the NHL, and they largely ignored the efforts of Thin Ice, other than to launch the occasional broadside.

For example, *Free Press* sports reporter and leading Jets/arena booster Scott Taylor wrote in December 1993 that while there had been much recent talk about the Jets deal, "Sadly for the most part, the talk has been misguided and ill-informed," in large part because of "people who refuse to see the Big Picture." His column on that day was intended "to educate those poor souls from Cho!ces who prefer not to read, listen or comprehend."[31] Taylor became known in particular as the voice of Barry Shenkarow. He and Shenkarow were in frequent contact, so that Taylor's columns were often first with inside information. Shenkarow benefitted by getting a "positive spin" placed on his version of the facts; Taylor benefitted by getting regular "scoops."

But the more standard media response to the case being made by Thin Ice was simply to ignore it. A Hal Sigurdson column in the *Free Press* calling for "unemotional number crunching" prompted a letter from Thin Ice. The letter went unpublished. Attempts in June 1994 to elicit interest from CBC Radio's *Morningside* and *The Inside Track* and TSN's *Inside Sport* produced no response. The Winnipeg story in a *Globe and Mail* series on Canadian NHL franchises made no mention of Thin Ice or of the grounds for our opposition.[32] A letter to the *Globe and Mail* expressing disappointment and setting out some of Thin Ice's objections to the proposed new arena went unpublished. The boosters would not debate the issues. They relied on slogans. Mayor Thompson asserted, "For those who are forward thinking and realistic, it isn't a debate." Barry Shenkarow said, "The public just isn't educated enough to see this as a sound investment rather than as a subsidy for millionaire owners and players."

Most significantly, the media's daily news and sports coverage provided a regular diet of Jets/arena stories. For example, in a detailed analysis of *Free Press* coverage of the Jets issue covering a two-week period in late June-early July 1994, Thin Ice member Todd Scarth "could find no articles written by *Free Press* staff which questioned the basic views of the government and corporate elite. It seems that one of the *Free Press'* main functions in this debate is to limit dramatically the range of discussion."[33] To the extent that Thin Ice reached the public, it did so for the most part by means other than the daily media.

The bias of the media could not, however, overcome the apparent unwillingness of the local business community to invest in the money-losing Jets and their new arena; nor could the many flawed consultants' reports and the harried decision-making process at city hall. By June 1994 it seemed that the risk and the cost to the public were too high; the private-sector commitment was too low; and, however distressing it might be, the plug simply had to be pulled.

5. Heroes, White Knights and the Kids: A Resurrection Story

Dale Cummings

Filmon's calm demeanour in the Legislature and before the TV cameras on Friday morning, June 24, 1994, belied the tension that had been building in the previous days. The long wait for the Burns Report had created a pressure-cooker atmosphere. Mayor Thompson acknowledged, "I was beginning to feel boxed into a corner." Councillor Glen Murray, speaking at a council meeting the day before the release of the Burns Report, said, "It's unfortunate that it's had to come down to the eleventh hour again." City councillors were kept in the dark, as usual. Premier Filmon, who had almost certainly been made aware of the contents of the Burns Report some weeks in advance, was about to roll the dice.[1] In the Legislature that day he announced that not a nickel of private-sector money had been found to save the Jets, and the government's option to purchase the Jets at $32 million was being allowed to lapse. Filmon said that $30 million of public-sector money would not be enough to build the arena, and that the full cost of the facility was now estimated at $111 million. "I cannot in good conscience expect Manitobans to fund a $111 million facility and also double their current spending on the Jets.... As the Burns Committee stated, no private sector investors have expressed interest in purchasing the hockey club because of the existence of excessive losses and the potential for continued losses in the future."[2]

As far as anyone could tell, the great arena debate was over. The members of Thin Ice congratulated each other in the halls of the Legislature. Who would have known that Filmon's announcement, his concession of defeat, was a ploy to bring a new set of players into the off-ice game? The death announcement was intended as a dash of cold water in the face of a private sector that had been watching from the sidelines, unprepared to risk private capital in what was clearly a marginal venture.

While publicly pulling the plug, Filmon was privately organizing a revival. Within hours of his announcement in the Legislature, the premier and his staff were on the phones, pulling together the key players. Phone lines buzzed all weekend. The premier had captured the private sector's full attention. As Terry Cristall, president of the Winnipeg Chamber of Commerce, put it, "Filmon forced everyone to react immediately instead of waiting. He deliberately or otherwise made people realize the time was now . . . and so we were keeping as close as we could to it by keeping the phone lines going."[3]

Two meetings in Filmon's office in the Legislative Building on Monday, June 27 produced the desired outcome. The Jets were saved from death. The meetings brought together in a single room for the first time all the major players in this long-running drama. The three levels of government were there, in the form of Mayor Thompson (along with Deputy Mayor George Fraser and Councillor Bill Clement), Premier Filmon, and federal Human Resources Minister Lloyd Axworthy (member for Winnipeg South Centre). Jets' president Barry Shenkarow was there, of course, as well as a representative of the private sector in the person of Jim Burns, chair of the Implementation Committee and executive vice-president of Power Corporation. Filmon also took the precautionary measure of including provincial NDP and Liberal leaders Gary Doer and Paul Edwards, although Doer and Edwards appear to have been excluded from any real decision-making and were not included in any further meetings or strategy sessions. Axworthy, who had been lying in the reeds watching, now indicated a willingness to commit federal money and play a leadership role. Reporter Scott Taylor labelled him "the hero."[4]

The Winnipeg media would consistently interpret the struggle over the next year in terms of "heroes" and "white knights," several of whom would ride to the rescue at future eleventh hours, only to stumble and fall flat in the face of the media's adulation. But for now, leadership—whether Filmon's or Axworthy's or both—had saved the day. By the end of Monday, June 27, 1994 a commitment was in place to build a new arena, to do so by means of "creative financing," to seek new or expanded ownership of the Jets and to put it all together by May 1, 1995. Filmon's gamble had paid off. The first resurrection miracle had been successfully performed. The patient, almost lost, had been given at least another ten months to live.

Some concerns were expressed publicly, and although they represented a minority view, they were prophetic. Bill Neville, a former city councillor and a particularly astute and thoughtful observer of city politics, commented that if Filmon's blunt announcement in the Legislature had been a deliberate strategy, it had worked. He added ominously, "But the last-minute panic, prompted by the Premier's judgement on a last-minute report, is a cause for concern: what kinds of decisions are being made in a swirl of last-minute activity, by 'heavy hitters' behind closed doors?"[5] Once again, whatever the quality of the decisions, the notion of "behind closed doors" aptly captured the essence of the decision-making pattern.

Winnipeg's Business Class, the Youth Corps and Questions of Property

The hesitancy of Winnipeg's business class to invest in the Jets has a history. Aggressively self-confident and entrepreneurial in the early years of the century, Winnipeg's business class had lost its drive by the post-Second World War period. In his *Manitoba: A History*, historian W.L. Morton noted that during the postwar era civic politics and private business in Winnipeg "were dominated by adherence to routine and precedent," and "not since the lamented death of J.A. Richardson in 1939 had the Winnipeg business community known creative leadership." Winnipeg's business leaders were, Morton argued, "canny, reactionary, untravelled, fearful of ideas and imagination."[6] Alan Artibise concurred, writing in his 1977 history of Winnipeg that in those years, "Winnipeggers lacked a concept of the city's future that might have instilled new energy into the community. . . . Even the city's anglo-saxon business community . . . was unable to provide the leadership it had provided before."[7] Peter Newman, in his book *The Canadian Establishment*, called Winnipeg's postwar business elite "comatose."[8] And as recently as 1990, a joint City Hall-Chamber of Commerce economic development committee struck to make recommendations about Winnipeg's economic future realized it had no ideas at all, after which it hired the consulting firm Price Waterhouse, which duly reported: "We have observed a very low entrepreneurial culture throughout our interviews . . . the entrepreneurial climate is poor." More specifically, the report said, "The absence of a focused and concerted effort on the part of Winnipeg's leaders has hampered the City's economic development." The Winnipeg Chamber of Commerce had said the same in its February 1, 1989, symposium: "Another challenge facing Winnipeg is leadership, or lack of it, in either the private or the public sectors."[9]

Not surprisingly then, the Burns Committee reported that Winnipeg businesspeople responded as usual to the enquiries. Winnipeg's business class had contributed not a nickel. Some six months of searching by the Burns Committee had yielded not a single local investor. The risk was too great. They wouldn't take a chance. But now, if Filmon's announcement was a deliberate wake-up call, an attempt to get them involved, the bait was grabbed. Within days of Filmon's dramatic announcement the media were announcing that "a mystery group" was prepared to acquire an option to purchase, at $32 million, the 64 percent of the Jets' privately held shares. The city's and province's option, good to June 30, 1994, had lapsed; the private sector was soon to acquire a new option exercisable at any time to

May 1, 1995; an additional ten months had been purchased.

The latest initiative would turn out to be a foolish and costly mistake, one of many to follow. The problem was not so much that Winnipeg's business class lacked entrepreneurial qualities. Rather, the young corporate executives about to ride to the rescue had no appreciation whatever of the economic reality of NHL hockey in Winnipeg—and their innocence of the changed economics of the NHLwould prove exceptionally costly.

The "mystery group," initially a handful of young businessmen, soon became the Manitoba Entertainment Complex Inc. (MEC), known briefly as the "Group of 44" and later as the "Group of 58." Its most distinctive feature was that it comprised the younger generation of Manitoba's business class: "the kids," as they came to be called; "the children," as the business community referred to them a year later when their efforts had collapsed. This younger generation of Winnipeg's business community—many of them the sons and nephews of the old business elite—had been stung by the Price Waterhouse report and embarrassed by Burns's failure, and in re-sponse had decided to seize on the plight of the Winnipeg Jets. They would Save Our Jets they pledged, and in so doing revitalize the business commu-nity's tarnished reputation.

They believed that the presence of an NHL franchise brought significant economic advantages to the city. Among other things, these young corporate executives argued, the Jets contributed to creating the kind of cosmopolitan culture that is a factor in attracting and holding middle-level and senior-level corporate executives. These corporate executives, almost all of them male, often use a knowledge of professional team sports as part of a common language of business relations, and many of them would use an arena's corporate luxury suites as a venue for business activities. The loss of an NHL franchise would remove such opportunities and would erode Winnipeg's status as a place for corporations to do business. Winnipeg would no longer be a "big league" or "world-class" city. It is not at all clear that this NHL presence would have any *economic* impact on the vast majority of Winnipeggers—claims about the broad economic benefits of professional sport teams being regularly exaggerated by the promoters of the franchises—but it is clear that many actors in the corporate sector consider a local NHL franchise to be symbolically and culturally significant for the conduct of business. MEC decided to save the city's NHL franchise.

The leaders of MEC were in their thirties and early forties, and most held senior corporate posts by virtue of family ties. The six-person executive was typical. John Loewen, MEC chairman, is the nephew of Bill Loewen, founder of Comcheq Services, long-time corporate philanthropist and one-time president of the National Party. Hartley Richardson is a member of the fifth generation of the city's most powerful family, the Richardsons. He is the son of George Richardson, the chairman of James Richardson and Sons Limited, and the grandson of James A. Richardson. Sandy Riley is the latest in a long line of Rileys whose fortune arose out of the insurance and finance industry—the family helped found the Great-West Life Assurance Co. One uncle, Derek Riley, raised the $7.8 million for the Capital Fund as part of the 1991 Interim Operating Agreement. Another uncle, Culver Riley, founded the Winnipeg Enterprises Corporation, which in the early 1950s built the stadium and arena at the Polo Park site. Robert Silver (no relation to the author of this book) runs the clothing manufacturing business passed on to him by his father. Stewart Murray, president of Domo Gasoline Corporation, is married to the daughter of Domo's owner, former Senator Douglas Everett.[10] The Oslers are also long-time members of Winnipeg's establishment. Cam Osler, president of MEC and later of Spirit of Manitoba, is the son of E.B. Osler, a Liberal MP first elected in Winnipeg South Centre in 1968. Their family fortune arose from the long-established financial services firm of Osler, Hammond and Nanton. For many years predecessors of Cam Osler, Hartley Richardson and Sandy Riley had served simultaneously on the board of directors of Great-West Life.

MEC clearly represented a passing of the torch from an older generation of business leaders, exemplified by Arthur Mauro and Jim Burns—who had *not* pulled the business class together to build a new arena and save the Jets—to a younger generation of business leaders who saw themselves, as Sandy Riley put it, as people "who have a stake in the future of the city."[11] Indeed, the MEC executive talked openly about their effort to save the Jets as a "passing of the torch."

For most of this younger generation this was their first, big public project, and not surprisingly mistakes were made. The group was narrowly constructed: it did not include senior and more experienced members of the local business class; it did not, at least initially, include Sam Katz of Nite Out Entertainment or any of the other concert promoters who would be users of, and crucial income generators for, any new arena. Many of those who were involved with MEC merely lent their names to the effort; they were not active participants. The group had little experience in dealing with a complicated and fractious city council. As chairman John Loewen later acknowledged, "It seemed, initially, there wasn't a great deal of trust between the elected politicians at City Hall and the business community, simply because I don't think we'd ever worked together as a group on a common project."[12] Yet civic politics was the level of government that Winnipeg's dynamic, turn-of-the-century capitalist class had directly and completely dominated. Of the 1874–1914 period, historian Artibise observed: "Winnipeg's commercial class dominated every elective office throughout the period. In the case of the mayor's office, the commercial group had a representative in office for 37 of 41 years, or 90 percent of the time."[13] In recent years the business elite had largely ignored city hall.

Business was no longer so locally oriented; it was increasingly continentalized and thus had little need of aid from local government. Thus when the inexperienced members of MEC came looking for support from city council in 1994–95, they were clumsy and ineffectual, and when they did not immediately get their way they became heavy-handed, resorting to private arm-twisting and pressure tactics, public misinformation and threats of capital flight.

The group was inexperienced in the economics of professional sport. None of the long list of reports—the Lavalin, Coopers and Lybrand, Mauro, Ogden and Burns reports—had analyzed NHL economics, and only Shenkarow had direct knowledge of the business. John Loewen had limited experience with professional sport. A former basketball player with the University of Manitoba Bisons and former assistant coach of the University of Winnipeg Wesmen basketball team, he had also been a shareholder of the Northern Basketball League's Winnipeg Thunder, which folded in July 1994, just as MEC was emerging.[14] It was an inauspicious omen for MEC's adventure in the new NHL.

In the end the leaders of MEC, powerful though their families might be in Winnipeg, would prove to be minor players in a corporate-driven NHL undergoing the same dramatic restructuring, with the same effects on smaller centres as was occurring in other increasingly continentalized industries. But whatever its members' shortcomings, MEC quickly and decisively took charge of one important decision—the site of the proposed new arena. The Mauro, Ogden and Burns reports all had recommended the Convention Centre site. Immediately after the release of the cautious Burns Report and Filmon's tactically bold statement in the Legislature, only one thing remained clear—the site. As *Free Press* editorial writer Jim Carr put it, "The only decision taken so far is that if a new arena is to be built it will be across the street from the Convention Centre."[15] This location seemed to be accepted by everyone involved: the consultants in their reports; the business community; the mayor and deputy mayor; the premier; the media.

Almost immediately the newly formed MEC, despite claims that "the Mauro and Burns Reports are the basis for MEC action," overturned the recommendation of those reports and restored the idea of building at the North Forks site.[16] Some of their public explanations for this shift bordered on the trivial. Cam Osler said the North Forks was preferable because it was a "signature site. . . . When they say it's a good signature site, they mean it's a good photo opportunity." Sandy Riley pointed out that an arena at the North Forks could incorporate a restaurant that overlooked the Red River. And John Loewen insisted repeatedly that the North Forks site was not at the Forks: "We've said all along this is not Forks land. The real tie-in is to Portage and Main."[17]

While the site was indeed not technically a part of the Forks, its development, as MEC itself acknowledged, was to be coordinated by the Forks Renewal Corporation.[18] More importantly, an arena at that site, given its bulk and height and the necessity for parking facilities and street changes to facilitate greater traffic flows, would constitute a northern barrier to the future development of the Forks. Loewen's claim that the site was "not in any way a part of the Forks and would not change any plans to leave the Forks green"[19] was extremely misleading.

More substantially, MEC stated that the cost of servicing the North Forks site was $7 million less than the cost of servicing the Convention Centre site. But as it turned out the group's estimates for the North Forks site were unrealistically low—more than $20 million lower than the costs later estimated by the city in April 1995.[20]

Cam Osler later stated that the earlier preference for the Convention Centre site was largely attributable to the presence of more credible proponents for that site than for the Forks site. He argued that when MEC emerged the group invited several architectural firms to make submissions, and these architects were unanimous in preferring the North Forks. This, Osler said, is not surprising—the beautiful North Forks site offers an architect much more scope for imaginative design possibilities than the more cramped downtown Convention Centre site. The predictable opinion of the architects weighed heavily with the relatively inexperienced MEC leaders.[21]

But an arena at the Forks site was inconsistent with the vision expressed by Winnipeggers in 1990 in *Future Directions for the Forks*, a vision that almost certainly accounts for MEC's dogged insistence that the site was not at the Forks but was rather an extension of Portage East. It was this claim—the insistence, as Loewen put it, that "the real tie-in was to Portage and Main"—that led to the suspicions held by many Winnipeggers about the real cause of MEC's shift from the Convention Centre to the North Forks site.

The Richardson family owns much of the land around Portage and Main, including the Portage East site of what is now called the Lombard Hotel. They had long been interested in developing the property adjacent to their Portage and Main holdings. The Richardson family, represented on the board of Great-West Life for a total of twenty-eight years between 1928 and 1970, would certainly have benefitted from the 1976 proposal by GWL and the CNR to construct a new arena as the centrepiece of a massive redevelopment of the Forks. And George Richardson had consistently supported Rick Koswin's superplex proposal intended for the Forks. In January 1994, at a time when everyone appeared to agree on the Convention Centre site, Richardson wrote to Koswin saying that he had "continually become more fascinated and impressed" with Koswin's "imaginative thinking," which he thought was "similar to the planning of those who developed Winnipeg initially." Richardson noted in particular that "The location you have suggested would make a dramatic impact on the whole city."[22] It is difficult

Richardson Family Portage and Main Holdings

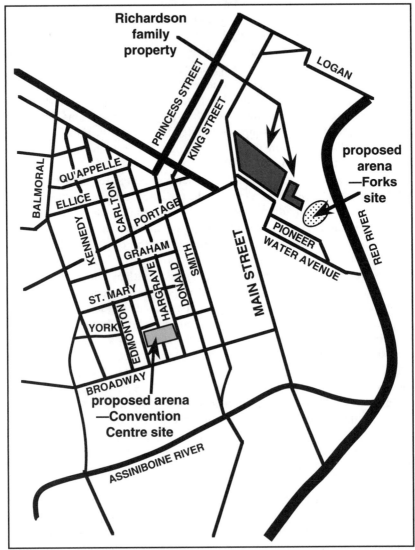

to know why Richardson would have been so enthusiastic about the Koswin proposal which inspired virtually no support from the rest of the business community, unless it was to keep alive the idea of developing the northern part of the Forks adjacent to the family holdings.

Certainly MEC's shift from the long-agreed Convention Centre site to the North Forks site prompted suspicions. Jets booster Taylor reported, "The group . . . changed the site everyone seemed to agree upon for reasons that some city council members feel are suspicious." Martin Eva, developer and promoter of an arena at the Convention Centre site, remarked that the arena location had become a struggle between those businesses with interests in the Forks area and other firms located closer to the Convention Centre. "There is every reason to believe a land play is going on," he said. Eva was not alone. A *Free Press* article pointed out, "Indeed, many in business circles are suggesting the 'Richardson Equation' is the reason the site north of the Forks is now being pushed instead of one across from the Winnipeg Convention Centre."[23]

Hartley Richardson "hotly" denied that the location of his family holdings explained MEC's shift to the North Forks. John Loewen insisted that the potentially huge appreciation in the value of the Richardson holdings at Portage and Main "had absolutely nothing to do with it. . . . Everyone has shelved their own interests."[24] Yet the alternative public explanations—that it was a "signature site," that it would cost less to service the site, that a restaurant could be built overlooking the Red River—are not convincing in light of the overwhelming pre-MEC support for the Convention Centre site. The later Osler explanation—that the inexperienced MEC leaders were swayed by the architects' fascination with the aesthetic possibilities afforded by the potentially beautiful North Forks site—is plausible and should not be lightly discarded. Still, the fact remains that the Richardson family would have benefitted handsomely if an arena had been built adjacent to their substantial Portage and Main holdings.

The Great Marketing Campaign: A Silencing of Opposition

In early October 1994 MEC applied to city council to use the money remaining in the Capital Fund—the $7.8 million raised in 1991 by Sandy Riley's uncle, Derek—for a marketing campaign to sell luxury suites and club seats in the proposed new North Forks arena. The first attempt failed. To gain the extra votes needed to get council approval, Mayor Thompson called a special "Public Meeting" of the Executive Policy Committee for Saturday, October 8, 1994, during the Thanksgiving long weekend.

There was at the time substantial opposition to public funding for a new arena. The Viewpoints Research poll of February 1994 had showed that almost three-quarters of Manitobans opposed public funding for a new arena, and the public was clamouring for the opportunity to express their views on the issue. Yet the so-called "Public Meeting" was designed to hear *only* from those with specific arena proposals. Opponents of public funding for a new arena were prohibited from speaking. When Thin Ice wrote to Mayor Thompson a few days before the "Public Meeting" asking to speak, the reply from the mayor, four days after the event, informed us that there was not enough time to hear everyone in a one-day public meeting. She added, "This meeting is the starting point for further future consultations with the public on issues relating to a new arena/entertainment facility."[25] No such consultation ever occurred. When I made a telephone call asking that Thin Ice be given a chance to speak at the "Public Meeting," the clerk of the Executive Policy Committee advised that he had been specifically instructed by the mayor that delegations opposed to public funding for a new arena were not to be heard. He also advised that he had been "swamped" with calls from people wanting to speak.

The mayor's explanation for the public's exclusion was that the meeting was called specifically so that councillors could consider all the arena proposals before voting on MEC's application for $1.5 million from the Capital Fund. Yet even this more limited purpose was little more than going through the motions. The mayor stated publicly that only the MEC proposal was being considered, and only MEC held an option to purchase the Jets. Other councillors concurred—the public meeting was a mere formality. As superplex promoter Rick Koswin lamented, "People won't listen. Let's face it. It's a done deal. The focus is on the Group of 44."[26]

The public meeting was held, and not surprisingly—given that it took place on the Thanksgiving weekend with members of the public prohibited from participating—it was reported that "hardly anyone was there to listen." MEC, however, seizing the public relations opportunity, announced that the public's absence was evidence of broad support for its proposal. "I think the public probably spoke by its absence," Loewen said. "I think the people are saying 'Let's get on with it. Let's move ahead.'" Sports reporter Taylor intoned, "Yesterday's session at the Convention Centre was a wonderful example of the politics of democracy."[27]

The next wonderful example of "the politics of democracy" took place October 14, 1994 on the floor of city council. On that date the council was scheduled to vote again on whether to allocate to MEC the $1.5 million remaining in the Capital Fund to mount a massive campaign to market luxury boxes and club seats in the proposed North Forks arena—despite the complete lack of public consultation and documented evidence of widespread opposition to the Forks site and to public funds for a new arena. But if councillors had any concerns about public opposition, those qualms were quickly allayed by a pre-emptive example of MEC's marketing talents. On the morning of the 14th a front-page headline in the *Free Press* announced, "Six of 10 Winnipeggers want new arena, poll says." MEC had commissioned an Angus Reid poll, timing its release to coincide with the important council vote. The *Free Press* was quick to accommodate the news. How could council say no in the face of such a dramatic shift in public opinion? Loewen, it initially appeared, was right. Winnipeggers just wanted MEC to get on with the job.

Yet the poll was extremely misleading. The question asked, according to the Angus Reid press release, was: "Based on what you may have read, seen or heard, do you as a Winnipegger strongly support, moderately support, moderately oppose or strongly oppose the construction of a new Entertainment Complex?" Some 59 percent of Winnipeggers strongly or moderately supported the idea of a new entertainment complex. But the *real* question was not asked—do you support *public funding* for a new entertainment complex?

Thin Ice asked whether the failure to ask the real question might be deliberate. MEC knew that the majority of Winnipeggers were opposed to public funding for a new arena. Asking the question as they did was akin to asking people if they'd like a new Mercedes Benz. The proportion saying "yes, I would like to have a new Mercedes Benz" would be much higher than the proportion who would say yes if asked whether they were able and prepared to *pay* for a new Mercedes Benz. Indeed, answers to a second question in the survey confirmed this analogy. Immediately after asking the respondents about their support for or opposition to a new entertainment complex, the poll asked them how much influence the cost of such a facility to the three levels of government would have on their answer. An Angus Reid spokesperson informed me that around 75 percent replied that the cost to the public would have a strong influence on their answer. Thus it is likely that if the more pertinent question had been asked—"Do you support public funding for a new arena?"—a significant majority would have said no. That, after all, had been the case with the Viewpoints Research poll of February 1994, and would prove to be the case again in November 1994 when a second Viewpoints Research poll commissioned by Thin Ice found 74 percent of Winnipeggers were still opposed to public funding for a new arena. John Loewen later admitted to Carl Ridd that he was embarrassed by having approved a tactic such as the carefully timed release of, and misleading construction of, the Angus Reid poll results.

On the morning of October 14, with councillors preparing to vote armed with the news that public opinion had shifted behind the MEC proposal to build a new arena at the North Forks site, I appeared as a Thin Ice spokesperson before council. Pointing out that the Angus Reid poll was misleading and that opposition to public funding for a new arena continued to be strong, I argued that the city council should not make any decisions without public consultations—of which there had to date been none, despite public demands and despite Mayor Thompson's promises—and that MEC had presented no convincing evidence of the merits of the North Forks site. MEC executive members Loewen and Robert Silver, who had been sitting in the council gallery, asked for the chance to respond and used the opportunity to enlighten councillors about the consequences of a "no" vote. Robert Silver was especially aggressive and emphatic, hinting that local companies would leave Winnipeg if council did not approve MEC's request for $1.5 million. Loewen added that a negative vote would put an end to MEC's efforts, and the Jets would be gone. In the end a majority of council was "persuaded," voting 8 to 6 in favour of allocating $1.5 million to MEC to begin its marketing campaign.

Winning this council vote had been a tough battle for MEC: it was no doubt one of the specific instances that made Loewen "surprised at the amount of effort and time it took to try to educate city councillors."[28] In the end, though, MEC's "educational techniques" carried the day. To respond to the shift from the Convention Centre site to the North Forks, Thin Ice began, in early September 1994, to pull together a resurrected Coalition to Preserve the Forks. The task proved more difficult than we had first anticipated. Key activist Kent Gerecke had died in 1993, and his group Greening the Forks, which had played a lead role in 1989, was virtually defunct. But local environmentalist Christine Common-Singh pulled together a small coalition that held a news conference at the Forks in late September, arguing for the overall goal of keeping the Forks green.

The media reacted angrily, insisting that the proposed arena site was *not* a part of the Forks and that Thin Ice was misleading the public. Yet, the Forks Renewal Corporation had the responsibility for planning the North Forks site, making it all of a piece. The construction of an arena in the North Forks would confine the Forks itself to a much smaller area than would otherwise be the case, and the increased traffic flow would add to the extent to which the Forks was dominated by the automobile.

Nevertheless, there was a clear determination to mute expressions of concern about the Forks. Common-Singh, a Heritage Winnipeg board member, was subjected to a finger-wagging verbal attack at the next board meeting when an irate businessman accused her of undermining the interests of Heritage Winnipeg by opposing the North Forks arena. Heritage Winnipeg withdrew from the coalition and abandoned opposition to a North Forks arena, a move that was almost certainly the result of pressure from the business community. A high-profile Winnipeg lawyer advised Thin Ice in November 1994 that all opposition was being silenced behind closed doors by powerful forces.

In the meantime, Thin Ice had asked economics professors Errol Black and Joe Dolecki of Brandon University to prepare an analysis of the Coopers and Lybrand Report—the source of the oft-repeated claim that the loss of the Jets would take $48 million per year out of Winnipeg's economy. Although Thin Ice could not afford to pay for the work, the professors readily agreed to the project, considering it a contribution to an important public debate. Submitted in October 1994, the Black and Dolecki Report was a devastating critique, showing that Coopers and Lybrand should have used a "net benefits" analysis and that the multiplier that Coopers and Lybrand used was almost double the one recommended by the Manitoba Bureau of Statistics. The Coopers and Lybrand Report was more pro-Jets

Tom Brodbeck, *Uptown*

Barry Shenkarow, part owner and President of the Winnipeg Jets. A clever negotiator, Shenkarow ended up with the prize: the huge capital gain from the sale of the Jets. As early as April 1995—before the massive Save Our Jets rallies—Shenkarow and his partners took steps to avoid paying Manitoba taxes on this capital gain.

Winnipeg Sun

Israel (Izzy) Asper, owner of CanWest Global Communications. The corporate spark behind the final effort to keep the Jets in Winnipeg, Asper battled with Jets owner Barry Shenkarow. When told Shenkarow was disappointed with an Asper-assembled offer to purchase the Jets, Asper replied: "Barry's upset? Oh, that's gonna ruin my day."

Ian Flett, *Uptown*

John Loewen, Manitoba Entertainment Complex Inc. Spokesperson for the group of young businessmen which failed in its attempt to buy the Jets. MEC was described by a Winnipeg journalist as having "a serious credibility problem when it comes to numbers—especially the ones with dollar signs in front."

Ian Flett, *Uptown*

Susan Thompson, Mayor of Winnipeg. The city's chief booster, Mayor Thompson remained "cheerily innocent of the details" of the complex Jets/arena conflict.

Ian Flett, *Uptown*

Gary Filmon, Premier of Manitoba. The premier insisted throughout the April 1995 provincial election that, if elected, his government would spend no more than $10 million to save the Jets. He knew all along that much more would be needed.

Ian Flett, *Uptown*

Save Our Jets rally, Portage Avenue and Main Street. One of many rallies of Jets' supporters, most of them young men, in late April and May 1995. This rally followed MEC's calculated attempt to blame their failure to save the Jets on NHL Commissioner Gary Bettman.

AP News / WorldWide Photos

Key members of Spirit of Manitoba Inc., the final attempt to save the Jets. From the left are Cam Osler, Spirit president; Alan Sweatman, Spirit chairman; Mike Sinclair, attorney; Gerry Gray, honourary chairman; and Steve Bannatyne, Spirit board member. The firms with which Osler and Sweatman were associated earned huge consulting and legal fees. In the end, Winnipeg's corporate sector would not invest its own money in the effort to save the Jets.

propaganda than hard-headed economic analysis; the Black and Dolecki Report threw into question the entire economic rationale used by Jets/arena boosters. Why spend huge sums of public funds on a new arena when the Jets contribute little in net financial terms to the local economy? Jets boosters might reply that keeping the Jets was important for reasons having to do with "community pride," but as Black and Dolecki argued:

> Given the limitations on resources, an argument—indeed, a strong argument—could be made that community confidence and community pride would be better served by putting those resources into reducing child poverty rather than the Jets. Surely a story in some future edition of the *Free Press* under the caption, 'A dramatic reduction in child poverty: Manitoba record Canada's best' would do as much if not more to boost community pride than retention of the Jets.[29]

The media response to the report was tepid at best. Ironically, the idea of preparing such a study had originated with *Globe and Mail* reporter David Roberts, but when we offered the report to Roberts on an exclusive basis he did not use it. Roberts, one of the most astute media analysts of the issue, later explained that he had to be "very judicious," otherwise "the phone would ring off the hook." In other words, MEC members would respond to any criticism of their efforts with a barrage of angry phone calls. They had done so on earlier occasions. Roberts did not submit to such pressure and continued to write insightful articles about MEC, but made only a single passing reference to the Black and Dolecki Report, some three months later on January 23, 1995.

In Winnipeg, news of the report was "buried" on page 16 in the October 15th issue of the *Free Press*. After mailing the report, with a cover letter, to numerous media outlets, we did get a phone call from Gare Joyce, *Globe and Mail* sports reporter. Joyce was excited about the report, spent more than an hour on the phone with both me and Errol Black, and said a story would appear the next week. It did not. When I phoned him, Joyce insisted the story would appear "next week." It still did not appear. I phoned again, and the response was again the same—it would appear "next week." The Black and Dolecki Report was never covered in *The Globe and Mail*, save for Roberts' single-line mention in January 1995 story. Only Frances Russell, a *Free Press* columnist, gave the report anything like the coverage its significance warranted.[30] The difference between the media's treatment of this important and professional study and the media's coverage of everything that MEC did or said is striking.

By mid-October the *Free Press* was completely on board the Jets/arena booster bandwagon. Even the editorials, which had been relatively balanced, had become gung ho. The sports reporters, led by Taylor, were one-sided, as might be expected given their self-interest, but so too was the news coverage. The completely uncritical front-page coverage of the Angus Reid survey on the day of the crucial council vote was a particularly blatant example of mindless boosterism. By that time some *Free Press* reporters were responding privately to Thin Ice's complaints by saying that some of the paper's editors were rewriting stories to produce a pro-MEC slant. Whether this was true or not, it was at the very least an inside acknowledgement that the *Free Press* did indeed carry a pro-MEC slant.

With the $1.5 million from the Capital Fund in hand as of October 14, 1994, MEC immediately began its campaign to market luxury suites and club seats. They hired Karen Theobold, a twenty-eight-year-old Floridian marketing consultant described by Taylor as "a firecracker" who is "at the top of a craft many people don't master in a lifetime."[31] They staged a gala marketing kickoff for their "Be a Builder" campaign that attracted six hundred people to the Westin Hotel. They ran full-page newspaper, television and billboard ads, all extolling the virtues of club seats and urging people to "Be a Builder." The ads, in common with oft-repeated MEC public statements, reiterated the marketing goal and deadline: "Club seats are only available until November 30! All 1,500 seats must be sold by November 30 to keep the Jets and the Manitoba Entertainment Complex alive in Winnipeg."

Soon hints about sales being slow started to appear. By the end of October Theobold was publicly complaining and insisting that if MEC didn't accomplish its two goals of selling forty suites and 1,500 club seats by the end of November, "There won't be any point." Taylor berated Winnipeg's business community: "The big time business giants in this community have not responded as many expected they would last month. . . . half the members of the very successful Group of 58 haven't stepped forward to buy a box or club seat."[32] In other words, MEC had demanded $1.5 million in public money to market seats that its own members were not buying.

MEC's newspaper ads focused on the luxury and privilege inherent in purchasing a club seat. One full-page ad, clearly a response to the Thin Ice-led campaign against spending vast sums of public money on a new arena in the child poverty capital of Canada, included a photograph of a multicultural mix of children over the caption "Build It and They Will Stay"—the clear implication being that spending public money on a new arena for the Jets would ultimately trickle down to the benefit of even the poorest in Winnipeg. Younger members of Thin Ice and Cho!ces, understandably outraged, responded by redesigning the ad, adding a single word to the caption: "Build It and They Will Stay . . . Poor."

On December 8, 1994, at a packed news conference complete with flip charts and graphs, MEC officially declared their Be a Builder campaign a success. Referring to the number of luxury boxes and club seats sold, MEC chairperson John Loewen gushed, "These are remarkable results." Marketing co-chair Stewart Murray called it "a little like running the mile in under two minutes." MEC executive member Robert Silver, pointing out that as yet there was no site and no building, added, "The most remarkable part of what we've done is we've sold air."[33]

The air they sold was hot air. The minimum targets had not been met. The failure to meet the target was especially significant given the aggressive tactics MEC used to try to get small businesses to purchase club seats: at least some small businesses feared that if they did not agree to purchase a club seat, they risked losing accounts. The Winnipeg *Sun*'s Glen Cheater, who had become one of the most perceptive analysts of the Jets/arena affair, pointed out the truth behind MEC's glossy charts: "Those who read the fine print in yesterday's press kit learned the 1,600 'premium seats' are really 1,096 club seats combined with the 528 seats in those 40 luxury boxes. In fact, MEC only got three-quarters of the way to its 'minimum' goal on club seats." Cheater added that although MEC was working hard, "the group has a serious credibility problem when it comes to numbers—especially the ones with dollar signs in front."[34] A local reporter told Thin Ice, "It's all a big scam."

Still, the media were not about to abandon MEC just because the organization was being less than honest with numbers. The *Free Press* editorial board stood by them faithfully, albeit cautiously, noting that the group had "marketed a hope and a prayer" and "should be encouraged to continue its crusade."[35] The appeal to faith was appropriate. Even the *Sun*, despite Cheater's critical observations, ran a front-page headline shouting "MEC is Winning 'Numbers Game.'" This would become typical of the *Sun*'s dual-personality coverage: analytically critical articles inside; boosterish headlines on the front page. No such doubts troubled Taylor, who, typical of the day-to-day coverage provided by the *Free Press*, positively exuded. "It really is a tremendous accomplishment. No other arena marketing plan has ever been this successful." And, as Taylor assured his readers, "everyone" knew it: "It was one of those rare moments in this community when everyone within shouting distance was upbeat. Good cheer abounded. People said, 'Hi, how are you?' with gusto. The Manitoba Entertainment Complex Inc. gave the city a little Christmas present yesterday."[36] What Taylor gave his readers, and would continue to give his readers, was what *Globe and Mail* reporter Roberts later described as "fatuous boosterism."[37]

In Thin Ice we attempted to counter MEC's marketing campaign with our own, but not having $1.5 million and media support, our marketing strategy reached fewer Manitobans. In addition to the "Build It and They Will Stay ... Poor" poster, which elicited no media response whatever, Thin Ice held a news conference in late November 1994 in front of a dilapidated and boarded up house in Winnipeg's inner city. Taking off on MEC's "Be a Builder" theme, Thin Ice asked "What is to be built?" Should money be spent on luxury boxes for a new arena—"Luxury and Privilege," as another of the offensive full-page MEC ads promoting sales of luxury boxes and club seats was headlined—or should money be spent building and renovating housing for those in need? The news conference drew only one media outlet, the *Free Press*, resulting in a small inside story with no photograph—even though the *Free Press* had sent along a photographer. The article was based on the striking visual image of the boarded up house, as juxtaposed to the selling of "luxury and privilege," but without a photograph the political message was lost. The electronic media did not cover the news conference. A third Thin Ice initiative did elicit a photograph, but no accompanying story. In October members of Thin Ice and Cho!ces staged a "Let Them Eat Pucks" luncheon in front of John Loewen's Comcheq office, with a member wearing a Mayor Susan Thompson mask promising "a puck in every pot" if a new arena were built and offering curious passers-by a "thin gruel of puck stew" from a large black pot filled with pucks and water. Later Loewen refused to talk to me when I contacted him about an interview for this book. He said that in staging the "Let Them Eat Pucks" luncheon in front of his office our group had treated him "disrespectfully."

In each of these instances of political theatre, Thin Ice attempted— consistent with its origins in Cho!ces—to make with humour the point that it was also trying to make analytically, namely that the large amounts of public money required to build a new arena would be better spent meeting the real needs of Winnipeggers. Then again, maybe, we thought, the solution was to refrain from humour and stick to analysis. So in late November Thin Ice staged a Town Hall meeting on the Jets/arena issue, filled the 220-seat auditorium of the Museum of Man and Nature to overflowing, and received an exceptionally positive response to a thorough and detailed analysis of the issue. The *Free Press* did not cover the event.

More Fun with Numbers, and City Hall Decisions

The "fatuous boosterism" of the media's coverage of MEC did serve to bolster that organization's *real* marketing effort, which was directed primarily at managing public opinion. Carl Ridd, writing on behalf of Thin Ice, said in a *Free Press* op-ed piece that MEC had a problem: "The public doesn't believe them, knows the risks of the new NHL, and has other priorities." He added: "Management of public opinion therefore became a problem." And he astutely described how MEC had attempted to manage public opinion: "They made a decision to start at the 'soft end' of their task, and work up from there: get the people enthused about the Forks site, 'sell' the fancy architects' drawings, sell luxury seats; do the easy stuff; and avoid to the bitter end the hard nut that everyone, early, thought MEC had arrived on the scene to crack. The one Jim Burns tried to crack and couldn't: private money to pay for capital costs of the arena and the purchase of the Jets. To this day, MEC has avoided that one. Its members have put up not a nickel of their own."[38]

Ridd also pointed to other problems. The Jets' losses were mounting, the public was paying, but the public watchdog, the Interim Steering Committee (ISC), was asleep. Mauro had resigned as chair in December 1993, and the ISC had not met between July and November 1994. Ridd reported that he had been informed by Loewen that MEC, not the Interim Steering Committee, was now in charge of monitoring Jets' spending. But despite the NHL owners' lockout that began in September, the Jets, unlike any other NHL team, had kept all but two of their forty-five full-time staff on salary during the lockout.[39]

Why had the Jets not laid off staff during the lockout? Because the Jets' staff was working for MEC in its marketing campaign. This drove up the Jets' costs and thus the size of the team's losses. But the public was paying for the losses. Thus the public paid twice for MEC's marketing effort: first, by contributing $1.5 million from the Capital Fund; second, by paying the salaries of Jets' staff who were working for MEC. And since MEC was now taking the place of the public watchdog, it was all too easy to turn a blind eye to that portion of Jets' spending that accrued to MEC's benefit. Even the *Free Press* editorial board expressed concern that the Interim Steering Committee was not meeting and "nobody in charge is asking any questions."[40] Ridd wrote: "Meanwhile, singing in high falsetto above the din are the almost daily voices of advocates, particularly Scott Taylor, John Loewen and Susan Thompson, calling for everyone to pull together as a community. It is the stuff of low comedy for those who can afford to laugh, and of tragedy for those who can't."[41]

Making matters still worse, the NHL player lockout ended in the second week of January 1995, with a new NHL-NHLPA collective bargaining agreement that included no meaningful salary caps and no revenue-sharing. There was only a *promise* by the NHL to study means of assisting small-market teams. The Mauro, Burns and Ogden reports had been clear: without salary caps and/or revenue-sharing, the already marginal Jets/arena deal would not work. Immediately prior to the lockout the *Free Press* editorial staff had concurred: "Unless players' salaries are brought into line, there isn't much of a future for big-league hockey in Winnipeg anyway." Gary Doer made the NDP's position clear: "No cap, no arena." Numerous councillors, including consistent arena proponents and even Mayor Thompson, expressed grave concern about the absence of salary caps and revenue-sharing. Reporter Taylor, however, remained true to the cause and assured readers that the new collective agreement did control salaries, and Loewen mysteriously concluded, "This deal certainly controls expenses." But it was obvious that

Winnipeg did not get from the NHL what everyone had agreed the team needed—effective salary caps and/or revenue-sharing.

It was equally obvious that the Jets' salaries were skyrocketing. At the start of the 1994–95 season, eight Jets' players were paid more than $1 million per year, and player salaries for 1994–95 totalled $18 million.[42] In 1989 the payroll had been $5 million. Team costs were out of control, the Jets played in the smallest market in the NHL, drew the smallest audiences, and charged the least for tickets, and in the absence of salary caps and/or revenue-sharing there seemed little chance that the numbers could work. And salary caps and/or revenue-sharing were simply not going to happen in the new, corporate-driven NHL.

In mid-January 1995, when it was clear there was to be no effective salary caps or revenue-sharing in the NHL, *Free Press* editorial writer Jim Carr publicly asked again about MEC's numbers—on which, as the *Sun* had pointed out in December, MEC had little credibility: "A business deal stands or falls on the strength of the numbers. The problem with this deal is that the numbers are not yet known to the politicians who are being asked to make decisions on behalf of taxpayers, many of whom do not share Mr. Loewen's enthusiasm for the project."[43] MEC was listening to Carr and to the many concerns being raised in the community. With an important city council meeting coming up on February 1, the MEC marketing team immediately undertook to do what it did best—the "management of public opinion." MEC's public relations strategy was identical to that used prior to the equally important October 14, 1994 city council meeting—leak favourable information to the *Free Press*. MEC gave Carr inside information on "the numbers." Carr dutifully checked the accuracy of the numbers with all three levels of government, and all three assured him that the numbers were correct. The *Free Press* ran the story. It was front-page, bold-headline material: "MEC finds $110 million for arena, Jets."[44] The article outlined how MEC would raise the $110 million, leaving about $32 million, the story claimed, to be contributed by the three levels of government.

But important questions remained to be asked. Could a new, "world-class" arena really be built for $110 million when no large arena in North America in recent years had been built for less than $150 million? What would be the cost of servicing the site and who would pay? If, as Carr wrote, the Jets' owners were to be paid $32 million for their 64 percent of the Jets' shares, why were there no numbers showing how much the public would be paid for its 36 percent of the Jets' shares? Thin Ice quickly prepared and distributed a "reality check" document showing how the MEC numbers reported by Carr made it evident that the cost to the public of the MEC deal would be at least $100 million. But the impression left by the front-page story was that the MEC had solved the money problem, and this was the impression held by councillors as they prepared for the February city council vote.

The most remarkable thing about this front-page news story is that MEC, having given the numbers to Carr and at least two of the three levels of government, which had confirmed the accuracy of the numbers, knew that the figures were false. MEC documents not made available until eighteen months later through an access to information request revealed that on January 11, 1995—ten days *before* Carr's story claiming MEC needed $32 million in public funds—MEC had filed an application for Canada/Manitoba Infrastructure Works funding in which the amount of public funds needed was stated to be $90 million. In short, at around the same time that MEC was telling Carr—and through him the public—that it would need $32 million in public funds, MEC was telling the federal and provincial governments that it would need $90 million in public funds. And it is clear that politicians at the highest level knew the real figure. On January 15, Lloyd Axworthy and provincial Finance Minister Eric Stefanson were briefed by a representative of MEC on the financial plan contained in the Canada/Manitoba Infrastructure Works application, which means they were made fully aware that MEC needed $90 million in public funds.[45] Yet, until *after* the April 25 provincial election, the public was consistently led to believe that the amount of public money needed was $32 million, or at most $40 million. None of them—MEC, the provincial government, or the federal government—took the steps necessary to inform the public of the real figure. The media ignored the Thin Ice analysis of late January 1995, which showed that $100 million in public funds would be needed. When city council met on February 1, most councillors assumed, because this is what they had been told, that the total requirement for public funds was $32 million.

That February city council vote was a crucial one because it would determine with certainty the question of site. As always, MEC exerted enormous pressure on councillors—continuing from its leak of inaccurate information to Carr and the *Free Press*. MEC representatives were relentless in their backroom lobbying of councillors, despite an earlier pledge made by Loewen to Ridd about being less aggressive in this regard. The day before the vote Loewen warned, as he had on October 14, 1994, that a "no" vote would kill the deal. Presumably referring to the January 21 *Free Press* front-page story, Loewen, who as MEC chair knew full well that the public and their city council representatives had been given false information, added, "The people asked for the private sector to step up and do their job, and I think everyone would agree they have done it."[46]

Everyone did not agree, and for good reason. MEC had not yet even produced a business plan. How the arena and the Jets were to be financed was unknown, save for a leaked, sketchy and, as would be later shown, completely inaccurate *Free Press* story. MEC wanted a commitment from council to donate the North Forks site and to service it at city cost, but five months after acquiring the option to purchase the privately held shares of the Jets, MEC was still *not* prepared to provide the public's representatives with a business plan. Nor had any form of public consultation taken place, despite the mayor's written assurances in October 1994.

Still, MEC demanded a commitment from council, and a majority of councillors were not prepared to be the ones to kill the deal. As Councillor Sandy Hyman put it in conversation with me, "Some pretty big powerful people are behind this."[47]

Since these "pretty big powerful people" had not yet produced a business plan, agreement was reached to propose a set of principles that would guide the process from February 1 to May 1. As Thompson explained to the media, she felt city council had to make a commitment, even without a business plan: "I can't keep putting the date off just because of not having this piece of information or that piece of information. . . . Because MEC can't come to us with a finalized business plan yet, we are feeling jammed. Therefore, we are proposing a set of principles."[48] In a memo to councillors dated January 30, Thompson acknowledged,"There are still many unanswered questions," but she added, "unfortunately, there is also great pressure to proceed further with the project."[49]

This, of course, was the decision-making model that would characterize MEC–city council relations. City council would never have the information necessary for making an informed decision. There would be no business plan, or the business plan and/or other crucial financial and legal information would be provided less than twenty-four hours before the vote. Enormous pressure would be exerted. The pressure would include an "information management" component: release a doctored public opinion poll on the day of a vote; leak a bogus story about how private funds will be raised ten days before a vote. And it would include good old-fashioned behind-the-scenes arm-twisting, sometimes called lobbying. Then MEC would announce publicly, the day before the vote, that if council voted "no," the deal was dead. But if council voted "yes," MEC was not *finally* committing itself to the project—this was just another step along the way. Not wanting to be the ones to kill the deal, and confident that there would be another vote at a later date on the matter anyway, a majority of councillors consistently voted yes. And by this piecemeal process, the deal blindly and mindlessly limped along. Clearly, little had changed at city hall since the 1970s when, referring to the long battle over the downtown Trizec project, David Walker observed that city politicians "were not in the same league" as the corporations they were bargaining with. "They were poor negotiators on point after point at high cost to taxpayers."[50]

On February 1, city council—in the absence of a business plan, with no effective NHL salary caps or revenue-sharing and with no public consultation—voted 10–6 in favour of a set of guidelines giving MEC approval in principle to build an arena at the North Forks site.

> The February 1, 1995, city council guidelines provided, among other things:
>
> ◆ that a business plan be presented and that there be a "reasonable period of time . . . for the city to carry out appropriate and sufficient due diligence with respect to its investment";
> ◆ that once a finalized business plan has been presented, and before council considers any required approvals, "there be full opportunity for public review";
> ◆ that the private sector pay all Jets' losses after exercising the option to purchase;
> ◆ that council be asked for no further funding;
> ◆ that council provide no financial guarantees for the project;
> ◆ that "should the project prove to be unsuccessful in the long term, there must be absolutely no financial liability left with the city";
> ◆ that "if the Winnipeg Jets leave Winnipeg the proceeds from the sale of the team or any assets of the team be directed as a first charge against any outstanding debt of the building."

If the guidelines had been complied with they would have provided the city with *some* protection. But despite Mayor Thompson's assurance that "they [MEC] have to work with those guidelines," it immediately became apparent that MEC had no intention of complying. MEC had its vote; it would jettison the guidelines. Loewen admitted to the media, "We have to keep working away with the City to determine exactly what they [the guidelines] mean. I'm not going to make any predictions now."[51] Loewen did make it clear that MEC would *not* cover the Jets' losses after exercising the purchase option. A delegation from Thin Ice met with City of Winnipeg Chief Commissioner Rick Frost on March 1 to clarify the intent and character of the guidelines and was informed that the guidelines were not binding and had never been intended to be binding.

The guidelines proposed to council by Mayor Thompson in lieu of a business plan and described by Jets/arena proponents as the means by which to protect the city's interests were worthless. This would become fully apparent very soon. In the meantime MEC had its North Forks site. The project had taken another giant step forward.

As a result, Thin Ice once again mobilized the Coalition to Preserve the Forks, which held a news conference at city hall on February 10 condemning the use of the North Forks site for the building of an arena and announcing that legal action would be taken if necessary to stop the project. Lawyer

Yude Henteleff, a partner in Buchwald, Asper, Henteleff, represented the Sierra Club of which Christine Common-Singh was president. Henteleff clearly and forcefully laid out the grounds on which legal action could be taken, emphasizing in particular the newly enacted Canadian Environmental Assessment Act (CEAA) and its requirement for public consultations. The news conference had an immediate impact. That night Common-Singh received a telephone death threat—"Stay out of the arena issue or you're dead."

Thin Ice would eventually take legal action, starting in April 1995. By then the organization would be left to act virtually on its own, supported only by the Point Douglas Residents Association. Other members of the Coalition to Preserve the Forks backed off at the prospect of legally challenging the powers-that-be. The Coalition to Preserve the Elms, which had its office in city-owned property and felt it ran the risk of being removed if it involved itself in court actions, withdrew from the Coalition. Other groups drifted away, offering various explanations. At the same time small Winnipeg firms were being tightly squeezed by MEC. The behind-the-scenes pressure to silence all opposition voices was powerful, and in most cases effective.

The case of the Coalition's lawyer, Yude Henteleff, is especially revealing. After the February 10 news conference Henteleff worked informally throughout March in preparing further legal action on behalf of Thin Ice and had agreed, in a letter of March 23, to act formally as legal counsel for Thin Ice. The next week Henteleff informed Thin Ice that he was dropping the case. He explained that a prominent firm had held consultations with Buchwald, Asper, Henteleff, and although no file had yet been opened with this firm—whereas a file *had* been opened with Thin Ice—a majority of the legal firm's executive committee agreed that the Thin Ice case had to be dropped. Buchwold, Asper, Henteleff did "not want to offend" its numerous large clients, many of them affiliated with MEC. Henteleff, a powerful and active human rights advocate, agonized over what to do but finally, and reluctantly, dropped the case. He informed Thin Ice that all the city's big legal firms would similarly refuse to represent the group. They were all linked to the big corporations that made up MEC. The establishment was tightening its grip. There is no doubt that in cases such as this the major law firms will inevitably find themselves in conflict and will, for obvious financial reasons, opt for the large corporation rather than the small community organization.

Thin Ice would later be directed to Rocky Kravetsky, who ran his own small law firm with two partners and had no connections with MEC, and Kravetsky and his law partner Sandra Hoeppner would provide outstanding legal counsel. But in late March it was clear that MEC was putting on the big squeeze to push the deal through in the final month leading up to the May 1 deadline. It was equally clear that if any within the established circles of power had misgivings—and indeed many did—they remained silent in the interests of class loyalty or out of fear of the consequences of speaking out.

Still, throughout February and March rumours abounded that MEC was having difficulties. It was being said in the business community that MEC was plagued with serious internal disagreements and that the organization might even be folding, but that MEC members were openly talking about the project as a "coming of age" test for the younger generation of business people who were the MEC leaders.

Part of the difficulty may have been attributable to the fact that former Blackwoods Beverage owner Gerry Gray, and Gray's legal counsel, Alan Sweatman became involved in the process in February.[52] Sweatman had been approached by some of the MEC leaders in early December 1994 to see if Gray might be prepared to contribute financially to the MEC project. Sweatman phoned Gray who was wintering in Palm Beach, and a short time later Osler, Riley, Loewen and Sweatman flew to Florida to see him, using the corporate jet that was time-shared by, among others, Investors, Great-West Life and Richardsons. Gray agreed to put $10 million into the project, and in mid-February had Sweatman establish a separate legal entity, MEC Management Ltd., as the means through which to exercise his involvement.

The promise of Gray's $10 million kept the struggling project alive, but it also contributed to an internal conflict. Gray's arrival coincided with a backing away from MEC on the part of Shenkarow. A pervasive influence in MEC, Shenkarow had played an active role in the marketing efforts and the design plans for the proposed new arena. But in February and March it became clear to him that he would not be running the show when the new arena was in place, and it was probably no coincidence that this realization dawned on him after Gray and Sweatman came on board. Shenkarow's intention had always been to maintain control of the Jets once the new arena was constructed, and when it became clear that such a role was not in the cards, Shenkarow withdrew. By late March, Shenkarow was letting it be known to MEC that he did not think the Jets could be made to work in Winnipeg, and the belief emerged in the minds of at least some of the MEC players that Shenkarow would not allow them to exercise the option and purchase the team unless a new arena was built and he remained in charge of the Jets. The ground was being laid for a round of bitter fighting between competing business factions.

In early March the three provincial party leaders, aware of the public concerns and anxious to position themselves for the forthcoming provincial election, announced they would not pay Jets' losses after May 1, 1995. In the *Free Press* Taylor lamented, "There would appear to be no political will when it comes to assisting the franchise in its efforts to become financially viable." He even concluded that "the city is doing everything covertly possible" to scuttle the deal.[53]

Far from trying to scuttle the deal, city hall was scrambling to meet the exceptionally tight timelines imposed on the process by the May 1 deadline—the date by which MEC had to exercise the option to purchase. "It's all rush, rush, panic, panic, for something you don't know will happen," said an anonymous senior city bureaucrat. "It's nuts," added another.[54] The pressure was on at city hall. Mayor Thompson continued to promise public consultation if council approved MEC's business plan, and MEC continued to report that it had, as yet, no date for tabling a business plan.

A February 22 motion "requested" MEC to present its "full and comprehensive" business plan to city council by March 17. MEC did not do so. A March 22 motion "requested" that MEC present its business plan by April 12. MEC still did not do so. No public consultation process had been implemented. No private-sector risk capital had been committed, other than Gray's promise of $10 million. Yet the entire project was a juggernaut—stumbling, squabbling and ineffectual in many respects, but for the moment, in late March 1995, a juggernaut nonetheless. There was but one month left to the May 1 deadline, and MEC would be pushing on many fronts.

The Ridd–Douglas Affair and the Blue Ribbon Campaign

The final month's push began Saturday, April 1. Late Friday afternoon *Free Press* business reporter John Douglas had telephoned Thin Ice member Carl Ridd, ostensibly for a casual chat about the Jets/arena issue. Douglas wanted to know, he said, what Ridd's thoughts were on the issue. The conversation was leisurely. In due course Douglas set out a hypothetical situation. What if, he said, a deal emerged that involved a one-time only public payment limited to $30–$40 million, with a guarantee of no further payout of public funds, and that guaranteed to leave Winnipeg with a debt-free arena able to pay all its expenses even if the Jets left? Would you support such a deal, Douglas asked?

At Thin Ice we had known for months that no such deal was possible. The group's "reality check" document in January showed that any deal was likely to cost somewhere in the order of $100 million, *not* $30–$40 million. MEC itself, it later became known, knew in January that $90 million in public funds would be needed. And Thin Ice had stated repeatedly that once an arena was built the Jets could continually threaten to leave unless they received ever more concessions, so that it was logically impossible to say that any deal could be crafted that could *guarantee* no further public payments. The hypothetical scenario painted by Douglas was, Ridd knew, purely pie-in-the-sky.

Ridd answered accordingly. To this purely hypothetical and thoroughly unrealistic scenario, he responded with multiple conditions and provisos and, appropriately, given that the whole exercise was merely "blue-skying," he responded off the record. When Douglas asked, could you support a scenario such as described, Ridd replied:

> I might. I'd rather put it more carefully, and there I don't really want to be quoted because I want to show solidarity with my colleagues. . . . The thing is that I could be you know. It would depend. I don't want to give a guarantee in advance of knowing what all the various conditions are.
>
> I could certainly say, 'Yes, I'm willing to go to $20 million, [and] I could be willing to go to $30 [million] or $40 million.' I've said this to John Loewen and I'm happy to say it to you although again I don't just at this point want to be quoted on that but if I were given more specifics, I might, at some early point, come right out and say, 'Yeah that sounds fine to me.'[55]

Ridd had said twice that he did not want to be quoted, and he had said twice that before actually answering such a question he would need more specifics. But Douglas had what he was after.

The next day, April Fool's Day, the front-page headline of the *Free Press* shouted: "A 'No-Lose' Arena Deal," with the subheadline declaring "Leading Sceptic Ridd Gives Qualified Support for MEC Proposal." Yet there was no "MEC proposal." There was no "no-lose arena deal." Douglas had accepted MEC claims about a proposed arena deal that had no foundation in fact, were completely unsubstantiated, and, less than a month later when MEC finally released its business plan to the public, would be revealed to be completely inaccurate. But Douglas had all he needed to produce a front-page story that started:

> The Manitoba Entertainment Complex group is putting the finishing touches on a deal that would see Winnipeg get a new arena for a total, one-time government cash contribution of about $40 million.
>
> 'If the people of Manitoba truly understand this deal, they couldn't vote against it,' Bob Silver, one of 70 business leaders behind MEC, said in an interview. 'This is a no-lose scenario.'

Exactly one month later, the one-time government contribution of $40 million would more than triple to a one-time government contribution of $131 million plus an ongoing annual government subsidy of $7.75 million.[56] How could the actual deal as revealed on May 1, 1995, be so different from what MEC claimed to be the deal on April 1, 1995? It is difficult not to conclude that MEC fed Douglas false information, as it had done to Carr some two months earlier.

False or not, "Done-deal Douglas," as he came to be known by some of his fellow reporters, appears to have been only too eager to report the good news as related by MEC. And even more valuable, a leading member of Thin Ice had given "qualified support" to "the proposal." Said Douglas: "When given an outline of the proposal yesterday, Ridd said it answers many of his concerns. He said he would be prepared to see up to $40 million in public funding go into the project if it were not connected to gambling and guaranteed it would put an end to taxpayer subsidies."

Ridd had been "sandbagged," set up in a classic divide-and-conquer strategy. The new deal was so good, Douglas's story implied, that even a leading member of Thin Ice was prepared to go along with it. If other members of Thin Ice continued to be opposed, they would only be demonstrating how very unreasonable they were. Thin Ice was split, Douglas would argue two days later, between those like Ridd, who were "pragmatic," and the rest of us who were "dogmatic."[57]

Thin Ice had finally managed to get some media coverage, but it certainly wasn't what we would have wanted. Douglas had inflicted considerable damage. The arena proponents were playing hardball. And there was a month to go to the May 1 deadline. The group scrambled to recover from what we feared would be a public relations disaster. Our entire campaign had been built around the slogan "no public funds" for a new arena or for continued subsidization of the Jets. Ridd immediately began phoning his many contacts throughout the city, and Thin Ice members began preparing a news conference for Monday, April 3, to set the record straight. At the news conference Ridd reiterated that there might be circumstances in which he personally would support public funds for a new arena, but he also insisted that he had been misrepresented by Douglas because he and Douglas had been discussing a completely hypothetical and unrealistic scenario, and not "the MEC proposal." Indeed, Cam Osler, president of MEC, would state publicly on April 5 that there would be no MEC business plan—no MEC "proposal"—until after the April 25 provincial election. Thin Ice reiterated its long-held "no public funds" position in the full knowledge that the real amount in public funds would be closer to $100 million than $30–$40 million.

The *Free Press* ran a long verbatim transcript of parts of the Ridd-Douglas telephone conversation and parts of the April 3 news conference. Careful readers were able to see how Douglas had sandbagged Ridd, and the use of the transcript was an implicit admission that the paper had handled the entire affair in a questionable fashion. Also questionable was the fact that Douglas himself covered the news conference that was called, in part, to level charges of journalistic impropriety against him. But the *Free Press* never did utter any explicit apology or admission of wrongdoing. On August 15, 1995, Douglas himself would subsequently be promoted, to business editor.

Two weeks after the Ridd-Douglas affair on April 16, Taylor, not to be outdone, used his column to launch yet another attack on Thin Ice, this time in the form of a highly personalized diatribe directed at Ridd and myself:

> It's ironic that the leaders of Thin Ice, the anti-arena, anti-hockey forces, are University of Winnipeg professors Carl Ridd and Jim Silver. While they rail against a public commitment to an arena, they collect publicly-funded paycheques every week.
>
> That's right. Jets' fans pay the salaries of the people who want to see their hockey team move to the United States. For all intents and purposes, Thin Ice is a publicly-funded organization.

Thin Ice received no public funding whatever. Legal costs of $8,832 incurred between April and October 1995 were raised entirely by donations from private individuals.

The evening before, between periods of a Jets game broadcast live on *Hockey Night in Canada*, Taylor had explained the problem in Winnipeg as the result of very powerful anti-arena groups that were preying on the people, and especially on the elderly, by telling them that health care would be placed at risk if public funding went into a new arena for the Jets. Perhaps not coincidentally, on the weekend of April 15–16, my University of Winnipeg office was vandalized—the first such incident since the inception of Thin Ice.

The next stage in the April public relations effort on behalf of MEC began two days later with the launching of a "Blue Ribbon campaign." Brothers Mark and Michael Dandenault, thirty-two and thirty years of age respectively, staged a news conference to announce their intention to spark a grassroots campaign to build support for public funds for a new arena and the Jets. They proposed to distribute blue ribbons and petitions at Jets games and throughout the province and to rally corporate support for the effort. The *Free Press* was only too eager to help, with a prominent story including a contact phone number for the campaign.

The campaign had a twofold focus: first, collect ten thousand signatures on a petition; second, involve the corporate community in the effort. Company owners were asked not only to display the blue ribbons in their places of business, but also to encourage their employees to sign the petition. That it might be inappropriate for company owners to be asking employees to sign a petition on such a highly charged emotional issue—would an employee who refused to sign be punished by an overly zealous Jets' fan and business owner?—went unremarked.

Some companies did clearly go well beyond what was appropriate. Perths, a local dry cleaning company, circulated a petition that read: "I, the undersigned, support the participation of all three levels of government to assist in the construction of a new entertainment complex in Winnipeg." Attached was a coupon offering a 10 percent discount on dry cleaning. The coupon offering the discount said: "Card must be completed to qualify." In short, qualification for the discount was contingent upon a person's signing a petition pledging support for a particular point of view. Put differently, at least one of the companies participating in the Blue Ribbon campaign was, in effect, paying for names on petitions, by offering lower prices to those who signed the petition. It is not known what percentage of the names on the Blue Ribbon petitions were secured in this fashion.

Thin Ice sent a photocopy of the Perths–Blue Ribbon petition-coupon to the *Free Press* suggesting that such methods by the Blue Ribbon campaign were worthy of a story. No such story appeared. As MEC's May 1 deadline drew near, The *Free Press* continued to see its role as being booster and cheerleader.

"Community Consultation" and a Provincial Election

On February 23, 1995, the city's Board of Commissioners had hired local consulting firm Jim August Associates to develop the integrated plan for the Forks. The community consultation component of the integrated plan, conducted in April, was of particular concern to Thin Ice. Would it open up to genuine public debate a process that had so far been characterized by last-minute, back-room deals; or would it be an exercise in going through the motions in order to create a veneer of public involvement?

None of the organizations that had participated in the news conference on February 10 to express concerns about the proposed North Forks development were consulted, with the exception of the Old St. Boniface Residents Association which expressed numerous concerns. The Sierra Club, the Greening of the Forks, the Point Douglas Residents Association, Cho!ces, Thin Ice—all were excluded from the process, despite their expressed interest in the matter. Thin Ice wrote to the City of Winnipeg Chief Commissioner Rick Frost on March 27, 1995, requesting permission to display information at the public open house that was billed as part of the community consultation process and was to be hosted by MEC on April 7 and 8. Permission was not granted.

The public consultation report inaccurately claimed that the Manitoba Federation of Labour was included in the consultation process. There was a meeting with three members of the MFL executive on April 13, 1995, but it had been called by Patrick Martin, business agent of the Carpenters Union, to discuss technical issues relating to the use and sourcing of steel. MFL participants were not made aware that the meeting would be claimed to be part of the consultation process. Once again, MEC had played loose with the truth.

The public open house of April 7 and 8 was more a public relations exercise than public consultation. No business plan was available for public review. No information was provided about the cost to the public of the proposed project, even though MEC had known since at least January that it would need some $90 million in public funds. The public at the time was being led to believe that the cost in public money would be much lower than MEC knew to be the case. Information at the open house consisted largely of architectural drawings and photographs. The consultation report made no reference to the *Future Directions for the Forks* document and the expressed desire of Winnipeggers to keep the Forks green, or of the extent to which the proposed arena would be inconsistent with that desire. Nor did the report make reference to the March 28, 1995 letter from the president of the Forks Renewal Corporation expressing concern about the impact of the proposed project on the Forks. In no meaningful sense was the community consulted.

By the time this "community consultation" process was completed, the province was well into a provincial election campaign which became a reason for the still further delay of MEC's business plan. In April, MEC advised: "Delays to date, and the provincial election on April 25, may preclude MEC from finalizing all business plan commitments during April. It is unlikely, for example, that any formal public review of MEC's business plan can occur until after April 25."[58] This was convenient, since it meant that MEC's requirement for some $90 million in public funds would be concealed from the public even longer and would not become an election issue. The myth that $30–$40 million was the amount of public money needed could be sustained until after the election. That would leave a mere six days after the election for presentation of the MEC business plan—which would finally have to reveal the real amount to be paid by the public—plus a public review of the business plan and the convening of a special city council meeting to vote on the matter. As always, councillors would get crucial and complicated information at the absolute last minute before having to vote. The public would have no real opportunity to analyze and comment on MEC's business plan. The February 1 guidelines lay in shreds and tatters, long since abandoned. Mayor Thompson wrote to the three provincial party leaders on April 7, 1995: "The City of Winnipeg is facing enormous time constraints in their deliberations with regard to a new arena facility. We appreciate the fact that you are currently engaged in a Provincial election and that the arena issue may be one best resolved when the election results have been confirmed."

In other words, don't raise this inflammatory issue during the campaign. Keep it under wraps until after election day and then we'll slam it through. The stage was being set, deliberately, for a pressure-cooker final week of April. And indeed, in the provincial election campaign throughout April, the contending party leaders tended to stay away from the Jets/arena issue. Whenever he was asked his party's position on the issue, Premier Filmon stuck strictly to what the Tories had been saying for a year—they would commit no more than $10 million to the project.

Still, the issue did come up on doorsteps during the campaign and appears to have been an important factor in south Winnipeg constituencies where the Liberals posed a threat to the Conservatives. The south Winnipeg seats were crucial for a Conservative majority victory, and somehow during the course of the campaign the belief arose—whether it was deliberately promoted by Conservative Party campaign workers is not known—that the only way to Save Our Jets was to vote for Filmon. Premier Filmon—his public utterances notwithstanding—would ensure that the provincial government would do what had to be done to keep the Jets in Winnipeg. The $10 million limit was for public consumption; the real limit was whatever was needed. Filmon, it appeared, was playing both sides of the issue.

The impact was significant. Liberal candidates could point to the very day that the issue became a factor in the election campaign. All of a sudden they were inundated with calls about the Jets. "Toward the end, the perception was that Mr. Filmon would do anything to save the Jets," and "For many people, it was the one issue that determined their ballots," said two unsuccessful south Winnipeg Liberal candidates.[59] It is not clear to what extent the Liberal collapse in south Winnipeg was attributable to Filmon's double-edged position on the Jets, and to what extent it was part of a broader, province-wide phenomenon. What is clear is that voters were being told that the way to save the Jets was to vote Conservative. The belief became sufficiently public that Taylor, while being interviewed between periods on *Hockey Night in Canada*, exhorted viewers in Winnipeg to vote for Filmon to Save Our Jets. He said the same in his column the day before the election. Vic Grant similarly urged his CJOB listeners to vote Conservative to save the Jets. There is even some suggestion, though it could not be proved, that those who had signed Blue Ribbon petitions and lived in constituencies where the race was expected to be close were targeted with phone calls and told that only Filmon could be trusted to do whatever was necessary to save the Jets. In the end enough votes were moved in south Winnipeg seats to secure victories there, and to help win a Conservative majority.

Immediately after the election then, a newly re-elected Premier Filmon entered the final, post-election pressure-cooker week of April with a contradictory mandate from the electorate. He had publicly pledged, consistent with his government's long-standing commitment, that the province would contribute no more than $10 million to saving the Jets, but he owed his majority to a widespread belief that he would spend what had to be spent to keep the Jets in Winnipeg.

The February 1, 1995 guidelines passed by city council included a commitment to *no* cash contribution whatever from the city. The federal contribution was unknown, but Axworthy's problem was that a large injection of federal cash into saving the Jets would trigger demands for similar contributions from other struggling NHL franchises in small Canadian cities—Calgary, Edmonton and especially Quebec. How could the federal government give money to Winnipeg, and not to Quebec, given the tensions of the sovereignty issue? And if they gave to Winnipeg and Quebec, and as would necessarily then follow, to Calgary and Edmonton, how could they justify their continued assault on Canada's social security system? Perhaps, once more, what was needed was a little bit of political theatre.

On April 27, the date on which MEC was finally to release its business plan, a "public information session" was convened at an Executive Policy Committee (EPC) meeting of city council in a large hall at the downtown Winnipeg Convention Centre. The place was packed with Jets' supporters anxious to hear the details of the business plan crafted by MEC to "save our Jets," but a nasty surprise awaited them. John Loewen, tall, gaunt, and with a glint of a tear in his eyes, reported reluctantly that he and his associates had given it their best, but it was not enough. "Unfortunately, I'm not here today to bring good news." MEC was throwing in the towel. Loewen was cheered heartily for all his hard work before yielding the podium to Mayor Thompson and then to provincial Finance Minister Eric Stefanson. Each of them spoke a few words of lamentation and "might-have-beens" over the now dying body of the Winnipeg Jets.

The National Hockey League was the villain in this first scene of elaborately staged political theatre. In a faxed letter received "only this afternoon," Loewen advised, the NHL had surprised MEC by imposing onerous and last-minute conditions that were so unreasonable that no option was left but to concede defeat. This claim, it turned out, was patently false. There *had* been a fax that afternoon from the NHL, but it contained no hitherto unknown conditions. MEC had for some time known the conditions—at least since an April 13 meeting of NHL vice-president Jeff Pash and representatives of MEC. But dramatic theatre requires the creation of a villain, even if only to serve as a smokescreen. The NHL had killed the Jets!

Despondent, their dream dashed, the Jets' fans made their way slowly through the doors at the back of the hall and out into the Convention Centre foyer before emptying into the twilight of a soon-to-be Jets-less city. Some of the fans were angry, and a few spoke harshly to the handful of Thin Ice members who had attended to make yet another presentation to the Executive Policy Committee. The Thin Ice members hesitated before leaving. The frustration and anger of the disappointed Jets' fans could lead to problems: better to let the crowd disperse. The hall slowly emptied, except for the members of EPC and MEC. Why were they staying behind? Thin Ice member Mike Gray called a cab to get the group out safely—but something didn't quite ring true. Maybe it was better to wait, just to see what was going on.

It soon became clear. EPC intended to hear delegations who had registered to speak about the business plan. MEC President Cam Osler was at the podium in a now almost empty hall, describing the details of the business plan. But this was bizarre. The deal was dead. Loewen had said so. Or had he? What *exactly* did he say? *Was* the deal dead? If so, why carry on with hearing delegations speak to a business plan that was now dead and that nobody had yet even seen, let alone analyzed? City of Winnipeg Chief Commissioner Rick Frost hurried past a group of us at the back of the almost empty hall. I asked Frost, "Why are delegations being heard if the deal is dead?" Without hesitation Frost revealed the plot. If NHL Commissioner Gary Bettman "should happen" to come to Winnipeg on the weekend, and if a deal should happen to be struck, we want to be able to say that the city has complied with the requirement for public consultation, he replied. EPC in short, was about to conduct, *knowingly and deliberately*, a sham public hearing.

The mayor, of course, had promised full public consultation, at least as long ago as October 12, 1994, in her letter to us. She had repeated the promise often, and it had been incorporated in the February 1, 1995 guidelines. Guideline 10 required "that there be full opportunity for public review." Guideline 1 stated, "A reasonable period of time must be allowed for the City to carry out appropriate and sufficient due diligence with respect to its investment." As Councillor Glen Murray asked the mayor in a letter dated April 26, "What will 'allowing time for due diligence' now mean?" Mayor Thompson replied the same day, in her inimitable fashion, the totality of her letter reading: "Further to your correspondence of today's date, I can indicate that from my perspective, reviewing and reaching some decision with regard to the MEC business plan, as a Council addresses the concern of finding 'resolution to the outstanding issues on maintenance of an NHL franchise in Winnipeg.'"[60]

The meaning of the mayor's convoluted response to Murray was, shall we say, not clear, but the meaning of the well-orchestrated EPC meeting of April 27 certainly was. EPC would go through the motions of public consultation, hearing from those few delegations still on hand—most had left. But there would be no discussion about the details of the business plan—it had not yet been made available to the public. So much for "full opportunity for public review."

In our Thin Ice group at the back of the hall, we quickly debated whether to participate in what was so obviously a charade. If Thin Ice and others participated, would we all be lending credence and validity to the "public consultation"? Our legal counsel Rocky Kravetsky advised the group to go ahead and speak, using the occasion to put on the public record what was truly going on. So I was delegated to go forward and inform the EPC and the handful of spectators left in the cavernous, echoing hall of our view: that the entire process was a deliberately crafted attempt to deceive the public. The media did not report my comments; their representatives, too, had gone home.

6. Save Our Jets ...
and Shift the Risks

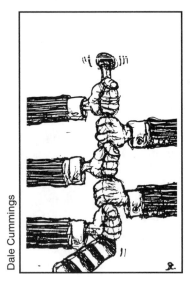

Dale Cummings

In the *Free Press* the morning after the Convention Centre meeting the front-page headline shouted, "Shafted by the NHL." The lead story opened: "The Winnipeg Jets are as good as dead unless the NHL backs down on a list of tough demands it made just 72 hours before a deadline to find new owners for the hockey club." The *Free Press* had bought the elaborate ruse: the story might just as well have been written by MEC. The paper said that "in a choked voice," John Loewen told the crowd, "The NHL has made it impossible for us to proceed." The NHL had "sabotaged" the deal, he explained. Mayor Thompson pleaded, "It is time for the NHL to stop this."[1] The cost in public funds was being obscured from public view by claims about the NHL's villainy.

Something closer to the truth of what was happening was revealed by Barry Shenkarow, who immediately convened a news conference to charge that MEC was "playing poker" with the NHL and wouldn't get away with it. He said the NHL was merely applying long-standing rules about ownership changes. The league feared, Shenkarow added, that MEC would purchase the franchise at the $32 million option price only to "flip" it later, when Jets' losses mounted, for a big capital gain. If there was to be a big capital gain made by selling the team out of Winnipeg, Shenkarow felt he deserved it, not the "Johnny-come-lately" MEC.

What is more, the NHL rules about ownership were known *almost a year before*. In a May 21, 1994 column, Scott Taylor quoted NHL vice-president Arthur Pincus regarding the prospect of someone buying the Jets from Shenkarow and then flipping the franchise for a profit. "That won't happen," Pincus had said. "In order to approve a new owner, we want to make sure he, or a group, is dedicated to keeping the team in the city in which it now plays." Taylor added: "According to one NHL Governor, if a government or government-controlled group wanted to buy a franchise cheaply and then flip it, it would be required to pay a franchise fee so high that it could be the entire amount of the profit." Taylor quoted the governor, who said, "If anybody is going to make money off our franchise . . . it's our present fraternity or the League itself."[2]

The NHL conditions had been laid out in detail in a letter from NHL vice-president Jeffrey Pash to the MEC dated April 13, 1995. They were intended to ensure that MEC meant to keep the Jets in Winnipeg. The Winnipeg *Sun* quoted an unidentified NHL source as saying, "The MEC people knew two months ago what the conditions were."[3] Despite the evidence, Loewen, Filmon, Stefanson and Thompson continued to insist that MEC first learned of the conditions on April 26.

The NHL required that the MEC commit to Winnipeg until the Jets had accumulated losses of $25 million while playing in the new arena; even then the league would impose a $15 million transfer fee. It was the large, inevitable future Jets' losses that stymied the MEC. Because nobody associated with the group was prepared to commit to covering those losses, MEC needed an escape hatch. Its members wanted to be able to move the Jets out of Winnipeg quickly when losses started to mount. If they could do so, they would not only have a hedge against rapidly rising losses but also be the group to benefit from the large capital gain earned by the sale. And as it became more clear to MEC that the Jets could not survive in Winnipeg, the issue became a struggle over which group was to reap the large profit just waiting to be had from the club's eventual sale.

It was a quick flip of the Jets by MEC that the NHL wanted to prevent. Ironically, far from being the villain, the NHL was, in effect, protecting Winnipeg's interests—though it was no part of the league's intention to do so. If the team was flipped in a way that allowed MEC to turn a quick profit, the city would then be stuck with an expensive new arena and no primary tenant—a virtual guarantee of future arena losses which Manitobans and especially Winnipeggers would have to bear. MEC, not prepared to pay the Jets' losses that they now, finally, acknowledged were inevitable, wanted the NHL to loosen its conditions. But to negotiate with the NHL's commissioner Bettman MEC needed some leverage, which could be provided by angry fans blaming the NHL for betraying a Canadian city in favour of U.S. relocation. The elaborate Convention Centre stage play and the casting of the NHL as villain would provide that leverage. Loewen himself gave away the strategy when a *Free Press* reporter asked him "if he had phoned Jets' President Barry Shenkarow to say the MEC would not exercise its option to buy the majority shares." Loewen told the reporter he hadn't done so, because "Monday midnight is the deadline. If the NHL comes to the table, maybe we can do something."[4] Loewen confirmed the strategy that Chief Commissioner Rick Frost had revealed to Thin Ice on the evening of Thursday, April 26 at the Convention Centre. The strategy was to bring Bettman into a pressure-cooker atmosphere in Winnipeg. The *Free Press* played along, probably unwittingly, running a front-page coupon and asking readers to fax it to Bettman. The coupon demanded that the NHL president "drop the conditions and let Manitobans decide whether the Jets stay or leave."

By Saturday the whole scam was clear to the *Free Press* sports writers, probably because Shenkarow saw what was happening and filled in Taylor, who informed Hal Sigurdson. On Friday Sigurdson had blamed the NHL, angrily calling them "a loose association of privateers motivated solely by self-interest," adding that the NHL "didn't particularly want Winnipeg as a partner in the first place." Accurate though this may have been, by Saturday Sigurdson had deciphered the plot and wrote, referring to Loewen: "His group wanted to be free to sell much sooner without paying a hefty transfer fee. . . . What that tells us is that MEC considered buying the Jets a huge financial risk. They wanted the safety net of a quick sale to avoid massive losses."[5]

Fans had rallied—some 1,500 strong—at Portage and Main on Friday morning, April 27, 1995 and had marched on the Legislature where Premier Filmon told the almost exclusively youthful crowd, "Gary Bettman and his little group of wealthy owners have no right to take Canada out of the game."[6] The next day, Saturday, Bettman was on his way to Winnipeg where angry crowds of Jets' fans saw him as villain.

For his part, Bettman was not about to be bullied. He demanded that Loewen apologize for his false accusations. He expressed serious reservations about MEC's capacity and commitment to keep the team in Winnipeg. He went so far as to say, on radio, that he never considered the MEC initiative to be serious, even ridiculing the MEC business plan. And he made it known that the NHL wanted someone who understood the economics of NHL hockey—MEC clearly did not—in charge of the Winnipeg franchise.

Bettman's pressure forced MEC to reach out to Shenkarow, who had taken his distance from MEC in February–March 1995. Robert Silver, MEC executive member, contritely offered, "Barry was excluded in error. It's our fault."[7] Now Shenkarow was back in charge. Bettman wanted him in and didn't trust MEC. Bettman saw that "the kids" intended to flip the team for a tidy profit when losses mounted. Shenkarow's hand was further strengthened when on the day of MEC's Convention Centre scam, Minneapolis-based health care entrepreneur Richard Burke along with partner Steven Gluckstern approached the Jets' owner with an offer to purchase the franchise. From here on in, Shenkarow would use the Burke and Gluckstern offer as a lever against MEC. MEC's star was fading fast.

Hectic meetings involving, at different times, some or all of the three parties—Bettman, Shenkarow and the MEC—filled the weekend. Shenkarow made certain the public knew that MEC's claim about new, last-minute demands from the NHL was false. In an interview he said, "Nothing was new.

The situation from the NHL's point of view has never been any different."[8] MEC scrambled for an extension of the midnight Monday, May 1 deadline, offering that Shenkarow could continue on as governor—an offer insisted upon by Bettman.

The extension was granted to May 3, but it was futile. An attempt to convince Filmon to move the Crystal Casino into the proposed new arena at the Forks failed. So did attempts to get a larger commitment from the federal government. One "exasperated" federal official said, "Every time we sat down we were being asked for more." MEC's option to purchase the Jets expired. A week of "arm-twisting," "fears" and "too much pressure" could not produce a solution. As MEC members explained afterwards, "The numbers were scary. It would have cost everyone too much in the long run." As the *Free Press* explained it in a perceptive editorial: "The aim of the last ditch negotiations over the past week should have been to unearth more money from the private sector. . . . Instead . . . the MEC spent the final days before its deadline for the purchase of the Jets inventing ever more creative ways to shift the risk onto the backs of the taxpayer."[9] This, of course, had been the pattern all along. The editorial concluded by observing about MEC, "There is not a genuine risk-taker among them." Bettman added, "People who don't want risks don't belong owning sports franchises." Taylor, ever the voice of Shenkarow, concurred, saying that MEC didn't have "the cleverness, the business savvy or the guts" to do the deal. Nobody in MEC was prepared to commit to paying the inevitable losses. As MEC's Silver put it, "There just weren't enough people who have the capacity to lose $5 million or $10 million a year with no end in sight."[10] Silver was right: the truth is that Winnipeg's corporate sector was simply not large enough to support a franchise in the up-market NHL of the 1990s. And so, as always, the strategy was to push the burden onto the public sector.

The MEC Business Plan, Filmon's Folly and a Funeral

With the help of four financial analysts associated with Cho!ces, Thin Ice spent the weekend of April 29–30 pouring over the MEC business plan. It became clear why MEC had for so long delayed making the plan public and why they had manufactured the story about the last-minute demands by the NHL.

The public funds required to save the Jets were wildly beyond what had been claimed. MEC's business plan asserted that the required public contribution would be $88 million; the Thin Ice analysis showed the real figure was $131 million in public funds up front, plus an ongoing yearly public subsidy of $7.75 million.[11] The private sector would invest $44 million, a mere 22 percent of the projected total capital cost, and even that amount, a well-placed source revealed, was not yet in place. Nor had MEC been able to find a lender for the $20 million bank loan shown in its business plan.

These holes in the strategy would ultimately have been filled with even more public money. Further, the entire foundation of the financing scheme was wobbly. It included wildly unrealistic assumptions about NHL salary escalation; imprudent assumptions about and improper accounting methods used for proceeds from the sale of premium seating and season tickets; and the use, once again, of the hugely exaggerated claims about the fiscal benefits of the Jets to the province.

The long-awaited business plan was a dud. MEC and its government allies knew that. They hoped the story about the last-minute NHL demands would distract public attention from the real issue—the skyrocketing cost in public funds of building a new arena, purchasing the Jets and paying their losses.

Thin Ice released the results of its weekend's analysis of the MEC business plan at a news conference at city hall on Monday, May 1. It turned out that the existence of the business plan, and its implications, had been obscured by the political theatre at the Convention Centre. The media made no attempt to analyze the business plan—indeed, they may not even have had a copy. Although city councillor John Angus sent the police in to try to stop the May 1 news conference—perhaps Councillor Angus, a former director of marketing for Comcheq (now headed by MEC's Loewen), felt better not knowing the facts—and although the media gave relatively little coverage to the Thin Ice analysis of the MEC business plan, the impact of the effort was significant. The broader business community was alerted to the collapse of MEC's efforts. Those who followed the media closely knew that Thin Ice was saying that the requirement in public funds was more than three times what they had been told up to that moment.

It was almost certainly the skyrocketing cost to the public that had prompted silence about the issue during the April provincial election campaign. There is no doubt whatever that Filmon knew that the cost in provincial funds would be far beyond the $10 million that he repeatedly insisted was his limit. Loewen admitted in May 1995 that MEC "had kept our partners informed all the way through since last July."[12] Filmon and his cabinet had known since October 1991 that the Jets' losses could be as high as $43.5 million. Filmon had admitted in the legislature on June 24, 1994, that the public sector would have to pay "the full facility cost, estimated to be $111 million."[13] And in January 1995 MEC's application for Canada/Manitoba infrastructure funding had included a request for public funds totalling $90 million—a fact directly communicated to provincial Finance Minister Eric Stefanson on January 15, 1995.[14] But it was feared that if the public knew during the election campaign how much it would really cost to save the Jets, the entire project might have been placed in jeopardy. This probably explains why Mayor Thompson wrote to the leaders of the three provincial parties on April 7, 1995 suggesting they not raise the Jets issue

...paign. All three parties—the NDP and Liberals ...was afraid to raise the issue, and the real cost was ...election.

...victory was in no small measure attributable to the ...that he would do whatever had to be done to save the Jets, ...rt began to collapse angry young Jets' fans blamed Filmon ...his promise. Filmon, determined not to be labelled the ...ately agreed to spend provincial funds far in excess of his ...$10 million. He had known all along he would have to. ...s May 3, the newly re-elected premier told the *Free Press* ...ed to spend not $10 million but $50 million in provincial ...ts.[15] His two-faced election strategy, though successful ...servative majority, would prove costly to the citizens of ...anitoba.

At a news conference Wednesday, May 3, it was announced, again, to "a whole collection of young people—aged eighteen to thirty—who were assembled at the Westin" that the deal was dead. Shenkarow cried. Mayor Thompson cried. Loewen continued to blame the NHL. But it was by this time apparent that the MEC—by its own admission—was not prepared to absorb the Jets' losses and had a contingency plan for selling the team out of Winnipeg. This led Bettman to reiterate: "We had some grave concerns about the Winnipeg group's commitment to keeping the team in Winnipeg."

As the young crowd left the Westin, one fan lamented, "We've been stabbed in the back by rich people." But others began to shift the blame to Filmon. They had voted for him because he said he would save the Jets. He hadn't come through. A *Free Press* story the next day was headlined "As the Dream Perishes, a Boy Cries on His Bed."[16]

The anger and the grief at the death of the Jets demanded a villain. The attempt to cast the NHL in that role was faltering. Filmon momentarily appeared a likely candidate, but soon proved unwilling to be thrust into the part. He was working the phones that night, just as he had immediately after his June 24, 1994 announcement of the death of the Jets.

The Jets were laid to rest on Saturday, May 6, at an emotional funeral in a Winnipeg Arena jam-packed with fans, most of them young, many of them heart-broken, some of them angry. There were cheers and tears, chants of "Save Our Jets" and "Bettman Sucks," and banners reading "Fire Gary, Hire Barry" and "What's the Future of Hockey in Canada?" Hockey commentator Don Cherry told the crowd that their franchise had been taken, but not "your heart and soul. You're the greatest." The emotion was intense. It was "a funeral for a dream."[17]

But the dream still would not die. The irrepressible Rick Koswin, long-time superplex promoter, called for a rally at Portage and Main on Monday, May 8. Then, saying, "Sure I know it's a long shot but I couldn't live with myself if I didn't try," Koswin announced another rally for the Convention Centre for the next Tuesday night. It attracted three thousand supporters.[18] The fans wouldn't let go.

Izzy and the Frenzy: The Stuff of Legends

Behind the scenes, plans were being hatched by a new group of high-rollers. On Thursday, May 4, the day after the death announcement at the Westin, Filmon was on the phone arranging a meeting in his office for the next day. On Friday, while arrangements for Saturday's funeral were being finalized, Filmon and Finance Minister Stefanson met secretly with Albert Cohen, owner of Gendis Corp., Israel "Izzy" Asper, founder and owner of CanWest Global Communications, and Shenkarow. On Sunday, May 7, Filmon spoke to federal Human Resources Minister Lloyd Axworthy about a new Asper/Cohen plan and informed Mayor Thompson of the discussions.

On Thursday, May 11, Filmon sent a letter to Axworthy and Thompson describing the outlines of the new plan. It would have the city, province and federal governments each contributing $37 million to the $111 million cost of a new arena, with the private sector contributing an equivalent $111 million to buy the Jets, pay off their debts and establish a pool of money to cover future losses. Shenkarow would continue to serve as president and governor. The next day the press quietly reported the existence of a rescue bid. That same day Shenkarow and his private-sector partners met and agreed to a purchase offer made by U.S. entrepreneurs Richard Burke and Steven Gluckstern, but at Filmon's request they agreed to give Asper and Cohen until noon, Thursday, May 18, to do a deal.

On Saturday, May 13, exactly one week after the Jets' funeral, some 1,500 fans in three separate groups "took over streets throughout the city's core" yet again, only the latest in a sporadic series of such protests. The newspapers were full of the plan to save the Jets, but the details were fuzzy and confused. Reporter John Douglas said the private sector had already assembled $100 million. On Sunday the amount reported was $85 million. As would later become clear, nothing remotely close to either of these amounts would ever be found in the private sector. That would not stop the media from reporting as fact whatever amount the private sector told them it had raised, nor did the fact that one day's number didn't match that of another day give some of the journalists cause to question, at least publicly, the credibility of their sources.

On Sunday the existence of a serious bid to rescue the Jets was public knowledge. A *Free Press* headline blared "Rescue Effort in Top Gear." But Asper was more cautious, chastising the media for raising people's hopes too high by means of "an hysterical media-induced frenzy" when the prospects of a deal were still "remote." He added, in a news release, "It's quite dangerous and damaging to all concerned to fan false hopes and toy with people's emotions, not to mention their political or private reputations."

Yet it could not be denied that it was *only* because of the fans and their refusal to let the issue die that a rescue bid was being attempted. And although Asper was concerned about the dynamic that could be created by the combination of an overly enthusiastic media and emotionally volatile fans, he hadn't seen anything yet. The frenzy was only about to begin.

If the period from the May 4 Westin Hotel news conference to May 14 had been, as the media described it, a "whirlwind" of efforts by the city's "movers and shakers" to revive the Jets, the week of Monday May 15 was to bring a wild mobilization of ordinary Winnipeggers, the likes of which had not been seen since the 1919 Winnipeg General Strike. Unlike the General Strike in which Winnipeg workers took to the streets to oppose the local business establishment, the remarkable mass mobilization of Jets' fans and Winnipeg boosters in May 1995 was in support of Winnipeg's business establishment and their efforts to Save Our Jets.

Radio station CJOB announced that, beginning at 5 a.m. Monday, May 15, it would abandon regular programming to run a twenty-four-hour-a-day, on-air fundraising marathon for the Jets. Talk show host Peter Warren had led a similar Save the Jets campaign in 1974, but it did not compare with the intensity of Operation Grassroots in May 1995. Millions of dollars poured in, with tens of thousands of Manitobans contributing. Children contributed their piggy bank savings, parents donated the funds set aside for their kids' education and grown men and women wept openly on radio. The Jets had to be saved.

The reputation of the city was at stake, it seemed, and everywhere people were saying, we can do it. The business community was, CJOB reiterated relentlessly, working tirelessly and selflessly to assemble the big corporate dollars. Izzy Asper and Gary Filmon were heroes, the city's saviours. Those who raised questions were thin-lipped naysayers—small people, with no vision for our great city. Many who called CJOB with critical questions were cut off. Rational debate became impossible, even dangerous: all effort had to be directed to saving our Jets.

Tuesday's *Free Press* headline declared "Millions Pour in to Save Jets." The *Free Press* announced that it would contribute $22,000 in free advertising to the campaign, and it eventually contributed far more. Dozens of stories detailed the contributions of ordinary Winnipeggers and of small businesses—dollar donations, percentage of sales donations, in-kind donations. Strippers at a local hotel contributed all tips to the Jets' campaign. Construction unions agreed to provide a dollar for every hour their members worked on the new arena—as much as $700,000—and agreed to a no-strike contract. The *Free Press* reported, "Money was coming in so fast and furious no one was sure how much was collected" although it appeared to be about

$1 million on the first day. The chairman of the Chamber of Commerce described the whole effort as "the kind of thing legends are made of. . . . They'll be talking about this for 50 years." The mayor, a relentless Jets' booster who remained cheerily innocent of most of the details of the Jets/ arena issue, offered her own, inimitable description: "There's a book I remember from my childhood. It's *The Little Engine That Could*. That's how I look at our city. We keep chugging and chugging."[19]

On Tuesday evening a Save Our Jets rally attracted a reported 35,000 supporters to the Forks. The newspaper reported, "They came in strollers. They came in Jets jerseys. They came in white. They came in painted faces. They came hand-in-hand. They came from work. They came from school. They came."[20] And they gave—a reported $100,000 to the Save Our Jets campaign. The mass outpouring of grassroots support had by this time attracted national and even international attention. The BBC World Service and *The Wall Street Journal* covered the Forks rally, and part of it was telecast between periods on *Hockey Night in Canada*.

The local media ran endless human interest stories, including many about concerned children breaking open their piggy banks to Save Our Jets. The May 17 *Free Press* announced that former Blackwoods Beverages owner Gerald Gray had contributed $10 million—though the amount had been committed to since January—and ran the story with a description of the $27.55 contributed by an eleven-year old boy. Said the *Free Press*: "The reward for both will be the same—a certificate and a charitable receipt—if a plan to save the NHL franchise is successful." The city was one, we were assured—corporate big shots and ordinary folks committed to the same goal, to Save Our Jets.

A social at the Convention Centre on Wednesday drew 2,500 supporters at $100 a ticket, and fifty corporate sponsors donated $40,000 in prizes. One of the organizers, a local sports doctor, described why he became involved. He had been at the Arena for the May 6 Jets' funeral with his three kids, aged six, eight and nine, when one of them looked up at him during a wave and said, "Dad, I just can't stop crying."[21]

The emotional intensity of this wild week in May was, indeed, the stuff of which legends are made. In the end, Operation Grassroots raised $13.5 million from ordinary Winnipeggers—an astonishing sum of money, and a tribute to a truly remarkable expression of community spirit.

The determination of the Jets' fans, and Filmon's fear of being labelled the villain, generated another effort—the most dramatic yet—to raise corporate money. MEC was widened beyond its original, narrow group of young scions of the Winnipeg establishment to include Asper, Cohen and Shenkarow, as well as a wide range of additional local businesspeople. Douglas referred to "the army of MEC members sent out to corral people's money," describing their efforts as "the largest mobilization of the Manitoba business community in modern history." The effort was coordinated out of the Jets' office by Mark Chipman, president of Birchwood Motors and son of establishment figure Robert Chipman; and Ross Robinson, president of Robinson's Lighting. Using membership lists of everything from chambers of commerce to trade associations and unions, and after dividing the province's businesses into seven groups "according to their ability to pay," the "army of MEC members" contacted thousands of Manitoba companies "in a complex web of networks aimed at hitting every entrepreneur in the province." And Manitoba companies responded—generously. Arne Thorsteinson, a Tory bagman and real estate developer said, "Companies that I've never heard of are faxing us pledge forms."[22] There is no question that small and medium-sized businesses donated generously, "according to their ability to pay." For example, forty-three companies associated with the Winnipeg New Car Dealers contributed $1 million, explaining in a full-page ad that they were "inspired by the enormous generosity of thousands of people throughout Manitoba." The genuine sense of community spirit that motivated so many donors was revealed by the text in the Winnipeg New Car Dealers ad: "This isn't just about hockey. The grass roots effort to build a new entertainment complex and keep the Jets in Winnipeg is not just about keeping the game we love in Manitoba, it's about *the future*. It's about moving forward into the twenty-first century with the vision of making our city and province places we will be proud to leave to our children."[23]

This no doubt noble objective was deeply supported by many. That it was essentially a false objective didn't matter. That it was at least partly the result of enormous pressure imposed by MEC on small and medium-sized businesses didn't matter either. All that mattered in May 1995 was the struggle to Save Our Jets. The noon, May 18, deadline loomed. And on Wednesday, May 17, the matter went to city council, where the councillors were overwhelmed, to say the least. They were being asked to approve the expenditure of $67 million to build the new arena to Save Our Jets—$37 million as the city's one-third share of the $111 million capital cost, and just under $30 million in related servicing and infrastructure costs. Councillors were in a no-win situation: they could be demonized for pulling the plug on the Jets when kids were pulling out their piggy banks to save the team, or they could find $67 million to subsidize NHL hockey at a time when they were cutting essential community services for want of money.

The details of the whole plan were still vague. Asper had met with councillors at 4 p.m. on Tuesday—less than twenty-four hours before the vote—to brief them verbally. There was still no business plan, and no detailed legal information. There had been no public consultations, as required by the February 1 guidelines. And the guidelines had called for no further financial contribution by the city: "As a point of principle, the city will not participate financially (property tax dollars) in the building of an arena." There was no rational basis upon which to say yes to the $67 million request. The amount of money raised by the private sector was still unclear. Although the *Free Press* had reported various private-sector commitments of $100 million and $85 million, Asper told the councillors on May 16 that he had written commitments for $32 million and verbal commitments for another $30 million. He told the media that if he got written commitments for $60 million, he would be prepared to go ahead, "and we'll get you the other 50 in the next year, 6 months, I'll gamble they'll deliver the rest."[24] There was a lot of gambling going on. But even the written commitments for $32 million were doubtful. A letter faxed to Winnipeg legal firms by MEC fundraisers, for instance, said all commitments were "subject to satisfactory legal, accounting and effective tax structuring." They were, in other words, highly conditional and probably unenforceable.

Thus, not only did councillors have no business plan upon which to base their $67 million decision; they had no way of knowing how much money, if any, the private sector had contributed. They had to vote blind. As *Free Press* columnist Bill Neville put it, city council was "adamantly insisting that it had no cash to give, but making a huge financial commitment, without a business plan and without knowing where the money would come from. Is this not a script from the *Twilight Zone?*"[25]

Twilight Zone or not, the $67 million city contribution passed, by a vote of 13–3, in a council meeting that, it was said, "resembled a World Wrestling Federation main event" more than a forum for reasoned debate. The council gallery was filled to overflowing with Jets' fans, mostly rowdy adolescents who cheered and booed and whistled, and to whom Mayor Thompson and a handful of councillors who had flipped positions on the issue played shamelessly. Those expected to vote no—and especially Councillor Rick Boychuk, a steadfast opponent of public funds for a new arena—were booed and jeered. So too was I when I appeared as a Thin Ice representative to oppose the motion, only to be cut off at the ten-minute limit, denied the customary extension of time to make concluding remarks, "with the loud approval of fans seated in the galleries." In debate on the motion to grant the extension, Councillor Mike O'Shaughnessey—who particularly hated Thin Ice and had previously expressed the hope that our member Barry Hammond would "rot in the gutter"—informed the Speaker that "if I listen to much more of this, I might have a heart attack."[26]

Nothing could be allowed to stand in the way. The deal had to be passed. And it was, as city hall reporter Nick Martin later put it, "with only a 10-page overnight report from Chief Commissioner Rick Frost." There was, Martin wrote, "No business plan, nothing in writing from the Province, from Ottawa, from MEC, from Israel Asper and his group, nothing from anyone. The Council Guidelines adopted with much fanfare February 1—including widespread public consultation, no cash beyond the basic land and services, a detailed business plan—appeared to have slipped the collective memory Wednesday."[27]

On the previous weekend Councillor Amaro Silva, who represented the lowest income ward in the city, had complained that "the City's been out of the loop on this." Councillor Jae Eadie, chairman of the city's finance committee, admitted, "I'm not aware of this new arrangement." Councillor Terry Duguid insisted, "I want to see a business plan."[28] Apparently the existence or not of a business plan didn't matter. There was pressure, intense pressure—"a tone of anger I've never seen," as Councillor Glen Murray put it, and it's "violent, ugly, ugly, ugly."

But in the end Silva and Eadie voted yes, as did Lazarenko and Reese, who had previously been opponents of the expenditure. "They've collapsed; it's a done deal," Murray told Thin Ice the evening before the vote. Also shifting to the "yes" side was Councillor Sandy Hyman, who had been subjected to intense and unrelenting pressure by big business and had long bravely resisted that pressure. Before the vote a battered Hyman remarked, somewhat confusingly, "I'm really excited with what's going on and the prospect the team could stay here, I feel so much tension because I can't respond to anything because we had nothing in front of us during the weekend."[29]

The thirteen councillors and the mayor acted on faith and under pressure. Several experienced a last-minute change of heart on the way to a "yes" vote. They did what they were told—all except Councillors Rick Boychuk, Glen Murray and Lillian Thomas. Now it was up to the private sector to finalize the deal. The deadline was the next day, May 18, at noon.

The next morning, some five thousand people gathered expectantly at Portage and Main, waiting for the noon announcement that the Jets were saved, keeping the faith. One fan remarked, "If anyone can do it, it's Izzy Asper. . . . He knows what he's doing." Izzy himself, getting caught up in the mood, called it "the miracle of Main Street."[30] But there was no miracle, no deal. The corporate money still wasn't there. The noon deadline passed, as did the two-hour grace period: still no deal.

Most of the fans at Portage and Main were young. It was a hot day, and some of them were drinking. As afternoon stretched into evening with no announcement of a deal, the crowd's disappointment turned to frustration. Police, fearing a riot, began to gather in numbers at Portage and Main. Glen Murray, one of the three councillors who had voted no, called for public protection for himself and me. At 6:30 p.m. on the advice of the police, the crowd was informed that no deal had been reached, negotiations were proceeding and they should go home and wait for the next day's announcement. The crowd dispersed without incident and the matter now reverted more fully to the back-rooms, where the real problems were occurring.

In fact, the back-room problems had started a day earlier when Shenkarow's legal counsel, Aikins MacAuley & Thorvaldson, had sent a fax to MEC indicating, among other things, that the $10 million deposit described in MEC's August 18, 1994 option to purchase as being refundable was actually non-refundable and that the option price specified in both the original Interim Operating Agreement and in the August 18, 1994, agreement as being $32 million was in fact $32 million net of tax, or about $54 million. Shenkarow was now saying that he and Asper had a verbal agreement to this effect, a point that Asper denied. The result was that the day before the option was to be exercised, the parties to the agreement disagreed on the option price. Shenkarow had moved the goal posts again.

MEC's legal people then scrambled, working through the night to prepare a signed affidavit from Asper and to line up a judge for the morning of May 18. Their intention was to seek an injunction blocking Shenkarow's sale of the franchise to Burke and Gluckstern in Minneapolis, and requiring Shenkarow to accept the $10 million deposit. Problems could then be worked out in court, but at least MEC would have met the deadline to exercise the option to purchase. The legal documents, including the Asper affidavit, were sent on the morning of May 18 to Aikins MacAuley, who were advised of the intention to seek an injunction. Aikins advised Shenkarow, who immediately went to see Asper. Shenkarow and Asper then spent the morning of May 18—while boisterous Jets' fans gathered in high expecta-tion at Portage and Main—sequestered in Asper's home, in conference and incommunicado. The character of their tête-à-tête and the agreements they reached are not known.

Asper finally called his office to arrange a meeting of all the would-be buyers of the Jets in the CanWest boardroom in the early afternoon. He "sauntered in" after everyone had arrived, asked Mark Chipman for the fundraising report, and said he wished more money had been raised. He had done his job, so what did the group intend to do? Chipman was enraged at Asper, and Hartley Richardson stormed out of the meeting. Sweatman tried to insist that the option had to be exercised, and/or the premier had to be informed of what was happening. A second meeting was arranged, this time to include Filmon, who was hustled out a back door at the Westin Hotel to avoid the increasingly restive late afternoon crowd at Portage and Main. Asper reiterated that he considered he had done his job; now Filmon was angry.

In the end the option was not exercised on May 18. MEC made an offer the next day at 10 a.m., well past the oft-extended deadline, and Shenkarow refused it, saying that it was not financially attractive and he had a $65 million U.S. deal to sell the Jets to Burke and Gluckstern if the Winnipeg bid did not come through.[31]

High-Stakes Poker and Fan Support

The problem in Winnipeg was that not enough corporate money had been raised. Asper tried to make light of the corporate shortfall: "There was never a realistic hope that in four days one could get commitments as opposed to expressions of interest."[32] But the result was that Asper had to make an offer to Shenkarow that was based on a promise that corporate money would be raised in the future. Shenkarow had to decide whether he could rely on a promise of future money raised in Winnipeg's corporate community, where Jim Burns had been unable to raise a cent for the Jets in 1994 and where MEC had since then been unable to raise enough to buy the Jets and cover their losses. In addition there was the element of Shenkarow's newly stated demand for a price of $32 million net of taxes.

Uncertainty reigned. MEC called a news conference and announced that negotiations were continuing. Shenkarow responded with his own news conference on Friday, May 19, announcing that since both the noon and 2 p.m. May 18 deadlines had passed without an offer, "Our position with [Burke and Gluckstern] is that we have an agreement in principle with them." But, Shenkarow added, he was not ruling anything out. He would still listen to MEC, though their offer was "subject to many, many conditions and has many, many problems." Asper's response was immediate: "We don't believe there's any deal with Minneapolis; talks with Shenkarow will continue."[33]

The truth was that neither of the two bidders had been able to assemble the money to close the deal. Burke and Gluckstern needed $20 million from the Minnesota state legislature, and they did not get it in the end. MEC and Asper needed, it appeared, something in the order of an additional $50 million in corporate money. Meanwhile, Manitobans were increasingly exasperated by the emotional roller-coaster. The deal was not done, all was confusion, and fans were frustrated, even angry.

But who was the villain? MEC? Asper? Shenkarow? Filmon? It certainly wasn't the NHL, which had not, as MEC had claimed, imposed onerous last-minute demands on April 26. Yet the NHL was not at all happy with developments in Winnipeg. The NHL wanted the Jets out of Winnipeg, and for two years Shenkarow had been promising that the Jets would indeed be leaving the city. But the league couldn't let its position be known publicly in the face of the massive mobilization of Jets' fans and city boosters in the streets of Winnipeg. So Bettman gritted his teeth, said with a forced smile how impressed he was with Winnipeg's support for the Jets, and privately steamed at Shenkarow and spoke contemptuously of "the children" at MEC. The layers of complexity and behind-the-scenes conflict were byzantine. Could Winnipeggers believe anything they were being told? What was really going on? Nobody knew. Some fans began to ask for their money back.

Even councillors who had voted "yes" were growing frustrated. Having coughed up their "yes" vote on May 17, they were no longer needed. They had been given no information before the vote, and now, not surprisingly, were being given none after. "No one wants to talk to us," complained Councillor Bill Clement. "We want to know what's going on. We're not in the loop," added Councillor Terry Duguid. "I don't want to be left in the dark," complained Councillor Amaro Silva.[34] But councillors who had been in the dark when they voted had given up their leverage with their "yes" vote. They had committed $67 million of city money, and now they were no longer needed. They would stay in the dark. The action had moved behind closed, corporate doors.

Negotiations the next weekend produced a highly tenuous and contentious agreement. Asper met Friday night, May 19, with Filmon and urged him not to release Shenkarow from the terms of the 1991 Interim Operating Agreement, which kept the Jets in Winnipeg until June 30, 1997, in return for which the city and province paid the Jets' losses to that date. Shenkarow had already persuaded Mayor Thompson to release him from the IOA so that he could sell to Burke and Gluckstern. Shenkarow had convinced Thompson that the Jets' losses would skyrocket to June 30, 1997, and the city would be on the hook for half of them. The city would therefore be best off, Shenkarow told Thompson, allowing him to sell to Minneapolis. That would stop the bleeding from the losses. Thompson agreed.

Now Shenkarow wanted Filmon to sign the same release. Asper insisted Filmon not do so. "But Barry wants it," the premier reportedly replied. Asper was insistent. He believed there was no firm offer from Minneapolis and that a deal enabling MEC–Asper to purchase the Jets at $32 million could still be hammered out—if Shenkarow was still bound by the IOA. Filmon agreed.

Asper then left the country on CanWest business, instructing three young MEC representatives to play hardball in negotiations on Saturday. Shenkarow, who said he was emotionally exhausted, called co-owner Harvey Secter in from Boston to take his place at the negotiating table.

The deal cut gave Shenkarow and his partners $32 million for their 64 percent ownership of the Jets and gave Shenkarow an ongoing role in the franchise. The deal also, however, left 22 percent ownership with Shenkarow and his partners, a condition justified by Shenkarow's agreement to keep the Jets in Winnipeg rather than sell for a higher price to Burke and Gluckstern. The 22 percent could only be realized if and when the Jets were sold away from Winnipeg. In effect, with the Shenkarow group's share of the Jets going from 64 percent to 22 percent, MEC would be buying the difference—42 percent of the Jets—for $32 million. The young MEC negotiators had made major concessions. Shenkarow got much more than the $32 million that had been the option price up to May 18, and he was still centrally involved, probably as the team's NHL governor.

Asper was enraged. Why make concessions to Shenkarow when the Minneapolis deal, Asper insisted, was a bluff? The children had panicked. Asper called their negotiating concessions "amateur night on the Red River."[35] He insisted that if "the kids" had stayed cool they could have stared down the Shenkarow people and done the deal for $32 million with Shenkarow out.

But with Shenkarow still in, Asper wanted nothing to do with the deal. He began to fade from the scene, amidst much anxious speculation about whether he was in or out of the deal, and in the end he never invested a nickel. He argued that he knew Shenkarow wouldn't hold costs down, a fear certainly borne out over the next year. But a more likely explanation for Asper's withdrawal is that two such large egos could not co-exist in a single NHL franchise.

A news release issued Sunday, May 21 did not clarify the details of the new arrangement and left many questions unanswered. How much private-sector money was in? How much was left to be raised? Was Asper in or out? Who was to own the franchise? Who would pay the losses? With negotiations continuing, it was said, the questions couldn't be answered just then, but a news conference on May 23 would provide details. When May 23rd rolled around, no news conference occurred and no further details were provided.

The frenzy of May had exhausted itself, replaced by confusion, frustration and unanswered questions. The deadline for completion of the deal was moved back yet again, to August 15. As a *Free Press* editorial put it: "The people of Winnipeg deserve something better than this. The tens of thousands who turned up at rallies and socials, the kids who broke open their piggy banks, the trade unions and employees' groups, the small businessmen—all those who, in the end, had kicked in more than $13 million to keep the Jets in Winnipeg—deserved a straight answer at week's end about where their efforts were heading. They did not deserve another dose of muddle and confusion."[36]

What the city did get out of the seeming chaos was the re-emergence of opposition to the delays, the missed deadlines, the secrecy, the in-fighting and the failure of the city's business elite to contribute their share of the financing. The time to close the deal had been during the days of the great frenzy, but the deal couldn't be closed then—the corporate money simply wasn't there. Soon the momentum created by the frenzy, by people on the streets, began to subside.

Pockets of opposition to the massive public spending needed to save the Jets were emerging spontaneously. In late May, a group calling itself Save Our Pride formed in response to a column by *Free Press* reporter Mike Ward. Headed by Janis Kaminsky, a retired lab technologist, the group ran press ads, staged public forums, distributed leaflets, made presentations at city hall and eventually had over four thousand names on its membership list. A great many smaller, individual efforts popped up all over the city and province. A woman and her daughter in Transcona prepared their own brochure and delivered it door to door. A shopkeeper in St. James handed out petitions in her store. Many individuals went door to door in their neighbourhoods with petitions they prepared themselves.

Given the public opinion surveys, Thin Ice believed that a majority of Winnipeggers and Manitobans were opposed to public funding for a new arena for the Jets and for the Jets' losses. But during the months of April and especially May, 1995, it seemed that a significant shift in public opinion had occurred in favour of the Save Our Jets campaign. Many people were moved by the remarkable sense of community spirit created by the Operation Grassroots campaign, and they expressed their support openly, demonstrably and tangibly. But the frenzy of early to mid-May could not be sustained in the long haul in the absence of corporate leadership. When it became apparent that such leadership was lacking, the support subsided and, as it subsided, the hard core of opposition to public funding for the Jets quietly and spontaneously re-emerged. The message long articulated by Thin Ice continued to express the views of the majority. The struggle to save the Jets would carry on behind closed doors for another three months, but the public enthusiasm created by Operation Grassroots was gone.

The Jets' fans had been magnificent in their support of the team. They had organized socials, attended rallies, flooded open-line radio shows with urgent calls for community solidarity and raised an impressive amount of money. Their contributions to the Save Our Jets campaign had been made without any expectation of personal financial gain, but rather out of a heartfelt commitment to the value of the team to the community. Their effort had truly been an expression of community spirit.

It has long been known that sport can contribute to a sense of community. The isolation and even alienation of city life, and what is for many the drudgery of work and day-to-day living, can be transcended through an identification with "our" team and its heroes. Sport can create for many both a sense of personal identity and the sense of being a part of something bigger, a part of community. Sport can create, in effect, "imagined communities"— communities that, however temporarily, cut across the divisions of money, status and power.

Sport also can create drama, heroism, victory, tragedy, myth—all of which generate intense emotional experiences. It is precisely these emotions to which advertisers appeal, seeking to identify their products with the myth, the drama of the game and its heroes. Sport produces audiences; the audiences are moved by the drama and the intensity and the heroism; and the advertisers identify their products with those emotions in order to sell to the audience. Though manipulated by the advertisers, the emotions are real, and for many are extremely rewarding and meaningful. As one Winnipegger put it in a letter to the *Free Press*:

> It wasn't just about hockey, it was about experiencing something that made us feel exhilarated as a community or down as a community.
>
> We live in a time where society is becoming fragmented and we're prone to feeling a little awkward at the simple task of saying hello to our neighbors, or making contact with a stranger passing us by. Yet we have no problem high-fiving someone at a hockey game, or weeping with them in the last moments of an era we couldn't believe was really ending.[37]

Such emotions sparked the collective community response to the Jets.

But for many Winnipeggers the roots of their collective response went deeper still. For many the mobilization of May 1995 was an expression of cultural nationalism. Our game, Canada's game, was being stolen by the Americans, and Jets' fans weren't about to let that happen. The fans saw their NHL franchise as part of our collective Canadian identity, as part of what makes us Canadian and, they in their struggle to save the franchise were expressing, in effect, a sense of Canadian nationalism in the face of the relentless expansion of U.S. cultural dominance.

For Winnipeg's business class, the Jets were less an expression of cultural nationalism than of their vision of Winnipeg's place in an increasingly continentalized economy. The Jets had to be saved, they argued, no matter the cost, because an NHL franchise put Winnipeg "on the map"—it made Winnipeg known in the United States—and was thus an essential part of a new, U.S.-oriented economic development strategy. With Winnipeg's historic, east–west role as railway centre and gateway to the West rapidly disappearing, if we are to be able to attract businesses to the city and find a new role in the emergent, post-Free Trade Agreement continental economy, then we must, as the business class insisted repeatedly, be a "first tier" city, a "world-class" city. The presence in Winnipeg of the Jets would be symbolic evidence of that status. It would make our city known in the United States, and help make the shift to a new north–south axis.

For many young people in particular, the struggle to Save Our Jets took on a symbolic significance rooted in their own profound sense of insecurity in a time of astonishingly rapid change and social and economic upheaval, and in a city transparently in economic decline. Sports writer Sigurdson accurately identified this phenomenon when he said about the Jets: "Somehow they became a talisman for a generation of young Winnipeggers. The team's future in the city became inextricably linked to their own." Many young people expressed the view "that if the Jets didn't have a future here, they didn't either." Columnist Christopher Dafoe, admitting, "Like thousands of others, I have a nagging feeling that people have been stampeded and blackmailed over all this and that the day of reckoning will come all too soon," immediately added: "Just the same, I think I can understand all that emotion and anger. Winnipeggers are simply fed up with being ignored, put down and dismissed by others. . . . There has been a distressing exodus from this city and an attitude in the rest of the country that Winnipeg is washed up . . . and ready to be closed down. . . . That expensive hockey team has become a symbol of our refusal to eat any more dirt."[38] It was the wrong symbol, but for many it was a noble fight.

This fight, it should be noted, was one that was engaged in primarily by men. Almost all of the actors in the conflict's corporate and political boardrooms and backrooms were men; and the majority of the people demonstrating in the streets and at the rallies were men, and, especially, young men. Although there is indeed a good number of women hockey fans, they remain very much in the minority, a condition reflected repeatedly in public opinion polling. In two such polls conducted on behalf of Thin Ice, four out of five women surveyed said they were opposed to significant amounts of public funds being used to build a new arena or to continue subsidizing the hockey club's losses—a significantly higher proportion of opposition than that reported among the men. A 1994 Winnipeg Area Study, conducted by the University of Manitoba's Sociology Department, found that only 12 percent of Winnipeg women (compared to 25 percent of Winnipeg men) considered a new arena to be important for the city. Similarly, *Chatelaine* magazine reported on another interesting survey of Canadian women in April 1994: in a study aimed at finding out which of fifteen factors the women considered important in determining the quality of urban life, the Canadian women ranked the presence of professional sports teams last. NHL hockey has developed in Canada primarily as a male preserve, and the struggle over the Jets was largely, though not exclusively, a male issue.

In the end the fans—both male and female—were betrayed. The "community" created by sport was only imagined. The transcendence of class and status and power differentials that can be created by sport was only temporary. While fans and citizens selflessly contributed their dollars to Operation Grassroots, corporate leaders waited to see if still more money might be squeezed from the public and then if they would get tax breaks for any contributions they might themselves make. Meanwhile Shenkarow and his private-sector partners had already taken steps, *before the May frenzy*, to ensure that they would pay no Manitoba tax on any capital gain realized from the eventual sale of the Jets. They made use of the legal tax loophole known as the "Quebec Shuffle." Companies incorporated in Quebec pay no capital gains tax on appreciated share values, while companies incorporated in

Manitoba do. In late April 1995, immediately after the provincial election, the Jets' private owners transferred the bulk of their shares in the Jets from Manitoba companies to companies newly incorporated in Quebec.[39] Their intention was to avoid capital gains tax when the Jets were eventually sold. Vast amounts of public funds may have been poured into the Jets to cover their losses and to pay a "management fee"—a guaranteed profit—to the owners, while the value of the owners' shares in the Jets appreciated, but these same owners felt no obligation whatever to return a small portion of their huge profits to Manitobans by paying Manitoba's tax on capital gains. Fans and citizens could risk their money, and indeed were urged to do so. Big business hung on to its money, and in the end the deal failed.

Questions were raised about MEC's competence—one very prominent Winnipeg lawyer observed that he was "appalled at their collective ineptitude." More questions were raised later when it was revealed that while the fans were struggling to save a part of their community, large sums of the public money pouring into the coffers of Spirit of Manitoba—the successor to MEC—were being funnelled straight into companies owned by Spirit's chairman and president.

The fans who tried to Save Our Jets were expressing an old-fashioned sense of community spirit. The business community was expressing an old-fashioned sense of class interest. The fans were struggling to save a franchise by contributing to the building of an arena whose seats would have been so costly that many of them would never have been able to attend, an arena in which the businesspeople would have enjoyed the comforts of viewing games and entertaining clients in luxury suites, the huge cost of which would have been, for them, tax-deductible. Sport, it is true, can create a sense of identity and of community, and that sense of community can even transcend, at least temporarily, real-world divisions based on wealth and status and power. But in the end, in Winnipeg, community gave way to power, and those who had poured heart and soul into the Save Our Jets campaign were left wondering why a handful of rich men were the only ones to benefit from all their effort.

Winnipeggers were also left to wonder about how they had been served by their local media. Important components of the media did not merely report on the story; they became central actors in the story. They climbed on the bandwagon to Save Our Jets, abandoning all pretence of objectivity, leading the cheering, becoming unabashed boosters. In the 1990s the attacks on arena opponents were, if anything, even more sneering, condescending and unreasoned than the attacks on Carl Ridd in 1977–78 that required the intervention of the Winnipeg *Tribune*'s ombudsman. But by now the *Tribune* was long gone and the *Free Press* had conveniently fired its ombudsman.

Media and the Lemon-Suckers in the Time of Frenzy

During the events of May the media as a whole were one-sidedly pro-Jets/ arena. They fed the emotional frenzy that roared like a tidal wave over the city. They parroted the MEC line, shut down the critics.

In the period May 15–21, 1995, the *Winnipeg Free Press* ran sixty-eight stories on the Jets, exclusive of editorials and letters to the editor. No more than six of the sixty-eight stories could even remotely be considered to be journalistically balanced. Claims made by MEC about amounts of private money raised were always reported without question, as if they were the truth by virtue of their source, even when the numbers jumped about wildly from day to day. The reporters most consistently assigned to the Jets' story were the sports reporter Scott Taylor and business reporter John Douglas. Douglas revealed his ideological sympathies through his open admiration for Ontario Premier Mike Harris, who had been a professional golfer playing out of the the North Bay Golf and Country Club when Douglas was assistant golf pro there. It is revealing of their approach to the issue that the *Free Press* chose to use sports and business reporters to cover the issue and not, for example, a social affairs reporter. Coverage noticeably improved when some of the paper's political reporters were assigned to cover the issue after the period of frenzy.

The continued presence of the Jets in Winnipeg had a direct impact on Taylor's income. He was a frequent and well-paid commentator on radio and TV on matters related to the Jets and the NHL and therefore had a vested financial interest in the Save Our Jets campaign. He was also on close terms with Jets' owner Barry Shenkarow, and some of the views he expressed in his columns and news stories are best understood as an expression of that relationship—Taylor often conveyed the Shenkarow line. When *Globe and Mail* correspondent David Roberts wrote, "Most of the local media coverage of the issue can only be described as fatuous boosterism,"[40] Taylor phoned Roberts and berated him, resulting in an angry exchange. When Thin Ice invited Taylor to a meeting to explain the origins of some numbers he had quoted as fact, Taylor was unable to make the explanation. When asked his opinion of the work of sports economist Robert Baade, Taylor dismissed Baade's highly respected work, although his comments suggested that he had not read it. In an April 24, 1995 column, Taylor called on Jets' fans to vote Conservative because only Filmon would save the Jets. Taylor, normally a competent sports reporter, became too emotionally involved with the issue and quite simply lost any sense of balanced perspective.

John Douglas was a similarly unabashed booster who appeared genuinely to have believed that saving the Jets was essential for the health of the local economy. In a column on December 31, 1994 he made his case particularly clear: the effort to save the Jets *cannot* be allowed to fail because that would be a blow to Winnipeg's young business leaders, and they in turn were the key to the city's future. Therefore these young leaders of tomorrow had to be allowed to succeed. He appears to have allowed this belief to colour his reporting on the issue. Perhaps not surprisingly, given that he was a business reporter, he rarely asked tough questions about the spin being advanced by business promoters of the various schemes to save the Jets. Even after the deal had collapsed around the MEC he announced, without a trace of irony, that the entire affair demonstrated that Winnipeg's business community had "met the test." He explained that "the failure of the Winnipeg Jets was a victory for Manitoba. The leadership torch has been passed into very capable hands."[41] The *Free Press* announced Douglas's promotion to business editor on August 15, 1995—the very day the Jets' deal finally collapsed.

The *Free Press* made little effort to hide its abandonment of the principle of journalistic objectivity. On May 18, 1995, the paper announced that it had donated $20,000 to the Save Our Jets campaign, in addition to contributing $40,000 worth of free ad space. One such ad, which ran May 15 might well be entered in the next "Stalinist realism in advertising" contest. Headed "One Community One Cause," the ad extolled the merits of "the new arena that will be the cornerstone of optimism, hope and vigilance as we march together towards the 21st century. Not in defeat, but with heads held high. . . . We have but four brief days in which to fan the spark into a bright and shining flame. A flame whose glow will be seen throughout North America."[42] During the week of the frenzy, May 14–18, the *Free Press* gave MEC daily full-page ads. Many of the "news stories" during that period might more accurately be categorized as advertisements.

Some balance was built into the *Free Press* coverage by means of letters to the editor and the paper's editorial coverage of the issue. In the period April 3 to June 3 the *Free Press* ran fifty-six letters on the Jets issue, forty-one of them, or 73 percent, opposed, and fifteen of them in support. In the same period the *Free Press* ran ten editorials on the issue, the tone of which was much different than the news coverage. The editorials were generally supportive of the Save Our Jets campaign, adopting a tone of quiet optimism, but were tempered by an insistence that Winnipeg was about more than an NHL franchise, and that it was important that the expenditure of public funds be limited. Occasional columns by Frances Russell and Bill Neville went further, raising important questions about the Save Our Jets campaign and even on occasion giving expression to the position of Thin Ice. Political reporters, when given the opportunity, provided more balanced coverage than the sports and business reporters whose views dominated. Many of Dale Cummings's editorial cartoons were masterful examples of political satire. On balance, however, the *Free Press* was overwhelmingly biased in favour of the Save Our Jets campaign, as expressed most importantly in its news coverage.

It is not an exaggeration to say that the paper did not serve the community well with respect to this issue. Had the paper provided its readers with a more hard-headed analysis in May, when it became apparent that the corporate sector could not raise sufficient money for the deal and that the cost in public funds would be wildly beyond what had been claimed, the city and province might have been saved from the unnecessary and futile expenditure of a great deal of money.

The coverage of the Jets/arena issue provided by the tabloid-style *Winnipeg Sun* was not as unbalanced as the coverage of the *Free Press*. The *Sun* sometimes offered a booster-like interpretation of the issue, but several of the paper's writers regularly produced articles that were more balanced than was the case in the *Free Press*. On many occasions the *Sun* asked critical and insightful questions.

The *Sun* quickly saw through MEC's attempt in late April 1995 to place the blame on the NHL. On April 29 a detailed *Sun* story made it clear that MEC had not received new and unreasonable conditions from the NHL only the day before the April 27 Convention Centre hoax. MEC had known the NHL's conditions long before, the *Sun* reported, because both the NHL and Shenkarow had been telling them. By April 30 the *Sun* was suggesting openly that "the NHL was being blamed to divert attention from MEC's business plan."

The *Sun* also provided slightly more coverage of Thin Ice activities. The paper ran a short but accurate page-two story on May 2 covering the Thin Ice analysis of MEC's business plan. While Thin Ice was virtually ignored for the rest of May, on June 3 the *Sun* ran a front-page headline, "Support for Thin Ice Gains Strength."

The *Sun* was also more explicit in blaming the failure to save the Jets on MEC for their unwillingness to assume the risk of covering future Jets' losses. For example, on May 4 a *Sun* headline blared, "Cold Feet: MEC Didn't Have Stomach to Handle Anticipated Losses." And on May 7 weekly columnist Doug Smith identified the irony of MEC's position: "It was strange to see the Winnipeg business community, in its guise as the Manitoba Entertainment Complex, argue for government funding. . . . These are the people who believe that governments should cut spending. . . . They have applauded successive efforts to reduce the size of the public sector. It would appear they are for fewer nurses, teachers and health inspectors, but more hockey players."

Nevertheless the *Sun* also got caught up in the campaign to Save Our Jets, especially during the mid-May period. Particularly revealing were the occasions when bold front-page headlines promoted a boosterish interpretation of the issue, while inside stories and columns raised important questions. Casual readers would see the front-page headlines; only the more careful readers of the paper would see the inside stories. Still, the *Sun* did provide coverage that was less unbalanced and sometimes more insightful than the coverage of the *Free Press*.

The reason for this difference in coverage is difficult to pin down. Perhaps the *Sun* didn't see the struggle over the Jets as "its issue"—the *Free Press* has seized that role. Perhaps the *Sun* sees itself as the paper of "the little person," as opposed to the increased business orientation of the *Free Press*. Still, sports coverage is financially important to the *Sun*, as it is to the *Free Press*, and the Jets were always a central feature of the *Sun's* sports pages. Circulation increased after a Jets game, and hockey action sometimes provided the *Sun's* front-page photo. Despite such considerations, the *Sun* did manage to raise key questions around the affair.

The same cannot be said for radio station CJOB, which played a particularly important role in the May frenzy. At 5 a.m., Monday, May 15, the station began the twenty-four-hour-a-day fundraising campaign known as Operation Grassroots. For four days listeners heard about nothing but the Save Our Jets effort. Callers declared their undying love for the team and insisted they would leave Winnipeg if the Jets did. Nothing was more important to the future of the city than to Save Our Jets. The occasional critic was cut off immediately. Opponents of the huge public expenditure needed to keep the Jets in Winnipeg were attacked. The two members of Thin Ice who taught at the University of Winnipeg, Carl Ridd and I, were condemned repeatedly for "sucking at the public teat," and listeners were urged not to contribute to the university's fundraising campaign. Opponents were called losers, naysayers and wimps, traitors to the great cause. Emotion was high. Some callers wept, some shouted, some attacked and threatened. After a man was arrested for threatening to kill Councillor Rick Boychuk, it was learned that the man had been listening to comments made about Boychuk—on CJOB. Members of Thin Ice received threatening calls from young men whipped into a frenzy by the station, which had abandoned all pretence of objectivity. CJOB ceased reporting on events and began participating in events, and the radio station became a particularly important player.

The station's initiative seems to have grown out of its response to the fans. CJOB's phone lines were jammed with calls from distraught Jets' fans following the May 6 Jets' funeral at the Winnipeg Arena, and when the Asper–Cohen initiative became public knowledge on the weekend of May 12–13, callers urged CJOB to rally supporters for one last push to Save Our Jets. Vic Grant, host of CJOB's evening talk show *Prime Time Sports*, says he received more than seven hundred calls on a single voice mail in the three days after the Jets' funeral, calls urging CJOB to do something; and that in the four days following the funeral CJOB had $53,000 in hand just from people walking into the station or sending cheques.[43] CJOB responded because it sees itself as a "community" radio station. It was at the time the only private Winnipeg radio station with a local phone-in show, with Peter Warren's morning phone-in show being especially popular. Warren deals with local, community issues in a distinctly populist, somewhat right-wing fashion—typical of radio phone-in shows. He had been a key figure in the 1974 Save the Jets campaign, using CJOB at that time as the means to rally emotional and financial support for the team. At a meeting of the talk-show hosts prior to the start of the 1995 campaign, discussion turned to financial targets. Some thought $500,000 seemed reasonable.[44] But the campaign took off: CJOB's efforts were like a spark that set off a raging prairie fire. At the end of the first day, May 15, it was being announced that Operation Grassroots had already raised $1 million; by the end of the campaign it had raised, in total, some $13.5 million. It was a remarkable achievement.

Remarkable though it was, it came at a cost. CJOB and its reporters and talk-show hosts gave up journalism to save the Jets. They did so by flooding the community with a unidimensional perspective—those not prepared to do whatever was needed to Save Our Jets were shut down. Claims about the benefits of the deal were wildly exaggerated—indeed were often factually inaccurate. The appeal was strictly to emotion, and emotions were sky-high. Reason was abandoned, debate was impossible, opponents were silenced, and in the end democracy was trampled. During the week of May 15–19 a mood of near-hysteria gripped the city, and CJOB fed that hysteria.

It is not clear to what extent CJOB's motives derived from its role as the broadcaster of Jets' games. It is clear that the right to broadcast Jets' games is a lucrative source of revenue for the station. It draws in precisely a male audience aged eighteen to forty-five, which advertisers love to target their messages, and once that audience has tuned in to CJOB for the games they are more likely to stay tuned for further programming. The right to broadcast Jets games provided programming for some eighty evenings per year, or about one evening in three during the season, and it created the basis for sports phone-in shows. The loss of the Jets would thus leave a huge programming hole to be filled, a hole unlikely to be filled by anything else so effective at attracting audiences and advertising revenue. But it would be overly cynical to attribute CJOB's efforts to save the Jets *entirely* to its "bottom line." Like many Winnipeggers, CJOB staff had come to believe that saving the Jets was about more than hockey—it was about the future of the city, about community and community spirit and local economic development and a "vision" for the future. CJOB staff and even owners were, in large part, well-intentioned victims of their own propaganda. The cost was the complete smothering of democratic debate on an important public issue plus the prolonging of a project that rational analysis repeatedly demonstrated could not work.

Local television coverage was not much better—and not surprisingly, given its links to professional hockey in Winnipeg. CKY-TV, the local CTV affiliate, is owned by Randy Moffat, a co-owner of the Jets. CKND-TV held the broadcast rights for Jets games and was owned by Izzy Asper's CanWest

Global Communications. MTN is owned by Stuart Craig, whose son Drew, MTN's general manager, became actively involved in the Save Our Jets campaign. And CBC-TV broadcasts *Hockey Night in Canada*. Add to this the extent to which the private stations' revenue is dependent upon advertising purchased by the very corporations that were behind the effort to buy the Jets, and there can be little remaining mystery about the one-sided coverage of the issue.

During this period there were occasional voices of opposition—buried behind the *Winnipeg Sun*'s boosterish front pages, or squeezed into the occasional CBC radio spot, but they were few. The CBC, for example, though providing Thin Ice slightly better exposure than other media outlets, was decidedly one-sided, and repeatedly excluded Thin Ice. In mid-May, for example, Thin Ice was pulled at the last minute from two national CBC-Television broadcasts when it became apparent that despite their funeral the Jets might not yet be dead after all. CBC-Radio's *Cross Country Check Up* did a show on the issue, but Thin Ice was not asked to participate. CBC-Radio's *Now the Details* did a show on the issue, and again Thin Ice was not asked to participate. Veteran CBC national sports broadcaster Don Wittman phoned Carl Ridd on June 2, 1995, and in anger and rage condemned Thin Ice for its opposition to public funding for a new arena and for the Jets. *The Globe and Mail* did a series on the perilous state of NHL franchises in small Canadian cities, including a story on Winnipeg, but did not contact Thin Ice. In these various ways, the public was denied access to the kind of information needed to make an informed judgement on an important public policy issue. It should not be thought for a moment that this is unusual—the media consistently give short shrift to serious voices of opposition to the dominant thinking of the day. In May 1995 the normal media bias was accentuated, and Winnipeggers paid more than the usual price.

Thin Ice did get some media coverage. On May 18, for example, Frances Russell wrote in her *Free Press* column that although civic boosterism had "gone mad and created a potent stew of hysteria, irrationality and rage," Thin Ice "has been proven right every step of the way" in its analysis of the public costs. Russell added that Thin Ice would also be proven right in its view that the cost of saving the Jets would add further to the erosion of Winnipeg's quality of life and the growth of poverty in the city.

Free Press columnist Tom Oleson responded the next day, May 19, in much more typical fashion. After condemning the corporate sector and politicians for "sitting on their wallets" while ordinary Winnipeggers poured heart and soul into saving the Jets, Oleson concluded: "Finally we should spare a thought for the lemon-suckers of Thin Ice and their ilk. Can they seriously believe that one more child will go hungry in Manitoba because governments build an arena? Will they now coalesce in Tippety-Toes, to oppose subsidies to the ballet, Sour Notes to fight grants to the symphony, Bad Quotes to subvert support for writers and publishers? All of that money could feed some hungry children in Winnipeg, but it wouldn't. That's an entirely different problem."

Of course, it wasn't an entirely different problem at all. What Thin Ice had succeeded in doing was to frame the issue as a social justice issue, as a matter of choices about how to spend limited public funds. Thin Ice had insisted repeatedly that the city was better off if the Jets stayed in Winnipeg than if they left, but not at the price of the huge expenditure in public funds that would be required to keep them. And Thin Ice had insisted repeatedly that if such huge sums of public funds were available, there were better ways to spend the money. There were more pressing needs in Winnipeg to which public funds could be applied than building a new arena that differed from the old one primarily in having luxury suites which would be the exclusive and tax-deductible preserve of the corporate elite.

This kind of analysis was anathema to the right-wing, anti-tax, anti-public spending organizations that might logically have been expected to oppose the huge expenditure of public funds on the Jets. Such organizations—the Manitoba Taxpayers Federation, for example—were virtually silent, only entering the debate in late May when the frenzy had long subsided and the issue was well into its lengthy and tortured denouement.[45] That such normally anti-public spending organizations had not opposed the vast expenditures in public funds needed to save the Jets is almost certainly attributable to their role as the servants of the corporate sector. Big business wanted to save the Jets and needed a huge expenditure of public funds to make it happen, so the Taxpayers Federation abandoned its normal opposition to public spending and remained silent on the issue.

The consequence was that a good many people who would normally be adamantly opposed to the social justice orientation of Thin Ice and its parent organization, Cho!ces—people who were in fact dyed-in-the-wool conservatives—became supporters of Thin Ice. There was no place else to go if they were to oppose the vast public expenditure on the Jets.

Indeed, the class character of the issue became very confused. Many working-class and low-income people who would normally be receptive to the views of Cho!ces and Thin Ice on public spending for health care, education, social services and job creation were lined up with the anti-Thin Ice side to save the Jets; many who were traditional conservatives were lined up on the side of Thin Ice because of their opposition to most forms of public spending. This sociological confusion notwithstanding, Thin Ice did succeed in framing the issue as a social justice and not an anti-tax issue and put a progressive spin on an issue that could just as easily have been seized by the political right. This social justice spin only added to the intensity of the media and corporate attacks, which in turn fuelled a certain amount of public abuse. The University of Winnipeg, for example, received numerous calls from angry Winnipeg businesspeople insisting they would make no further financial contributions to the university so long as Thin Ice members Ridd and myself were employed there. Both the president and the dean of the university were on the receiving end of angry harangues from anti-Thin Ice Jets' fans. Threatening phone calls, including at least two death threats, were received by Thin Ice members, and certain members of city council were verbally abusive—although to Winnipeggers' credit, not a single act of physical violence was ever directed at a member of Thin Ice.

What *did* affect the efforts of Thin Ice was the story about Carl Ridd written by *Free Press* reporter John Douglas and published on April 1. Ridd spent the next four days totally immersed in phoning and writing, trying to undo the political damage to Thin Ice and recover from an emotional and psychological hurt. After that he stepped back somewhat from public roles, fearing that his and Thin Ice's credibility might otherwise be damaged. What had been "joyful" to him—the genuine delight he derived from working with Thin Ice, the community-based group that dared to question the high and mighty of the business establishment—had become painful, something he stuck with out of a sense of duty but without the sense of fun and commitment and enthusiasm that had been there before. He had been injured, he later acknowledged, by the "manifest ugliness" that had enveloped the whole conflict. It was an exceptionally painful experience for Ridd and demonstrates in one more small way the enormous influence exerted by the media.

If Ridd had been guilty of anything in the entire episode, it was political naiveté. He had striven, as an individual, to remain on friendly terms with those who were determined to silence Thin Ice. They betrayed his trust.

The Business Class

The key players in the drama were, of course, leading members of Winnipeg's corporate community, and the events of May throw much light on them. At one level, the activities of MEC demonstrated once again, for those few who might not already have known, just how powerful the business class is. MEC completely dominated the local media, even more than business normally does, leaving many individual journalists upset and even ashamed of the role they were required to play. MEC used strong-arm tactics and various forms of threats to win votes at city council. Its members exerted enormous pressure on small and medium-sized businesses to contribute to the campaign: at least some businesses purchased club seats for fear of losing accounts if they did not. Even those businesspeople who doubted the wisdom of MEC's efforts—and there were many—remained silent, never publicly expressing their concerns, even when urged to do so by Thin Ice. For them, class loyalty came before the public interest. Most law firms were prevented from working for Thin Ice. Even leaders of community and social service organizations, who knew their funding could be jeopardized if huge amounts of scarce public funds were committed to the Jets, were reluctant to be publicly identified with Thin Ice for fear of the consequences for their organizations. MEC played rough, exerting their influence in a myriad of ways.

But in the end, MEC could not save the Jets. The young leaders of Winnipeg's business community were, in fact, out of their league. Extolled as the best and the brightest when they emerged in mid-1994, "the children" had spoken openly and repeatedly in the business community about their effort as a "passing of the torch" to a new generation of business leaders. Such claims could not obscure the truth conveyed by the evidence: the younger generation of Winnipeg's business leaders, despite all their strong-arming and public relations ploys, had failed.

Some might say—"Well, at least the young business leaders of MEC tried." Yet when the sheer financial magnitude of the Save the Jets effort finally dawned on them, when they finally saw how much money would *really* be needed to keep the Jets in Winnipeg, MEC's leaders scrambled to ensure that all the costs and risks would be borne not by them but by the public sector. At the same time they struggled to ensure that the large capital gain that would be earned when the Jets inevitably left the city would accrue to their benefit, and not to the benefit of either the city or province or of long-time owner Shenkarow. The struggle to save the Jets became a cynical struggle to seize the huge capital gain to be made from the sale of the Jets, and in this undignified scramble for money the MEC became a pale and even pathetic shadow of the still more powerful corporate forces now in control of the NHL.

MEC's efforts, far from enhancing the tarnished reputation of Winnipeg's business class, had worsened it. They had dropped the torch. It would be picked up for one last tortured, expensive and ultimately futile effort by a new configuration of business leaders who took from the frenzy of May the name the Spirit of Manitoba.

7. The Spirit of Manitoba

Dale Cummings

The Spirit of Manitoba Inc. included the MEC but reached beyond to bring in many of the city's older, more established businesspeople—those who had said no to Burns and had left the project to "the kids" in the summer of 1994. Now they emerged to bail out the kids and save the Jets in the summer of 1995. They took the name Spirit of Manitoba to reflect the fact that this final attempt owed its existence to the remarkable spirit of Winnipeg Jets' fans, whose determination and refusal to give in had resurrected the Jets from the dead. However, the corporate Spirit again would prove unable to live up to its community namesake.

The Spirit of Manitoba initially held out the prospect of success primarily because, unlike the MEC, a handful of its leaders were experienced, successful entrepreneurs. They were people who had built their own companies and made their own fortunes. They included, among others, Albert Cohen and, most importantly, Izzy Asper. One of Asper's corporate objectives was to make the aggressive and rapidly expanding CanWest Global Communications into a third Canadian television network. He had no particular interest in hockey as such, but he recognized the well-established connection between newly formed television networks and pro sport franchises: at least eight NHL franchises are currently owned by communications companies.

An NHL executive explained: "Cable and broadcasting companies will own most of the major-league sports franchises in North America and/or will have a major involvement of some kind. Sports is the cheapest, most spontaneous, direct-type of programming in the world. Turn the lights on and there you are. No script, no nothing. Just players and the facility. There's nothing like it when programming demands exceed inventory."[1] Professional sport not only offers lots of programming to a television network, but it also produces a large, demographically specific audience for which advertisers are prepared to pay large sums. The combined ownership of a new Canadian television network and an NHL franchise makes good business sense. Asper is a very good businessman.

It is not clear to what extent, if at all, this television network-pro sport synergy drove Asper's involvement in the Save Our Jets effort. It is clear that he was also motivated by a combination of genuine community spirit and a large personal ego. A former corporate lawyer who had been leader of the provincial Liberal party from 1970 to 1975 and had founded CanWest in 1976, Asper is an ambitious, hard-driving, larger-than-life character, a chain-smoking, baggy-eyed jazz aficionado with a genuine commitment to Winnipeg. His involvement in early May and the hopes he inspired were the catalyst for the week of frenzy, and for the establishment of the Spirit of Manitoba. Asper's role was to be chief private-sector fundraiser. In a letter to Premier Filmon dated May 12, 1995 he precisely set out his commitment: "I will undertake to lead the drive to put in place the private sector's equal contribution, capped at your estimate of $111 million. The private sector funds, like the governmental funds, will, of course, be advanced on a non-profit basis." Asper's commitment to raising funds "on a non-profit basis" would later be used as the reason for his abandonment of the Spirit of Manitoba when Spirit sought to raise funds on an equity—or "for-profit"—basis.

Tough Negotiations in Late May–Early June

In the weeks following the extended May 18 deadline for the purchase of the Jets, the newly formed Spirit of Manitoba struggled behind closed doors to structure the intricate financing needed to do the deal. Its members sought to minimize both the amount that the private sector would invest, and the risk that the private sector would incur. They wanted the public sector to pay the cost and bear the risk, and they struggled over what degree of ownership and what managerial role would accrue to Shenkarow. It was by now a four-cornered conflict: Asper and his new people; Shenkarow and his partners; the remnants of "the kids" from MEC; and the Gray–Sweatman interests.

Asper had been enraged with what he took to be the amateurish negotiating of the MEC representatives on the weekend of May 19. Shenkarow was an exceptionally tough negotiator with a well-deserved reputation for moving the goal posts just when a deal appeared done. If the franchise was going to stay in Winnipeg, Shenkarow wanted a continued, and major, share in its ownership and management. MEC had offered him, on the May 19 weekend, $32 million, plus a 22 percent stake in the team, plus a seat on the team's board of directors, plus a two-year contract to work with whomever was to take over day-to-day operations. Shenkarow wanted more: "He wants to be the team's president and governor for at least two years. If he can't do both, he doesn't want to do either." Former Blackwoods Beverage owner Gerry Gray and his legal counsel, Alan Sweatman, were equally adamant that they would not have Shenkarow involved in the club's day-to-day operations.[2] All recognized, however, that Shenkarow had to be involved in some way; otherwise the deal would not get NHL approval.

Only Asper could deal with Shenkarow's ever-escalating demands. "Izzy is the best deal-maker in Canada. He's the only guy in town who can sort out this mess," one prominent "mover and shaker" said. But for most of May and for periods in early June Asper was out of Winnipeg negotiating CanWest projects overseas. The result was fruitless bickering and rancorous conflict behind closed doors. As Scott Taylor, Shenkarow's public voice in these matters, put it, "In corporate terms, there is a war going on."[3]

Public support began to erode, the spirit of mid-May to subside. People grew angry with the delays and the in-fighting. In the wake of the wild mobilization of mid-May, it was hard to accept the truth—professional sport no longer cares about fans. As Roy MacGregor put it in *The Ottawa Citizen*, the Jets had been saved in mid-May "by the very people professional sports has been abusing, ignoring and taking for granted now for more than a decade—the home-town fans." Now Winnipeg's business class ignored the home-town fans while they quarrelled among themselves over the intricate details of high finance. The longer they quarrelled, the greater grew the resentment.

By late May–early June, the mood had fully turned. Even the media were fed up. On June 2, John Douglas lamented that talks had become "a contest of control." On June 4, in a news story, the Winnipeg *Sun* ran a phone number for Thin Ice and an address to which cheques for Thin Ice could be sent. The three WIN councillors who had voted against the May 17 deal were inundated with congratulatory phone calls. Councillors Lazarenko and Hyman, "yes" voters on May 17, called for an enquiry into the whole affair on June 7. Councillors who had voted "yes" increasingly expressed concern and even outrage at being kept in the dark.

In the provincial legislature, newly elected NDP MLA Tim Sale relentlessly pounded the Filmon government with pointed questions about the long-delayed deal. By the time the session ended in mid-July the NDP would have asked over 130 questions about the Jets deal in the legislature and dozens more in legislative committee meetings. Premier Filmon, struggling to find a reasoned defence of his government's position, was reduced to the type of comment he made on June 25, 1995 when he denounced Thin Ice and Cho!ces as "loony left-wing organizations."

The provincial Tory caucus was badly split on the issue. One usually reticent government backbencher described the mood in the Tory caucus by saying, "It's awful," adding that every day in his own caucus meetings Finance Minister Eric Stefanson took a pounding over the Jets issue. Rural Tories in particular were angry and became more so when Thin Ice ran radio ads in the Tory heartland of southern Manitoba, setting rural funding cuts against the vast public costs of the Winnipeg Jets and urging listeners to call their MLA to express their views. In July Thin Ice addressed a well-attended public meeting in Brandon and got favourable front-page coverage the next day in the *Brandon Sun*.

Rumours abounded that disgruntled contributors to Operation Grass-roots, the frenzy having long subsided, were now quietly withdrawing their contributions. A third public opinion survey conducted by Viewpoints Research for Thin Ice revealed that by early June, 61 percent of respondents were opposed to public funds for a new arena for the Jets; 49 percent of respondents were strongly opposed. While businessmen were holed up behind closed doors fighting and bickering over the finances and managerial control, public support for the effort had melted. The whole situation was in disarray.

Upon his return from Europe in early June Asper brushed aside the young MEC people for whose abilities he had little regard, and on June 9 made an aggressive offer to Shenkarow on behalf of Spirit of Manitoba. Shenkarow would get $32.45 million for his 64 percent of the team, plus an additional $22 million that would be payable only if and when the team was sold out of Manitoba, and that would be paid even then only if and when all other claims had been met. Shenkarow would no longer be in charge of day-to-day operations and would have only a non-voting seat on the Jets' Board.

Shenkarow was not amused. Even while new Spirit of Manitoba chair-person Mal Anderson was describing the terms of the offer to a news conference, Jets' personnel were distributing Shenkarow's hurriedly pre-pared news release to the assembled media. When told that Shenkarow was disappointed with the offer and was complaining that it did not live up to agreements already reached, Asper replied, "I don't give a damn who's disappointed," adding sarcastically, "Barry's upset? Oh, that's gonna ruin my day."[4] Mayor Thompson and city council, apparently emboldened by Izzy, sounded equally tough, insisting that if Shenkarow rejected the offer the city would no longer cover the Jets' losses.

This promise from the mayor, like so many she had previously made, would soon be forgotten, but in the meantime Shenkarow had seemingly been checkmated. If he said yes to the offer, he would be giving up his asset for far less than the going market price—the Quebec Nordiques had just sold for $75 million US—and he would, against his will, be squeezed out of the team's management. If he said no he would be painted the villain, the one who sold the Jets away after refusing an offer that would have kept the team in Winnipeg. After having his way for the past three weeks with the neophytes of MEC, Shenkarow had apparently met his match upon Asper's return. Once again, Izzy the deal-maker was the talk of the town, the saviour.

Shenkarow paused, then called Asper's bluff. On June 13 Shenkarow offered the Jets to Spirit for $32 million, with no role at all for himself, and subject only to NHL approval. It was a master stroke. The Asper offer had been subject not only to NHL approval, but also to a favourable Revenue Canada ruling regarding a proposed endowment fund. Shenkarow was saying: the franchise is yours for the $32 million specified in the option to purchase; you take the risk that you'll get a favourable Revenue Canada ruling; you raise the $32 million to purchase the team, plus $8 million in outstanding franchise debts, plus enough to create an endowment fund large enough to pay the Jets' very substantial losses.

The ball was now squarely back in Spirit's court. All Spirit had to do was raise the corporate money. But *that*, of course, had been the problem all along. Shenkarow was taking the calculated risk that Spirit—like MEC before it, and like Jim Burns before MEC—would be unable to find the corporate money. If Spirit could not find the money, they and not Shenkarow would be the villains, and Shenkarow would have another year with the city and province paying his losses while he shopped around for the best deal—and while the value of the franchise continued to grow.

Spirit had to put $10 million down by the following Friday, June 16. Tellingly, they could not. They had to borrow $5 million from the province. Spirit's and MEC's repeated claims, echoed endlessly by the media, that they had raised $50 million in private money—or $60 million or $80 million or $111 million, or whatever amount they happened to claim on a given day—must not have been true. It appears that they had only pledges to commit money—pledges that were conditional upon a favourable tax ruling. They retreated again behind closed doors to work at getting a favourable Revenue Canada ruling and to find a way to raise the corporate money.

Exit Izzy

By July Spirit was in chaos. Mal Anderson had resigned as chairman after serving less than a month, and no prominent business leader would take his place. Three were asked directly—Arthur Mauro, Robert Chipman and Jack Fraser—and all of them said no. A source told the *Free Press*: "None of the old names in this city will stand up. These guys are worried about getting exposed."[5] In the end, seventy-four-year-old Alan Sweatman—who had to that time been the paid legal counsel for potential $10 million contributor Gerry Gray—was forced, by default, to assume the position effective July 5.

In-fighting among business factions had reached the danger level. The whole deal was at risk of spinning wildly off the tracks. "I think we're at the falling apart stage," said Sweatman. "What we've been fighting over—and believe me we've been fighting—is the fundamental question of who is going to run this show. That's always been the problem, but now it is finally being recognized that is the problem."[6]

It had been the problem since February 1995 when Gray had arrived with his $10 million and Shenkarow had realized that he would not be in charge of the franchise once the new arena was constructed. Spirit believed that probably from late March or April, and certainly from May 3, Shenkarow had been determined that he would not sell the Jets to a local buyer. In their

Reply to the Statement of Defence in a legal dispute in October 1995 over the disposition of Spirit's $10 million deposit, Spirit pleaded: "The Defendants [Shenkarow and the majority owners of the Jets], after May 3, 1995, were not prepared to sell their interest in the Winnipeg Jets and, while publicly offering to sell their interest in the Winnipeg Jets to the Plaintiff [Spirit], were covertly taking steps to make it impossible for the Plaintiff to complete the purchase under the terms and conditions of the Option Agreement." Among these covert steps, it was later revealed, was the "Quebec shuffle," the perfectly legal tax loophole involving transfer of ownership shares to newly created Quebec companies to avoid paying Manitoba taxes on capital gains. This ownership shift was effected, for the most part, in late April 1995. Spirit also charged, in their *Reply to the Statement of Defence*, that Shenkarow had written a letter to NHL Commissioner Bettman "in which he denigrated the Plaintiff's business plan and the ability of the Plaintiff to maintain the Winnipeg Jets in the City of Winnipeg," and that Shenkarow had "supported and encouraged Scott Taylor . . . in his campaign to denigrate the abilities and integrity of officers and directors of the Plaintiff."

Shenkarow's perception was that "what these guys want to do is steal my dream away from me." And fears were growing that Asper might walk away from the whole mess "after getting a close up look at all the machiavellian manoeuvring." Mike Bessey, Filmon's Jets negotiator and close confidante, lamented, "People are always saying that government should run more like a business. Well, if this is how business is run, heaven help us."[7]

In the midst of this chaos, a fateful business decision was made. Spirit would seek to raise $50 million in private equity in the form of limited partnership units. Investors would potentially earn a 5 percent rate of return. Private-sector money would be raised, in short, on a for-profit basis. Spirit approached the Manitoba Securities Commission in early July—MEC had made a preliminary submission in early April—to seek regulatory approval for such a share offering. The shift in direction was enough to make Asper jump ship. In a news release on July 19 Asper announced that the non-profit basis of his original May 12 agreement with Premier Filmon had been breached, and as a result he would no longer serve as Spirit's fundraiser. The organization has lost not only its chief fundraiser but also its driving force. By that time as well, Spirit was unable to convince a single prominent businessperson in the city to serve as its chair and the *Free Press* was reporting, "Most of the big players have little interest in a hands-on ownership position."[8]

Back to City Hall: The July Flip-Flop

Meanwhile, no progress was being made in arranging for contributions to a proposed endowment fund to be tax-deductible. Without a tax deduction there would be no chance whatever of raising the remaining $61 million—

that is, over and above the $50 million in limited partnership units—in non-profit private-sector money. The corporate sector would contribute to the save the Jets effort *only* if if got a tax deduction, but getting a tax deduction required approval from one of the three levels of government. The province had emphatically said no, and Spirit had not even bothered approaching Revenue Canada, knowing its response would be the same. The only level of government that might be coerced into issuing tax deduction receipts was the City of Winnipeg. For so long ignored and kept in the dark after its May 17 vote, city council was suddenly needed again. So it was that the conflict turned once more, as it had so many times before, to the council, where MEC and Spirit had always been successful in getting their way.

On July 26 Spirit of Manitoba appeared before city council to ask for approval of a scheme that would have the city issue tax receipts to those who contributed to an endowment fund. The endowment fund would be owned by a new entity, which would in turn be owned by the city and the province. Thus the city and province were, in effect, to own the endowment fund. Therefore any contributions to the endowment fund, Spirit argued, were gifts to the city. The city had the authority—subject to Revenue Canada approval—to issue tax receipts, but only for "gifts to the city," so this scheme was intended to entitle the city to issue tax receipts to the donors, making the gifts tax-deductible. Donors would therefore get a 20 percent tax deduction, which would enable Spirit to begin its fundraising drive.

The document outlining this proposed arrangement, called the "Relationships" document, was complex. It was, in typical fashion, made available to city councillors for the first time on the morning of July 26—the day of the vote.

Spirit then insisted that council had to approve the complex scheme that day, or the deal was dead. Spirit president Cam Osler threatened councillors that if they did not approve the scheme that day, he would recommend to the board of Spirit that the whole project be abandoned. Fundraising could not begin in earnest until tax receipts could be issued to contributors, and city council's approval of the proposed scheme as set out in the "Relationships" document was necessary before Revenue Canada would rule on the acceptability of the scheme. As Chief Commissioner Rick Frost advised the councillors, "Without this decision there cannot be a fundraising campaign." Individual Manitobans and small businesses may have contributed over $13 million in May 1995 without any expectation of a tax receipt, but the corporate community had no intention whatever of doing so—no tax receipt, no corporate contributions to the Save Our Jets effort. And council's decision, as always, had to be made *now*.

The scheme described in the "Relationships" document—a document that Frost described as the "cornerstone" of the whole Save Our Jets effort—was in fact an elaborate money-laundering scheme. It had to get money to the Jets, but it had to make the money contributed to the Jets *look* like "gifts to the city."

This is how it was to work. The endowment fund would use interest earned on the money contributed to the fund to pay the operating costs of the arena and would borrow against the principal amount in the fund to make loans to the Jets to cover the team's operating losses. The amount loaned could be as much as the lesser of $30 million or 25 percent of the market value of the franchise. Any surplus earned by the arena would be paid to the Jets. It was likely that the arena would earn a surplus: it would have no debt-servicing charges to pay because the construction cost was to be donated by the three levels of government; it would have minimal operating costs because these would be paid by the endowment fund. And all revenue from the sale of club seats and luxury suites was to go directly to the Jets. Thus the arena, in this scheme, became a part of the means by which to sluice money into the coffers of the Jets.

What is more, only $61 million was to be raised by the endowment fund; the other $50 million was to be raised by means of the limited partnership offering which was to pay a 5 percent rate of return to investors. Thus the scheme would be redirecting money through the arena to the limited partnership investors.

Finally, the plan was to raise only $30 million of the $61 million in the endowment fund by August 15, the remainder to be raised in future. The very real likelihood existed that the $30 million would be consumed within a year or two by cost overruns on the arena and the payment of Jets' losses. Since the city and province would own the endowment fund, the public would then have ended up being responsible for paying the operating costs of the arena. When questioned by councillors on some of these contingencies, Spirit chairman Sweatman conceded, "It's all a leap of faith."[9]

Council balked. Once again they had been given almost no time to consider a complex scheme. It was the product of what Chief Commissioner Frost described to them as "the most difficult and complex negotiations I've ever experienced."[10] Yet councillors had to decide immediately. It was a rerun of the May 17 council meeting. Spirit had had sixty-eight days since that meeting, and now council had less than twenty-four hours.

What had they been doing all that time, some councillors asked? Why was this complicated scheme before them without a business plan? Why should they approve a plan that would see the city's tax number used to benefit the Limited Partners? What happened to the original Asper scheme to raise money on a non-profit basis? Why is it, an angry councillor Jae Eadie asked, that "the private sector to this day has not shown us the colour of its money"?[11]

As it began to appear that council might reject Spirit's request, Premier Filmon hurriedly called a news conference to reiterate that if council did not pass the motion before it that day, the whole deal was dead. Councillors were being squeezed from all sides. Why, some councillors asked, was city council always voting "with a gun to our head?"[12]

In the end, despite that "gun to their heads," council rejected the complex tax scheme. Some councillors who had been supporters all along, in particular finance committee chair Eadie, one of the key members of the conservative majority on council, had finally said enough is enough. "I guess I was tired of being pushed around," Eadie said. "I've lost my tolerance and my patience for the delays on the private sector side."

The deal, it appeared, was dead, killed by the city council. One angry Spirit member revealed how the business community had viewed council all along, saying, "I'm not surprised. This council is a big joke. They are a walking satire." Chairman Sweatman informed the media that the Spirit board would meet the next day to see "if someone has a rabbit we can pull out of our hat," but he conceded, "We've come up with a lot of tricks so far, but I don't have one this time."[13] Spirit did, however, have one old trick left that had worked well before—apply strong-arm tactics to individual councillors. Hyman and Duguid had frequently before been their targets. This time it would be Eadie.

One week later, on August 3, council met again to reconsider the matter. Why? Because on July 26 Spirit did not get the vote it wanted. Spirit exerted pressure; the mayor agreed that council would vote again. Spirit was more likely than usual to get away with such tactics because, as a *Free Press* editorial concluded, "As time moves on, fewer and fewer people care."[14] The public had been worn down by the issue.

Spirit began its pitch to the specially reassembled council with a thinly veiled threat. Give us this vote, Spirit spokesperson Paul Robson told council, so that businesspeople who volunteer time in so many ways will be encouraged to continue. "Sending a strong, positive message to this community is essential," Robson advised, clearly implying that otherwise businesspeople would withdraw from the community[15]. Steve Bannatyne, chairman of Winnipeg Enterprises, reiterated the now mandatory threat, most recently issued a week earlier, of give us the vote today or the whole deal is off.

Spirit chairman Sweatman then proceeded, in the most revealing performance to date, to lay bare the tensions and contradictions tearing at Spirit, while he simultaneously tried to draw a veil of secrecy over Spirit's innermost workings. First, he asserted that Asper could never have raised the promised $111 million in the non-profit way originally intended. Asper was, Sweatman noted, "talking through his hat." Next, Sweatman advised that Spirit could not now meet the August 15 deadline—"That's not possible." Deadlines, it had long since been made clear, were firm or not as suited the immediate needs of corporate leaders. For further clarity he added,

"There's no significance to August 15 in any meaningful sense."[16]

Sweatman was then asked by Councillor Golden for a list of all fees paid to law firms involved with Spirit, including Thompson Dorfman Sweatman, and all fees paid to Spirit president Cam Osler's InterGroup Consultants. "I don't know whether that's really a concern of this Council," Sweatman replied.[17] Yet council, as Sweatman knew, was paying half of those costs. Days before Sweatman had been asked to say who advanced the down payment on Spirit's purchase of the Jets. Sweatman replied, "I'm not going to tell you that. That is private information." Half the amount, $5 million, had been advanced by the province. As the *Free Press* remarked, "There ought to be nothing private about that."[18]

Councillor Boychuk asked Sweatman who was responsible for cost overruns. "We do not have an answer as yet,"[19] Sweatman acknowledged. This meant that the public sector would be expected to pay for cost overruns. When it was stated explicitly by Councillor Golden that the proposed scheme would have the new arena serve as a conduit for funds to be directed to the Limited Partnership, Sweatman, whose law firm was the key designer of the elaborate scheme by which this would happen, replied, "I don't think there is any conduit."[20]

Spirit was desperate. The deal was in chaos. They would do and say whatever needed doing and saying to secure council's vote.

I addressed that same council meeting on behalf of Thin Ice, pointing out that endless problems remained unsolved. There were still no salary caps or revenue-sharing in place in the NHL. The Mauro, Ogden and Burns reports had all insisted that without salary caps and/or revenue-sharing the Jets were not likely to be financially viable in Winnipeg. NHL Commissioner Bettman had advised Spirit in a letter received July 25 that they were overestimating league revenues to the Jets by about $2 million and underestimating salary costs by some $7 million. This would add dramatically to the Jets' losses, resulting in a still more rapid depletion of the proposed endowment fund, thus hastening the date by which the Jets would be forced to leave Winnipeg. What few financial projections Spirit had provided—there was still no Spirit business plan—were as unreliable as the MEC numbers of April 1995.

Further, I pointed out that Spirit had received the Bettman letter the day before the July 26 council meeting, but had not made its contents known to councillors at that meeting. That letter set out several conditions necessary for NHL approval, including an endowment fund level of $111 million, of which at least $80 million must be available to cover losses. Why didn't Spirit reveal these conditions to councillors, particularly since they had abandoned those targets as unachievable? Why had no Winnipeg businessperson stepped forward as personal guarantor of any shortfalls in the endowment fund, as the NHL was calling for? Why were councillors even considering the city's issuance of tax receipts—for "gifts to the city"—when it was patently obvious that the proposed contributions were intended to save the Jets? Why did they think Revenue Canada would be fooled into thinking such contributions were "gifts to the city"? What kind of precedent would be set by agreeing to use the city's authority to issue tax receipts for money contributed to a for-profit enterprise? And why was Spirit itself in such disarray, with Asper gone and no businessperson prepared to serve as chair?

The questions posed by Thin Ice went unanswered, but it didn't seem to matter. What mattered was that corporate leaders wanted the vote. Jae Eadie, who had delivered a surprise "no" vote on July 26 because he was "tired of being pushed around" by a private sector that had "not shown us the colour of its money," caved in. He explained his flip-flop with the unlikely comment that as a result of the no-vote on July 26 Spirit had finally come to see "that we can't be taken for granted any more, and their comments over the last few days indicate they are willing to be open and honest with their partners."[21] Their comments had, of course, indicated no such thing. But as Eadie himself put it, the pressures of the past few days had not "been the most pleasant of experiences."[22]

The tax scheme devised to launder money so that contributions to the Jets looked like gifts to the city had passed. The deal, though on life support, was still alive. Nobody wanted to be the one to pull the plug, even though it was clear by August 3 that the deal could not be salvaged. Revenue Canada was extremely unlikely to approve the city's use of its tax number for contributions to the Jets. And the NHL was emphatic in its insistence that at least $111 million had to be in place in the endowment fund to secure NHL approval. In a letter to Sweatman dated August 3, Gary Bettman repeated the general thrust of his July 25 letter:

> A critical condition is that an endowment fund of at least $111 million be in place at the time the proposal is put to the [NHL] board. I was troubled by recent press reports suggesting this represents a bargaining position and the Spirit's plan is to come to the League with only $80 million in place and a proposal to raise an additional $31 million over the next two years.
>
> My views expressed on July 25 are certainly not a bargaining position. In fact, I do not believe that the Board of Governors would find an $80 million proposal acceptable particularly in the absence of any personal or corporate guarantee.

Furthermore, it was at least questionable whether Spirit could get environmental approval quickly enough to start construction at the North Forks on schedule. Thin Ice had erected a number of legal barriers, and Spirit would need more time than it had to navigate through the legal tangle that awaited them.

Legal Procedures

In early April 1995, after retaining lawyer Rocky Kravetsky, Thin Ice had embarked upon a three-pronged legal strategy.

The move into the legal realm had been taken only after prolonged internal debate. For almost two years the organization's efforts had been broadly political—preparing independent analyses of the various corporate proposals and attempting, by a wide variety of means, to make the public sector and elected representatives aware of the real consequences of these proposals. For this kind of work Thin Ice had considerable experience and expertise and could, through Cho!ces, marshall an impressive array of supportive talent. Shifting a part of the focus to the courts meant giving up a good deal of control to lawyers and the courts, who would apply their own logic to the process. Once drawn into this process, all of an organization's time and energy can be consumed by its demands at the expense of the original political purpose. In addition, the legal costs could quickly run beyond a small group's financial capacities. The corporate sector could, and did, spend vast sums on legal bills—most of which in this case were paid by the public sector. Thin Ice had extremely limited funds. Even worse, certain legal actions—injunctions, for example—could result in individual members of Thin Ice being held liable for damages. The financial consequences for individual members of Thin Ice and their families were potentially crippling. The corporate lawyers knew this, and would use this factor as leverage if at all possible. The risks were great. And the chances of victory in the courts were relatively small—after all, most judges were part of the city's legal–corporate establishment. Intensive internal debate preceded the decision to add a potentially costly and risky legal component to the overall Thin Ice strategy.

In the end the Thin Ice members somewhat reluctantly concluded that the risks simply had to be taken; the money simply had to be raised. The corporations that now controlled the Save Our Jets campaign had no regard for public opinion, nor were they concerned about the ever-increasing financial burden they were imposing upon the public sector, and they almost completely controlled the public's political representatives. Thin Ice was running up against the real-world limits of community-based political action. Forcing the corporations into the courts could at least slow them down and increase the likelihood that their efforts would collapse under the weight of their own internal contradictions. Besides, court actions afforded some possibilities for attracting media attention.

The primary effort in the three-part legal strategy was at the civic level and was aimed at reversing what Thin Ice held to be the improper zoning of the Forks to enable the construction there of an arena. Thin Ice, which eventually lost this case in court, contended that the amendment to the Downtown Zoning By-Law had been processed improperly: it had started at Planning Committee rather than Community Committee and had done so, Thin Ice argued, solely for the purpose of avoiding Community Committee, where considerable opposition could be expected; it violated the February 1 council guidelines requiring that a business plan be presented and public hearings be conducted before any approvals be processed; it violated Plan Winnipeg, and particularly Plan Winnipeg's provisions with respect to riverbank protection, because the arena would be built too close to the riverbank; and it had been enacted in bad faith because it had effectively rezoned about 20 percent of downtown Winnipeg to enable the building of an arena anywhere in that rezoned area, when it was clear that its real purpose was to accommodate the desire of MEC to build an arena at a very specific north Forks site.

On April 4 and April 11 Thin Ice made its case on the bylaw amendment to Planning Committee, at this stage still acting on behalf of numerous other organizations. April 11 was an interesting example of why it is difficult to fight city hall. Thin Ice and its legal counsel Rocky Kravetsky were scheduled to speak at 9 a.m. and were finally heard at 1:55 p.m. The Community Committee dealt with a related matter at 5:30 p.m., and Thin Ice was finally heard on this matter at 8 p.m. Virtually the entire day was spent waiting to be heard—an expenditure of time that most citizens cannot afford. MEC was represented at both hearings by legal counsel and consultants who were present all day and paid for their time—out of the public purse. The next day, April 12, the matter heard the evening before was hurried through Planning Committee, where committee chairman Mike O'Shaughnessey, upon noticing that Thin Ice had addressed Community Committee the evening before, launched into a highly personalized and venomous attack on individual members of the group for having the temerity to speak again at a public meeting. Such personal attacks did not deter us, but the mood of hostility created at city hall may well have caused others who were concerned about city council's behaviour to remain silent.

In May, in the midst of the frenzy, Thin Ice put its intended court challenge on hold. A rational discussion of why a court challenge was being launched would then have been impossible. By June 2, with public frustration grown as a result of long delays, back-room dealing, and internal bickering among business groups vying for control of the Jets, we organized a news conference at the Legislature announcing the initiation of legal proceedings against the city with respect to the zoning amendment. The news conference attracted more media attention than almost anything Thin Ice had done to date—a reflection of the growing mood of frustration.

By the end of June, drawing on the expertise of Cho!ces' environmental activist Don Sullivan, we had also written to the provincial minister of the environment contending that the proposed arena at the North Forks site was a Class II project as per the Manitoba Environment Act. If it were a Class

II project it would be necessary for the contractor to file a proposal and obtain a valid licence, neither of which had yet been done; or for the minister to exercise his discretion under the act to exempt the project from these requirements. When no satisfactory reply was received from the minister and demolition work was begun at the proposed arena site, Thin Ice and Sullivan commenced a second set of legal proceedings under the terms of the Manitoba Environment Act. A summons was issued to the city and to Paragon Industries, a subcontractor on the arena project, and a court date was set for August 3.

At the same time Thin Ice, along with Sullivan and Christine Common-Singh of the Sierra Club, continued to monitor developments regarding the federal Canadian Environmental Assessment Act. Under the provisions of the CEAA, no federal money could be committed to a project until an environmental review had occurred, and subsequent to that the minister could require a reference to mediation or a panel review if there was sufficient public concern about a federally funded project. Neither MEC nor Spirit had, by early July, fulfilled the requirements under the CEAA, even though federal money had already been committed to the project. In short, the federal government was already in violation of CEAA requirements. We let it be known that if more federal money were committed without those requirements being fulfilled, a third set of legal proceedings would follow.

Thus by late July–early August Spirit still faced a number of major obstacles. It had to convince Revenue Canada that contributions to an endowment fund intended to save the Jets were really "gifts to the city." It had to get NHL approval even though it was clear that Spirit could not meet several of the NHL's conditions. And it had to work its way through a tangle of legal obstacles. In addition, and by far the most difficult obstacle, Spirit had to begin corporate fundraising. Remarkably, until the council meeting of August 3, 1995, Spirit had not even begun the process of corporate fundraising.

To Council Yet Again

The entire matter came back to council one final time, August 9, when councillors finally got the opportunity to evaluate Spirit's business plan and the so-called "due diligence" reports prepared by four City of Winnipeg committees. Composed of senior personnel, these committees were to identify and monitor the risks and costs to the city arising out of the Spirit deal. In what had become standard practice, the due diligence reports were presented to council August 4 and the Spirit business plan August 8—the day before the August 9 meeting.

These and associated documents revealed that Spirit's financial projections were seriously flawed. On the cost side, Spirit projected salaries to remain largely flat for five years and to grow by 20 percent over the next nine years. Yet since 1991–92 the Jets' salary costs had risen 25 percent *per year*.[23] In his August 3 letter to Sweatman, Bettman had said:

> We continue to be quite concerned that the projections regarding player costs are unrealistic and do not accurately reflect the likely operation of the club. Even if player cost increases were held to ten percent, which would represent a very substantial reduction from the last four or five years, Spirit's projections would be off by nearly $10 million in simply three years. It may be that your player costs can be controlled more effectively than other teams, but I think there is no reasonable base for expecting your costs will grow by only 20 percent in the nine years from 1996 to 2004.

Revenue projections were similarly flawed. Attendance was projected to increase substantially, even though by July 24, 1995 only 40 of 48 luxury suites (83 percent) and 1,100 of 2,649 club seats (41 percent) had yet been sold. This was despite MEC having strong-armed council into giving them $1.5 million on October 14, 1994 to market these seats, and despite MEC's announcement two months later, in December 1994, that its marketing of the club seats and luxury suites had been a remarkable success—"a little like running the mile in under two minutes," as they had then disingenuously announced. Spirit's revenue projections also included the optimistic expectation that 2,300 more seats would be sold per game than during the previous year, even though ticket prices would rise substantially and some season ticket holders would be required to pay an additional advance seat fee.[24]

With all of this in mind, the city's Financial Due Diligence Committee reported that if costs turned out to be 10 percent higher than projected, or revenues 10 percent lower, or if cost and revenue projections were off by some combination that totalled 10 percent, the result would be a "deficiency of financing being reached within two or three years," which would "more than likely necessitate the sale of the team being considered."[25] In short, the city's own financial analysts were finally acknowledging publicly the virtual certainty that the Jets would need to be sold within two or three years.

The gist of their analysis was confirmed in a report prepared by the NHL and sent to Spirit on August 10. The NHL had asked their Montreal-based controller, Joseph DeSousa, to prepare a written analysis of Spirit's July 24 business plan. DeSousa concluded that Spirit's financial projections were overly optimistic by as much as *$14 million per year*. NHL vice-president Jeffrey Pash advised that the results of DeSousa's analysis served "to reinforce the views expressed by the Commissioner in his last letter to Mr. Sweatman—namely that an endowment fund of *at least* $111 million must be in place for Spirit to expect the Board seriously to consider any proposal. In light of this report, I suspect that many members of the Board would be looking for a larger endowment fund or additional back-up guarantees."[26] Spirit's numbers simply did not work; unless *someone* was prepared to absorb inevitable large losses, the Jets would soon be forced to leave Winnipeg. That someone, it was clear, was to be the public sector.

Thin Ice had already demonstrated that to attempt to keep the Jets in Winnipeg would cost in excess of $200 million in scarce public funds,[27] and in the end such an expenditure would not be enough to save the Jets. To a majority of councillors, none of this mattered. They passed the acceptance of Spirit's business plan and the Due Diligence reports, so the deal was still alive. At least some councillors had again voted "yes" because they "knew" that the deal would not get Revenue Canada or NHL approval anyway. At a lunch meeting intended to try to move Councillor Lazarenko's vote to the "no" side, Thin Ice was informed by the councillor that "someone has to be blamed, and it's not going to be me." This had long been the view of at least some councillors. They knew the deal would die, but with voters to account to they did not want to be seen to pull the plug. The result was that the Jets were not sold in time for the start of the 1995–96 season. The public picked up their losses for another year, plus the substantial costs incurred by Spirit of Manitoba. The political cowardice of some and the blind faith of others came with a price tag of at least an additional $30 million.

Spirit scrambled for a few days after August 9 to raise the corporate money, but with no success. The money still wasn't there, not surprisingly because it had never been there. Councillor Jae Eadie's plaintive cry on July 26, 1995 that "the private sector to this day has not shown us the colour of its money" remained true to the bitter end. On August 10 the NHL advised Spirit that their projections were out by as much as $14 million per year and reiterated that the proposed endowment fund had to reach at least $111 million. On August 15, the same day that the *Free Press* announced that John "Done Deal" Douglas had been promoted to Business Editor, Spirit of Manitoba chairman Alan Sweatman issued a news release announcing that the board had decided the day before that the project "should now be firmly and finally terminated." The deal was finally dead.

The Public Cost of the Save Our Jets Effort

The effort to keep the Jets in Winnipeg proved expensive. *Most* of the costs incurred by MEC and Spirit of Manitoba were paid by the public, and *all* of the expenditures undertaken by the Interim Steering Committee and the Capital Fund were paid by the public, as were the Jets' losses.

Audited financial statements reveal that from June 30, 1994 to September 30, 1995, MEC and Spirit spent $6.9 million, $6.1 million of which was paid by the three levels of government. The province contributed $3 million, the city $1.6 million and the federal government $1.5 million. Of the amount spent by MEC and Spirit, $830,407 was paid to Thompson Dorfman Sweatman,

Spirit chairman Sweatman's legal firm, and $610,943 was paid to InterGroup Consultants, Spirit president Cam Osler's firm. Sweatman and Osler, in short, led an organization that dragged out the attempt to save the Jets long past the point when informed observers knew the attempt was futile, and all the while they kept the meters of their firms running.

Some of the specific charges are revealing. Thompson Dorfman Sweatman billed Spirit $160,000 for legal work on the ill-fated attempt to convince Revenue Canada that a gift to the Jets was a gift to the city. A second legal firm, Gray & Brown, charged $141,938 for its work on this scheme. The City of Winnipeg also hired legal counsel, the firm of Taylor McCaffrey, to advise them directly on the intricacies of the tax deduction scheme. The amount billed by Taylor McCaffrey was not made public. Therefore, the attempt to get the tax break insisted upon by would-be corporate contributors to the Jets cost more than $301,938, most of it paid for by the public—many of whom had already contributed to the Save Our Jets campaign in May without any expectation of a tax break.

Thompson Dorfman Sweatman also billed Spirit $140,000 for legal work on the attempt to raise money by means of a limited partnership. This was the initiative that sought to raise $50 million in limited partnership units without providing potential investors with financial projections. It was also the initiative that led Asper to abandon Spirit.

Thompson Dorfman Sweatman and InterGroup Consultants charged Spirit and MEC $672,252 and $136,517 respectively for "Financial Plans and Related Work." The total cost of this work was $1.4 million. These charges included costs for the preparation of business plans. Both the MEC and the Spirit business plans were submitted long after the agreed deadline, and only one day before the council meeting at which they had to be approved. The MEC business plan included a public contribution so far above what MEC had been claiming that it became necessary to divert public attention by means of false claims about last-minute NHL demands. The Spirit business plan was estimated by NHL controller Joseph DeSousa to be inaccurate by as much as $14 million per year. For such financial plans, consultants and legal firms charged $1.4 million.

The real cost in public funds of the MEC proposal—$131 million up front plus a $7.75 million ongoing annual subsidy—was revealed by Thin Ice, who asked four financial analysts associated with Cho!ces to evaluate the business plan. Their devastating critique of the MEC business plan cost Thin Ice, and the public, not a nickel. Nor did government contribute a nickel to the legal costs incurred by Thin Ice. The grand total of $8,832 was paid in its entirety by Thin Ice and its individual supporters.

There were additional costs to the public incurred as a result of the efforts of MEC and Spirit that do not show up in their audited financial statements. For example, Aikins MacAulay & Thorvaldson was the legal firm representing Shenkarow and the Jets in their complex negotiations with Spirit. It is likely that all or part of Aikins MacAulay & Thorvaldson's costs would have been paid by the Jets and added to the Jets' losses, which were paid by the public. Thus the public paid the many lawyers representing both sides—both MEC/Spirit and the Jets. Total billings by Aikins MacAulay & Thorvaldson are not known: the public pays the Jets' losses, and thus paid this legal cost, but the Jets' financial statements continue to be private.

The province and especially the city incurred additional costs as a result of the effort to Save Our Jets. Many civic employees spent a great deal of time working on various aspects of the project. As a senior city bureaucrat said in mid-March: "It's all rush, rush, panic, panic, for something you don't know will happen."[28] The dollar cost of this work is not revealed in the audited statements and is not known to the public.

The audited financial statements of MEC and Spirit reveal details of further costs incurred in the effort to save the Jets. For example, in the period July 1, 1991 to September 30, 1995, the public paid $279,108 for costs incurred by the Interim Steering Committee; $8.4 million for expenditures made out of the Capital Fund, as required by the Interim Operating Agreement; and $25 million for losses incurred by the Jets. *Additional* Jets' losses to June 30, 1996, would probably fall somewhere between $15 and $20 million, making total Jets' losses paid by the public in excess of $40 million. Expenditures made out of the Capital Fund include guaranteed management fees to Barry Shenkarow and his partners Marvin Shenkarow, Harvey Secter and Randy Moffat, totalling $6.3 million to September 30, 1995.

A conservative estimate of the public-sector contribution to the effort to save the Jets would be $6.1 million to MEC and Spirit; $0.3 million to the Interim Steering Committee; $8.4 million to the Capital Fund (this amount includes the $6.3 million in management fees); and $40 million to cover the Jets' losses. This total of $54.8 million in public costs is less than the actual cost to the public because it does not include costs for which numbers cannot be obtained or the amount of provincial tax revenue lost as a result of the "Quebec shuffle" tax avoidance scheme—an amount estimated at $3 million—and it includes only minimal estimates for the period after September 30, 1995. The attempt to save the Jets was expensive.

Some of this public expenditure will be recouped because the city and province must be paid for their 36 percent of the Jets' shares at the same rate that Shenkarow and his partners are paid for their 64 percent of the Jets' shares. This requirement was one of the positive features of the 1991 Interim Operating Agreement. The city and province will receive 36 percent of $65 million U.S., or about $30 million Canadian, once the sale of the Jets to Phoenix is closed. The net cost to the public of the effort to save the Jets will be at least $25 million.

The cost would have been much higher had plans proceeded to build a new arena for the Jets. The cost of the proposed new arena was estimated at $111 million but, given the cost of comparable arenas built in recent years in North America, it is almost certain that the arena would have ended up costing at least $150 million—and Spirit had no intention of paying for cost overruns. The cost of servicing the North Forks site, which the city agreed to pay, was estimated at $29 million. And if the new arena had been built and Spirit had exercised the option to purchase the Jets, the plan was to purchase only the 64 percent of the Jets' shares owned by Shenkarow and his partners. The publicly owned shares would have been "contributed," and thus their $30 million value would have been foregone. The cost to the public of building the new arena to save the Jets would therefore have been at least $209 million ($150 million for the arena; $29 million to service the site; $30 million in foregone sales proceeds for the publicly held Jets' shares), plus the costs incurred by MEC and Spirit, plus the Jets' losses until such date as Spirit began to pay them. The total would have most likely exceeded $250 million or some ten times the actually incurred cost. And the Jets would have left Winnipeg within a few years anyway.

8. Conclusion

Dale Cummings

The final chapter in the long Jets saga proved expensive indeed. The mass mobilization of fans and boosters in May 1995 ended with a whimper when the corporate sector refused to commit any of its own money and fell instead into bickering and fighting over control of the prize. The prize of course was valuable: since it had become clear that the Jets would have to leave Winnipeg in a few years even if a new arena were built for them, the question had become which group of business leaders would get the benefit of the huge capital gain that would be made when the inevitable sale of the Jets occurred. Ever more outlandish financing schemes were devised by various legal firms and corporate consultants who did quite well by their efforts. These schemes, called "creative financing" by those who devised them, were in fact little more than attempts to maximize the public sector's financial contribution and risk and minimize the corporate sector's financial contribution and risk. This in itself is not unusual. More interesting and revealing is that these schemes were, by the end, a façade behind which contending factions of the local business community, unable to compete in the financial big leagues with those powerful corporate interests who now controlled the NHL, fought bitterly with each other over who was to secure whatever financial benefits might be gained from an adventure that competent businesspeople must have long known was doomed to failure.

Throughout the twenty-year period during which Winnipeg's always financially marginal Jets slid ever more deeply into economic difficulty, the city's corporate business leaders proved repeatedly unwilling to invest in the Jets. As early as 1974 Jets' founder Ben Hatskin commented publicly on the Winnipeg business establishment's fear of the risks associated with the Jets, and in 1982 sports writer John Robertson reminded Winnipeggers: "We have NHL hockey here today because Michael Gobuty was soft enough to lead with his heart while the cold, calculating old money people in this town sat on their collective assets, afraid to take a chance on Winnipeg, for Winnipeg."[1] The old money people and their offspring still sat on their assets in the 1990s: Winnipeg's corporate leaders scrambled for more and more *public* money, while refusing to risk their own money on the Jets.

The result has been more than twenty years of demands by Jets' owners for government assistance—to build an arena, to cover losses, to pay large management fees. As the NHL changed, the cost to government of keeping the Jets in Winnipeg rose rapidly. To have kept the Jets in Winnipeg permanently would have required propping the doors of the government vault wide open in perpetuity. In a city in economic decline, in which a myriad and growing number of social and economic needs go unmet, this was indefensible.

Nor were developments in Winnipeg unique to this city. The relentless quest for greater profits is making the NHL un-economic in all but the very largest Canadian cities. What remains to be determined in each of the smaller centres that still have teams is the precise character of, and who will benefit from, the "creative financing" schemes that will be devised by various business groups in response to relocation threats, and how much public money will be lost in the process.

Was it right to have tried to save the Jets? The answer is yes—unequivocally. The Winnipeg Jets were a valuable community asset, not so much economically—these claims were always exaggerated—as culturally and emotionally. The presence in the city of an NHL franchise added to the texture and variety of the city's culture. The Jets were an enjoyable pastime for many people. For some they were more: the Jets enriched their lives, became a part of their identity—although this is notably more the case for men than for women.

The loss of the Jets had broader symbolic importance too. Their departure reflected the acceleration of the city's long economic decline and the erosion of local opportunities. It was a particularly visible manifestation of the growing extent to which we are subject to vast corporate forces beyond our control, forces that care not one whit for our interests or even our needs. It represented another major step in the stripping away of our heritage and the Americanization of our culture. For all these reasons, it was important to try to save the Jets.

Did Jets' supporters go too far in trying to save the Jets? The answer again is an unequivocal yes. The effort was pursued long past the point when it was rationally defensible. The total cost as a result was needlessly high. Some would argue that this misses the point, that the determination to save the Jets was an admirable expression of community spirit of which Winnipeggers and Manitobans can be proud. At one level this is true. The Save Our Jets campaign of mid-May 1995 was a truly remarkable expression of community spirit. However, the cost to the public purse by mid-May had grown so large that it forced upon the community a consideration of fundamental questions that are not only political and economic, but also ethical. Is it appropriate to spend tens and even hundreds of millions of dollars on professional sports when—to take but one of many relevant examples—children are lining up at food banks? Communities have to make such choices; their choices express the values and the character of a community. How are such choices made? Who makes them? It is here that an analysis of the long struggle over the Winnipeg Jets proves most revealing and most disturbing.

Power

There has been a long debate about the exercise of power in local communities. Is power widely held in the community, as one might think it ought to be in a democracy, or is it concentrated in the hands of an elite and, in particular, a corporate-dominated elite? Does corporate business have a privileged position in terms of power? If so—and the evidence that emerges from this analysis of the conflict over the Jets suggests that this is the case—then is it local corporate leaders who occupy a privileged position or is it broader corporate forces beyond the community? The evidence of the Winnipeg Jets story suggests it is both. The broader corporate forces impose their own necessities upon local communities—it was the changing economics of the NHL, driven by giant infotainment conglomerates, which created the Jets' financial crisis in the 1990s and forced a response upon Winnipeg—but within Winnipeg that response was largely structured by the local corporate community.

The disproportionate power of the corporate sector was revealed repeatedly and most transparently at city council, where councillors and thus the citizens of Winnipeg were subjected by corporate leaders associated with MEC and Spirit to strong-arm tactics, economic threats and the withholding and even deliberate manipulation of information. Council repeatedly gave way to their demands, and repeatedly did so without an adequate consideration of the accuracy of the claims being made or the implications of their decisions for the community. Indeed, the decision-making process at city hall was revealed to be very seriously flawed.

The Filmon government acted similarly, seemingly prepared to spend any amount of money asked of them by the corporate leaders of MEC and Spirit with whom they were so closely associated—though for a long period the administration was not prepared to acknowledge this publicly. Indeed, the provincial role was consistently dualistic: the real action comprised deals behind closed doors covered by a veil of secrecy; the more benign public face consisted of repeated assurances that expenditures would be limited. In the end, corporate demands were always met, corporate business interests were afforded privileged consideration by our elected representatives. This observation is consistent with the historical experience: business has long dominated the politics not only of Winnipeg, but of other Canadian cities as well.[2]

Some might argue that this is as it should be: corporate leaders have firsthand knowledge of how the economy works and of how to get things done, so governments *should* listen to them. But the case of the Jets casts doubt upon such thinking. MEC and Spirit were repeatedly shown to be economically mistaken and even ineffectual, as were their various well-paid corporate consultants. They directed the bulk of their efforts to maximizing the risk and the cost to the public sector and minimizing the risk and cost to the private sector, while proving consistently unable to raise corporate money.

The complexity and the scale of the new NHL—the industry they wanted to enter—appear to have been beyond the comprehension and the capacity of both MEC and Spirit. Although they had a preponderance of power locally, they did not have the competence or the wherewithal to prevail, as had previous generations of Winnipeg's corporate elite. They were minor players in a new, continental corporate power structure that clearly leaves smaller population centres on the margins.

As the businessmen fought their battles behind closed doors over who would benefit from the Jets conundrum, the public paid the costs—lawyers' fees, consultants' fees, architects' and engineers' fees and an additional year's losses because of the delay in selling the team. Indeed, had Winnipeg's corporate community been successful in saving the Jets, it would only have been because they had squeezed even *more* money out of the public sector. Yet the same businesspeople who fought this battle at public cost and who had repeatedly *demanded* multimillion dollar investments of public money in the Jets and a new arena had written an open letter in February 1993 calling upon the mayor to scale back essential community services in order to reduce public spending. Such evidence reflects badly on the motives of the local business class and on the merits of their proposals for economic development. It suggests that their interests may well be different from the interests of the community at large. These corporate leaders demanded public money for themselves—indeed, the centrepiece of their financing strategy was to make the public pay; they took all the legal and financial steps necessary to ensure that their own financial interests were protected, including elaborate measures to avoid paying their share of taxes; at the same time they insisted vociferously that public spending to meet the economic and social needs of the community *had* to be cut. The whole affair suggests that there would be value in a closer scrutiny of, and more informed debate about, the claims and demands being made by the corporate community.

Dominant though they were, however, it was not *just* the corporate sector that had an impact on the outcome of the struggle over the Jets. Too often, little is said about those people who are *not* part of the elite. Yet in the conflict over the Jets, Winnipeggers and Manitobans who were not part of the elite played an important role. It is clear, for example, that it was the determination of Jets' fans that kept alive the possibility of saving the franchise in May 1995. This episode revealed, with dramatic clarity, the capacity of sport, with all its emotional intensity, to mobilize people. When combined with the power of old-fashioned civic boosterism, the events created a potent ideological brew, an astonishing display of people power.

Still, the mass mobilization of May, remarkable and impressive though it was, did not typify public opinion on the issue. Public opinion polls revealed repeatedly and consistently that a majority of Winnipeggers and Manitobans, and an even greater majority of them who are women—four out of five according to the Viewpoints Research polling results—opposed significant public funding for a new arena and for the Jets. Yet this majority was passive, at least compared to the people who took to the streets or went to rallies and socials to save the Jets. They opposed public funding for the Jets, but the issue was seemingly not important enough to them to do much about it. Thus they exerted relatively little influence on the issue.

By contrast, for many of the minority who supported significant public funding for the Jets, *no* issue was more important. The Jets *had* to be saved. This certainty gave this group enormous leverage—any politician who voted to kill the Jets ran the risk of being targeted for electoral defeat by the efforts of a highly focused and concentrated group of Jets' fans. Civic politicians who knew the deal would eventually die voted to keep it alive not just because of the intense pressure from the corporate elite, but also because of their fear of the electoral consequences of crossing these dedicated fans. Conversely, a politician prepared to spend what was necessary to save the Jets would benefit from the same phenomenon—witness Filmon's success in the provincial election campaign of April 1995. It was the combination of a sustained and aggressive corporate pressure plus the narrowly deter-mined, sometimes even almost rabid single-mindedness of a portion of the public for whom no issue was more important than saving the Jets, that created the intensity of the pressure on politicians, especially those at the civic level.

Contradictory conclusions can be drawn from this experience. On the one hand, it suggests that the mobilization of large numbers of committed people can have an important impact on political outcomes. One can imagine the potential of such people power as a means of promoting social justice and as a corrective to the abuse of power by self-interested elites. On the other hand, this mobilization of people occurred in support of a local elite who, the evidence suggests, were abusing their power, and it was attribut-able to an ideological fervour that, at its peak in mid-May, bordered on being thoroughly irrational. Democracy is imperilled when such certainty and intolerance are loosed on the community, and particularly when it occurs on behalf of those who already wield the bulk of the power.

Also of significance was the unusual way in which people aligned themselves on the Jets issue. For example, the majority who opposed significant funding for the Jets were not only politically passive, but also ideologically mixed. Many were opposed because they saw the issue as a social justice issue—large amounts of public funds for the Jets would be better spent meeting real needs in Winnipeg. That was the Thin Ice position. But many others were opposed because they were opposed to public spending, period. They were old-fashioned conservatives. But as conservatives, they had no place to go organizationally because those organizations with whom they shared an ideology were the very organizations demanding, or giving way to the demands for, ever more public funding for the Jets. Many, therefore, supported Thin Ice—with whom they might not otherwise have been associated.

On the other hand, many of those who might have been expected to support the Thin Ice position did not, or did so only reluctantly and tepidly. Organized labour, for example, was split. Public-sector unions were concerned about the huge public costs that would inevitably be incurred in the attempt to save the Jets. The result, they rightly feared, would be greater pressure on wage levels and job security, and an erosion of public services. But many private-sector unions, and especially the building trades, focused on the much-needed jobs that would be created in building a new arena. The result was that for most of the conflict organized labour straddled the fence on the issue, finally coming out in support of building a new arena in late spring 1995 when it appeared that a deal was inevitable. Various community organizations who stood to lose as the result of the huge public cost of saving the Jets and who based on past experience, might in any event have been expected, to align themselves with the social justice orientation of Thin Ice, also stood on the sidelines—the result, for the most part, of a fear of the consequences of being seen publicly opposing the local establishment. Thus the potent ideological brew that generated the mass mobilization of May also created a strange and atypical alignment of forces for and against public spending on the Jets.

Given this environment, Thin Ice helped to give voice to a largely passive majority. Though the effort to save the Jets ultimately failed because the corporate community was not prepared to risk its own money in a venture that made no financial sense, it is at least possible that in the absence of Thin Ice it might have "succeeded"—it might have pushed the public sector into contributing even more money and assuming even more risk. The Thin Ice connection to Cho!ces proved especially valuable. Cho!ces is an organization with access to an impressive array of creative and analytical talents, and Thin Ice was a part of this creative network. This connection with a broader community amplified the talent and energy of the small group directly involved with Thin Ice. People ought to be able to consider and choose from alternatives in a democracy, and Thin Ice contributed to making that possible. By the end of the long and protracted conflict over the Jets, a significant majority of Winnipeggers were supportive of the position consistently advanced by the group.

Thin Ice's sustained presence was especially important given the role played by the media. Many media analysts have argued that the media tend to reflect the existing balance of power and thus to reproduce the status quo. In practical terms this means the media tend to reflect the interests of the corporate elite and to be dismissive of those who are critical of the elite. This should not be surprising. The primary source of media revenue is corporate advertising, and most newspapers, for example, are owned by a handful of Canada's wealthiest businessmen. *The Winnipeg Free Press* is owned by the Thomson interests—Kenneth Thomson is generally considered to be one of Canada's two or three richest people. It would be naive to expect that such media corporations would be anything other than sympathetic to the corporate community of which they are a part. This was certainly borne out in the Jets case. Much of the media treated the claims and actions of MEC and Spirit in a largely uncritical fashion, and for the most part ignored the message that critics were trying to put out. The result was that—with some partial exceptions—the Winnipeg media served the community badly. What MEC and Spirit said was too often accepted at face value and even promoted; those who suggested the emperor might be naked were generally ignored. The public and their representatives were thus denied the kind of information— save for the constant efforts of Thin Ice—needed to make informed decisions. Much was done on faith, on a blind belief in the capacities and the goodwill of the corporate sector—a faith that in the end proved to have been misplaced.

It is not at all unusual for the media to treat large and costly urban development projects positively and uncritically. Indeed, this kind of coverage is the norm. The media have a structured bias rooted in how they operate, a bias that leads to uncritical and boosterish reporting.

Media companies, after all, are businesses. Their profits are linked to the growth of the economies they operate in, and often this means the success of local businesses. Most of their revenues—about 80 percent in the case of newspapers—comes from advertising, and most of that advertising is placed by firms with a local presence. As a result the local media in all cities tend to be uncritical backers of urban development projects—it is in their economic interest to assume this role.

Not surprisingly, when it comes to technically complex financial arrangements involving the expenditure of many millions of dollars, local media tend to be especially uncritical. For one thing, most reporters don't have the technical skills, much less the time, to do detailed financial analysis. They tend to accept the information provided by a project's promoters. This certainly happened in the case of the Jets. Business reporters are more likely to be familiar with financial analysis, but they have little incentive to be critical of business-led projects: business executives, after all, tend to be their news sources, much as figures in the sports worlds—whether players, owners, managers or coaches—are the sources of sports reporters' stories. Moreover, there is little audience appeal in numerical analysis. Readers are more likely to respond positively to news stories featuring the symbolic aspects of such projects, such as their impact on the city's image.

Journalists similarly tend to accept at face value the reports of "expert" consultants hired to evaluate large projects. Yet an unexamined faith in the accuracy of consultants' reports can be a dangerous thing. A consultant with a major U.S. firm explained, "The pressure is immense to say what they want you to say—to give the go-ahead for the project."[3] This element too is consistent with the Winnipeg experience.

Further, the beat structure of newspaper writing is fragmented: someone covers the business beat, someone covers city hall, someone covers the legislature and still others cover sports. Coverage of a complex project like the Jets and the arena becomes broken up into different areas of responsibility; no single journalist sees and writes about the project in its entirety. In the case of the *Free Press*, according to one of the paper's reporters, those covering the team's story from their several different beats *never once* met to discuss how to tackle news about the project as a whole. Given this beat structure, the complexity and totality of the project can thus overwhelm the paper's capacity to provide adequate coverage.

At television stations the problem is even more extreme. Because there are no beat assignments, on a given day a reporter is likely to cover numerous stories, only one of which may be the large and technically complex development project. Then a different reporter may cover that issue the next time it makes the news. And the turnover among TV reporters tends to be high. Television reporters are thus more likely to arrive at a news conference with only a slight background knowledge about the project, and they are even more likely to accept what they are given based on the authority of the source. Indeed, they often develop a routine dependence on the "news sources" whom they deem to be "authoritative."

TV reporting has its own built-in structural bias, especially apparent in the desire—the very *need* of the medium—to get good, quick visuals and short sound bites and the tendency to simplify matters in terms of heroes and villains—a snappy clip from both sides—in order to personalize stories and "add colour and drama." This bias makes it unlikely that TV reporters will stop to evaluate complex economic details and arguments.

The flawed media coverage of the Winnipeg Jets was, for all these reasons, typical of the media coverage generally afforded to large urban development projects.

CONCLUSION

Democracy and the Authority of Riches

The long struggle over the Jets raises questions about the democratic process. Should large corporations exercise such a preponderance of power? Should the media be so uncritically accommodating to corporate elites? Should our elected representatives exhibit such apparently boundless faith in the often self-interested claims of big business? Should those who raise questions or express criticism or alternative views be silenced, as was attempted in so many ways during the struggle over the Jets? It would be reasonable to conclude that the answer to all of these questions is no, and that democracies cannot thrive when power is abused in this fashion.

In this regard, Winnipeg's Save the Jets campaign is not an aberration. It is widely claimed in Canada today that business knows best, that corporate leaders have the prescription for the public's economic health, that the earning of greater profits will accrue to the benefit of us all. Those who express doubt, who dare to criticize, are marginalized.

John Ralston Saul made this a central theme of his 1995 Massey Lectures. We have fallen victim, he argues, to what Adam Smith called "the authority of riches." We have need, Saul argues, of more doubt, more criticism, less ideologically inspired certainty. The new ideologues of global markets and corporate wisdom are certain they are right, and act accordingly: "It isn't a matter of democratic debate with all the compromise that involves. They have the truth. The aim of the ideologue is therefore to manipulate, trick or force the majority into acceptance." It is precisely in such an environment, Saul argues, that criticism is most needed: "Criticism is perhaps the citizen's primary weapon in the exercise of her legitimacy. That is why, in this corporatist society, conformism, loyalty and silence are so admired and rewarded; why criticism is so punished or marginalized."[4]

Winnipeg's corporate leaders were, at best, terribly wrong about the economics of the campaign to save the Jets. As that became increasingly the case, they resorted to bullying and manipulation because they *insisted* they were right. They were not.

Might the broader corporate sector, with their "think tanks" and political and media allies, be equally wrong about economics in Canada generally? Should, for example, health care be privatized and social assistance slashed as corporate leaders insist is necessary? Are they any more correct about these matters than they were about the economics of the Jets? Are we any better off pursuing a U.S.-oriented economic strategy as embodied in the corporate-led North American Free Trade Agreement than we have been as a result of the NHL's corporate-led U.S. Sunbelt strategy? Or might a greater measure of doubt and criticism be as warranted in these matters as it was in the case of the Save Our Jets campaign?

As the NHL's new marketing-oriented, U.S. Sunbelt strategy takes effect, Canadians are losing a part of our heritage, a part of our culture. We are, with respect to NHL hockey, the victims of the very corporate forces that are insisting that we abandon our collective heritage as embodied, for example, in our publicly run, not-for-profit health-care system. Some large corporations benefit; most of us are made the poorer.

The loss of an NHL franchise is no small matter. It has proved deeply painful to many in Winnipeg, a prairie city that boasts a long, cold winter and a long hockey history. To most of us it seems an absurdity that an NHL franchise would move from a city like Winnipeg to Phoenix, Arizona, a city in which there is no hockey history whatever. Yet Winnipeg's hockey history—indeed hockey as part of Canada's cultural heritage—means nothing to those who control the business of the NHL, whose motivation after all is the pursuit of profit. It may serve the interests of profit to move the Winnipeg Jets to Phoenix, or it may not. That remains to be seen. It does not serve the interests of hockey fans or of Winnipeg more generally. Yet the contradiction is that, given the corporate-driven character of the new NHL, the interests of Winnipeg would not have been served by *keeping* the Jets here either. The astronomical public costs of attempting to keep the Jets in Winnipeg would have damaged even further an already struggling local economy. Winnipeg generally, and especially the poorest and weakest among us, would have been the worse for the effort. Thus the terrible irony is that one way or other, whether the Jets stayed in or left Winnipeg, the drive to make greater profits from the business of NHL hockey was bound to imperil the interests of Winnipeggers. It will have the same effect elsewhere in Canada.

The fate of the Jets is an instance in microcosm of the plight of Winnipeg. The same powerful market forces that marginalized the Jets in a rapidly changing NHL are marginalizing Winnipeg in an increasingly continentalized economy. The failure to save the Jets is a symptom of Winnipeg's economic decline and provides further evidence of the perilous state of the city's corporate business class. As Spirit chairman Alan Sweatman put it, the fear of being identified with failure "permeates the institutional people in Winnipeg."[5] And this defines Winnipeg's problem: Winnipeg is an economically marginalized and declining city with a weak, fragmented, and fearful business class—a class lacking in leadership and in a coherent vision and sense of direction for the city.

It may no longer be prudent to rely so exclusively on this group for economic direction. On the contrary, it is probable that those cities that give voice to a wide variety of ideas about how to build communities battered by powerful economic forces will be the most likely to give birth to the creative energy that will generate economic and social vitality. This story of the struggle over the Jets suggests that Winnipeg is *not* now an environment in which such creativity is encouraged. The conflict over the Jets produced evidence that a weak and fearful corporate elite is not prepared to tolerate honest debate about the city's future if doing so means calling into question corporate dominance of economic ideas. So long as this continues to be the case, further economic decline, with its predictable social corollaries, will be the almost certain result.

The struggle over the Winnipeg Jets and the bitter contradictions that struggle created can perhaps be seen as a symbolic representation of the many losses and conflicts being imposed upon us by powerful corporate forces and their supporters who insist—no matter the evidence—that they know best. The story suggests though, that they may not know best. It suggests that there may be good reason to doubt the accuracy of their claims and the merits of their prescriptions. It suggests that these powerful forces may be pushing us, metaphorically, onto thin ice, and that the greater goals of democracy and of our collective economic and social well-being might be better served if critical voices were not so invariably pushed aside by the ideological certainty of those who now wield power.

Afterword

Throughout the saga of the selling off of the Jets and the selling out of both Jets' fans and Manitoba taxpayers, the one voice of reason was Thin Ice. It was the only group that consistently asked the tough questions, the only one whose numbers could be relied on, whether on the economic and fiscal impact of the Jets or the cost to taxpayers of bailing them out. It was the only group attempting to make sense of the impending departure of Winnipeg's professional hockey team within a broader analysis of trends within the NHL *as a business*; the only group that took the trouble to analyze experience elsewhere in the use of arenas and sports subsidies as a vehicle for community economic development. It was the one group attempting to identify the often complex interests of the media and different segments of the business community in the Jets/arena deal.

Jim Silver's book captures all of this admirably, as well as the politics of it all. It also pays suitable tribute to the small group of volunteers who led Thin Ice throughout the lengthy and often acrimonious campaign. The one weakness in the book, and an understandable one to those of us privileged to know and work with him, is Jim's modesty about his own role in Thin Ice. Jim pushed himself to the point of exhaustion in providing intellectual and political leadership to the group. He was the main public spokesperson, a key political strategist and one of the main sources of intellectual insight. In public meetings he was incredibly effective, bringing a clarity and depth of knowledge to what became a very complex issue of public policy. At one memorable full-house gathering at the Planetarium in Winnipeg, the audience insisted that he carry on speaking, well after his allotted time, a rare compliment indeed!

But so powerful were the pro-arena forces that Jim, together with Carl Ridd, were vilified in the local press, by journalists and others, and in public forums such as city council. He and his family were harassed and threatened. But still he stood his ground. Throughout it all, the political message that he and others were trying to get across remained clear; that in a time of mass unemployment, growing poverty and budget cutbacks to essential social services, giving the owners of a professional hockey franchise large cash handouts in the form of subsidies and a new arena did not make sense in terms of social justice. We all owe Jim Silver an enormous debt of gratitude for his insights, activism and commitment.

John Loxley
Winnipeg
August 1996

Notes

In the interest of trying to leave the text uncluttered with reference details I have used a series of endnotes to direct the reader to the source of the reference. Endnotes which have multiple sources listed are in sequential order as they appear in the text. Full details of each reference can be found in the Bibliography at the end of the book.

Abbreviations used in these endnotes are as follows:

G & M—Globe and Mail; WFP—Winnipeg Free Press;
WS—Winnipeg Sun; WT—Winnipeg Tribune

2. The Business of NHL Hockey

1. Gruneau and Whitson, 1993, p. 101.
2. Dryden and MacGregor, 1989, p. 266.
3. Houston and Shoalts, 1993, pp. 41–42.
4. This and the next two quotations, including that from *Sports Illustrated* (S.I.), are from: Cruise and Griffiths, 1991, pp. 38, 35 & 42.
5. Smythe, 1981, p. 191.
6. Cruise and Griffiths, 1991, p. 43.
7. Nagler, 1964, p. 21.
8. This and the following quotations are from: Cruise and Griffiths, 1991, pp. 45–46, 49 & 51.
9. Nagler, 1964, p. 114.
10. Dowbiggin, 1993, p. 78.
11. Houston and Shoalts, 1993, p. 43.
12. Dowbiggin, 1993, p. 239.
13. Houston and Shoalts, 1993, p. 44.
14. Houston and Shoalts, 1993, p. 40.
15. Dowbiggin, 1993, pp. 47–48; Cruise and Griffiths, 1991, pp. 88 & 90. (References in this and subsequent multiple source endnotes are in sequential order as they appear in the text.)
16. Dowbiggin, 1993, pp. 51–52.
17. Houston and Shoalts, 1993, pp. 49–50.
18. Dowbiggin, 1993, pp. 51 & 53.
19. Dowbiggin, 1993, p. 163.
20. Mills, 1991, p. 191.
21. Dowbiggin, 1993, p. 52.
22. Dowbiggin, 1993, pp. 199 & 200.
23. Houston and Shoalts, 1993, p. 51; Dowbiggin, 1993, p. 200; Houston and Shoalts, 1993, p. 209.
24. Dowbiggin, 1993, pp. 237 & 219.
25. Dowbiggin, 1993, pp. 204–205.
26. Conway, 1995, p. 23.

27. Houston and Shoalts, 1993, pp. 126 & 204; Dowbiggin, 1993, p. 241.
28. Conway, 1995, pp. 72–73.
29. Conway, 1995, p. 157.
30. Houston and Shoalts, 1993, pp. 103–104.
31. Conway, 1995, pp. 199–201.
32. Dowbiggin, 1993, p. 246.
33. Dowbiggin, 1993, p. 251.
34. Dowbiggin, 1993, p. 296.
35. Conway, 1995, pp. 32–33.
36. *G & M*, March 1, 1996.
37. Dowbiggin, 1993, p. 195.
38. Houston and Shoalts, 1993, p. 208.
39. Cruise cited in Houston and Shoalts, 1993, p. 208.
40. MacGregor, 1993, pp. 40–41; Fischler, 1995, p. 40.
41. Jhally, 1984, p. 45.
42. Gorman and Calhoun, 1994, p. 55.
43. Helyar, 1994, p. 67.
44. Gorman and Calhoun, 1994, pp. 58 & 117–118.
45. Katz, 1994, p. 32.
46. Gorman and Calhoun, 1994, pp. 55 & 61.
47. Welling, 1987, p. 40.
48. Gorman and Calhoun, 1994, pp. 75–76.
49. Helyar, 1994, pp. 15 & *passim*.
50. Gorman and Calhoun, 1994, p. 155; Gruneau and Whitson, 1993, p. 127; Welling, 1987, p. 40.
51. MacGregor, 1993, p. 92.
52. *Hockey News*, April 5, 1996.
53. Gruneau and Whitson, 1993, p. 126; MacGregor, 1993, p. 37.
54. MacGregor, 1993, pp. 3, 38 & 96.
55. MacGregor, 1993, p. 89.
56. Fischler, 1995, pp. 81 & 86.
57. DeGeorge, 1996, p. x.
58. Fischler, 1995, pp. 13 & 99.
59. DeGeorge, 1996, p. 164.
60. Guterson, 1994, p. 39.
61. Katz, 1994, p. 33; MacGregor, 1993, p. 39; Gorman and Calhoun, 1994, pp. 134–135.
62. Whitson, 1994, pp. 9 & 13; McGrath,1994, pp. 49–50; DeGeorge, 1996, p. 238.
63. Helyar, 1994, p. 70; Gorman and Calhoun, 1994, p. 130; Katz, 1994, p. 27; Brooks, 1994, p. 32.
64. *WFP*, Dec. 4, 1995; Brunt, Jan. 18, 1996.
65. MacGregor, 1993, p. 182; Katz, 1994, p. 36.
66. Katz, 1994, pp. 69 & 10.
67. Sklar, 1995, pp. 40–41.
68. Deacon, 1994, pp. 51–53.
69. Deacon, 1994, p. 51.
70. *New York Times* as quoted in Gorman and Calhoun, 1994, p. 160.
71. Helyar, 1994, p. 73; *G & M*, Mar. 4, 1996; Gorman and Calhoun, 1994, p. 109;

Fischler, 1995, p. 220; Whitford, 1993, p. 121.
72. Whitson, 1994, p. 10.
73. Gruneau and Whitson, 1993, pp. 99–100.
74. Campbell, Jan. 6, 1996.
75. Whitson, 1994, p. 13.
76. MacGregor, 1993, p. 96; Cook, 1995, p. 211.
77. MacGregor, 1993, p. 107.
78. Cook, 1995, pp. 207–208.
79. Fischler, 1995, pp. 105–107; Cook, 1995, p. 209.
80. Fischler, 1995, p. 98.
81. Fennell and Jenish, 1990, p. 43.
82. MacGregor, 1993, p. 108.

3. On the Margins: Pro Hockey in Winnipeg

1. *WT*, June 14, 1952.
2. *WT*, Aug. 17 & Dec. 31, 1953.
3. *WT*, Dec. 31, 1953; Jan. 8 & 14, 1954.
4. *WT*, Sept. 8, 1950; Nov. 13, 1951; Mar. 8, 1954.
5. *WT*, Oct. 18, 1955.
6. This, and the next five paragraphs, are derived from: Mott, 1994, pp. 9–12.
7. *WT*, Jan. 10, 1958.
8. *WFP*, Oct. 19, 1990.
9. Davidson, 1974, p. 143.
10. *WFP*, Oct. 1, 1988.
11. Beddoes et al., 1973, p. 336.
12. Davidson, 1974, pp. 210 & 226.
13. *WFP*, Mar. 16, 1974.
14. *WT*, Apr. 18, 24, 25 & 27, 1974.
15. *WT*, Apr. 27, 1974.
16. Fenson, 1982, p. 63.
17. *WT*, Dec. 10 & 24 & Mar. 27, 1975.
18. *WT*, Dec. 10 & 24, 1975.
19. *WT*, Dec. 24, 1975; Mar. 25 & 26, 1976.
20. *WT*, May 27, 1977.
21. *WT*, Dec. 11 & 29, 1976.
22. *WT*, Apr. 22 & Dec. 15, 1977.
23. *WFP*, Jan. 9, 1976; Nov. 8, 1977.
24. *WT*, Nov. 18 & 19, 1976.
25. *S.I.*, Oct. 17, 1977, p. 49.
26. Letter from Zuken to Ridd, Dec. 22, 1977.
27. *WT*, Dec. 22, 1977.
28. Letter from Ridd to Schreyer, Mar. 16, 1974.
29. Gammons, 1976.
30. Ridd, presentation to Finance Committee, City Council, Dec. 23, 1975; Ridd, *Uniter*, Mar. 1978.
31. *WT*, Dec. 15, 1975.
32. *WT*, Jan. 17, 1976.

33. *WT*, Jan. 6, 1976.
34. Ridd, presentation to Finance Committee, City Council, Dec. 23, 1975.
35. Letter from Ridd to Filmon, Jan. 15, 1978.
36. *WT*, Jan. 21, 1976; Jan. 6, 1978.
37. Ridd, draft article for *Uniter*, Mar., 1978.
38. Finkel, 1970.
39. *WT*, Jan. 17 & Mar. 26, 1976.
40. *WT*, May 3, 1978.
41. *WFP*, Nov. 8, 1977; *WT*, July 6 & Dec. 22, 1977.
42. *WFP*, Jan. 19, 1978.
43. *WFP*, Feb. 15 & 27, 1978.
44. *WFP*, May 6, 1978.
45. *WFP*, Feb. 27, 1978.
46. *WFP*, Mar. 2, 1978.
47. *WFP*, May 6, 1978.
48. *WFP*, Jan. 24, 1978.
49. *WT*, May 1 & 26, 1978.
50. *WT*, Aug. 17, 1978.
51. *WT*, Sept. 21, 1978.
52. *WFP*, Jan. 27, 1979.
53. *WT*, Jan. 10, 1979.
54. *WFP*, June 3, 1981; *WS*, Apr. 19, 1982.
55. *WFP*, Oct. 21, 1983 & June 3, 1981.
56. *WFP*, Aug. 14, 1983; *WS*, Oct. 19, 1983.
57. *WFP*, Oct. 20, 21 & 26, 1983; *WS*, Oct. 26, 1983.
58. *WT*, Oct. 20, 1983.
59. *WFP*, Jan. 11, 1984.
60. *WFP*, Jan. 12, 1984.
61. *WFP*, Jan. 16 & 17, 1984.
62. *WFP*, Mar. 22, 1984.
63. *WFP*, Dec. 5, 1984; Jan. 7 & 9, 1985.
64. CBC, Oct. 28, 1994.
65. Houston, 1989, pp. 187–189.
66. *WFP*, May 16, 1985.
67. *WFP*, June 7, 1985.
68. *WFP*, May 18, 1985.
69. *G & M*, Mar. 1, 1989.
70. Quotes in this and the following paragraphs are from: *WS*, Feb. 13, 1990.
71. *WFP*, Mar. 21 & June 3, 1991.
72. *WS*, July 7, 1991.
73. *WFP*, Aug. 25, 1991.

4. To Build or Not to Build. . .

1. *WFP*, Nov. 16, 1989.
2. *WFP*, Nov. 24 & Dec. 7, 1989.
3. *WFP*, Nov. 17 & Dec. 3, 1989.
4. *WFP*, July 5, 1991.

5. *WFP*, July 12 & 25, 1991.
6. *WFP*, May 21, 1991; Jan. 16, 1993.
7. *WFP*, Oct. 22, 1992.
8. *WS*, April 11, 1992.
9. *WFP*, Jan. 5, 1991.
10. *WFP*, Nov. 18, 1995.
11. *WS*, July 5, 1991.
12. *WS*, June 8, 1994.
13. *WFP*, Aug. 7, 1992.
14. *WFP*, Nov. 15, 1991.
15. *WFP*, Oct. 26, 1991.
16. *WFP*, Nov. 19, 1991.
17. *WS*, Dec. 2, 1991.
18. *WFP*, Nov. 17, 1989; May 22, 1991; *WS*, July 24, 1993.
19. Baade and Dye, 1990, p. 13. See also Baade 1987 and 1994 and Baade and Dye, 1988.
20. Mauro, 1993, p. 33.
21. Ogden, April, 1994; Burns, June, 1994, p. 9.
22. Mauro, 1993, p. viii.
23. *WFP*, July 29, 1993.
24. *WFP*, Dec. 16, 1993.
25. Burns, 1994, p. 5.
26. Burns, 1994, p. 10.
27. *WFP*, Nov. 19, 1991; Cho!ces, June 30, 1992.
28. Quirk and Fort, 1992, p. 175.
29. *WFP*, Feb. 28, 1993.
30. Viewpoints Research, Feb., 1994.
31. *WFP*, Dec. 28, 1993.
32. *G & M*, Jan. 6, 1994.
33. Verbal report to Thin Ice from Todd Scarth.

5. Heroes, White Knights, and the Kids: A Resurrection Story

1. *WFP*, June 24 & 25 & July 10, 1994.
2. Manitoba Legislative Assembly, *Debates*, June 24, 1994.
3. *WFP*, July 10, 1994.
4. *WFP*, June 28, 1994.
5. *WFP*, June 30, 1994.
6. Morton, 1967, p. 465 and pp. 501–502.
7. Artibise, 1977, p. 212.
8. Newman, 1975, p. 212.
9. Price Waterhouse, 1990, pp. 56 & 83; Winnipeg Chamber of Commerce, Feb., 1989.
10. Wells, 1995, p. 65.
11. *WFP*, Aug. 25, 1994.
12. *WFP*, Jan. 8, 1995.
13. Artibise, 1975, p. 25.
14. *WFP*, July 12, 1994.

15. *WFP*, June 30, 1994.
16. MEC, Aug. 24, 1994.
17. MEC, Oct. 8, 1994, p. 6; Winnipeg, April 25, 1995.
18. *WFP*, Sept. 24, Aug. 25, Sept. 22, 1994.
19. MEC, Oct. 8, 1994, p. 3.
20. *WFP*, Sept. 28, 1994.
21. Osler, personal interview, May 27, 1996.
22. Letter from Richardson to Koswin, Jan. 25, 1994.
23. *WFP*, Sept. 24, Dec. 7, and Oct. 2, 1994.
24. *WFP*, Oct. 2, 1994.
25. Letter from Thin Ice to Thompson, Oct. 5, 1994; Letter from Thompson to Thin Ice, Oct. 12, 1994.
26. *WFP*, Oct. 1, 1994.
27. *WFP*, Oct. 9, 1994.
28. *WFP*, Jan. 8, 1995.
29. Black and Dolecki, 1994, p. 8.
30. *WFP*, Oct. 20, 1994.
31. *WFP*, Nov. 2, 1994.
32. *WFP*, Oct. 29 & Nov. 2, 1994.
33. *WFP*, Dec. 9, 1994.
34. *WS*, Dec. 9, 1994.
35. *WFP*, Dec. 10, 1994.
36. *WFP*, Dec. 9, 1994.
37. *G & M*, Apr. 17, 1994.
38. *WFP*, Dec. 29, 1994.
39. *WFP*, Dec. 13, 1994.
40. *WFP*, Jan. 7, 1994.
41. Ridd, *WFP*, Dec. 27, 1994, unedited version.
42. *WFP*, Sept. 4, 1994.
43. *WFP*, Jan. 17, 1995.
44. *WFP*, Jan. 21, 1995.
45. MEC, "Canada/Manitoba Infrastructure Works, Description For MEC Project," no date, but received by Western Economic Diversification Office Feb. 2, 1995; MEC, "Response to Questions Regarding Project Proposal and Financial Statements," no date, but prepared in late January or February, 1995; letter, Mr. Bruce Birdsell, Senior Program Manager, Canada/Manitoba Infrastructure Works, to Mr. Cam Osler, MEC, Jan. 17, 1995.
46. *WFP*, Jan. 31, 1995.
47. Hyman, telephone conversation with author, Jan. 22, 1995.
48. *WFP*, Jan. 26, 1995.
49. Thompson memo to Council, Jan. 30, 1995.
50. Walker, 1979, p. ix.
51. *WFP*, Feb. 2, 1995.
52. This and the next paragraph are based on personal interviews with Alan Sweatman and Cam Osler, May 7 and May 27, 1996.
53. *WFP*, Mar. 3 & 16, 1995.
54. *WFP*, Mar. 15, 1995.
55. *WFP*, Apr. 4, 1995. Verbatim transcript.

56. Thin Ice, May 1, 1995.
57. *WFP*, Apr. 3, 1995.
58. MEC, April, 1995, p. 11.
59. *WS*, Apr. 29, 1995.
60. Letter from Murray to Thompson, Apr. 26, 1995, and Letter from Thompson to Murray, Apr. 26, 1995.

6. Save Our Jets ... and Shift the Risks

1. *WFP*, Apr. 28, 1995.
2. *WFP*, May 21, 1994.
3. *WS*, Apr. 29, 1995.
4. *WFP*, Apr. 28, 1995.
5. *WFP*, Apr. 28 & 29, 1995.
6. *WFP*, Apr. 29, 1995.
7. *WFP*, Apr. 29, 1995.
8. *WFP*, Apr. 30, 1995.
9. *WFP*, May 3, 1995.
10. *WFP*, May 5 & 6, 1995.
11. Thin Ice, May 1, 1995.
12. *WFP*, May 6, 1995.
13. Manitoba Legislative Assembly, *Debates*, June 24, 1994.
14. MEC, "Response to Questions Regarding Project Proposal and Financial Statements," submitted to Canada/Manitoba Infrastructure Works in January or February, 1995, p. 6.
15. *WFP*, May 30, 1995.
16. *WFP*, May 4 & 6, 1995.
17. *WFP*, May 7, 1995.
18. *WFP*, May 8 & 10, 1995.
19. *WFP*, May 16, 1995.
20. *WFP*, May 16, 1995.
21. *WFP*, May 17, 1995.
22. *WFP*, May 17, 1995.
23. *WFP*, May 18, 1995.
24. *WFP*, May 17, 1995.
25. *WFP*, June 1, 1995.
26. *WFP*, May 18, 1995.
27. *WFP*, May 21, 1995.
28. *WFP*, May 13, 1995.
29. *WFP*, May 15, 1995.
30. *WFP*, May 19, 1995.
31. Sweatman, personal interview, May 7, 1996.
32. *WFP*, May 19, 1995.
33. *WFP*, May 20, 1995.
34. *WFP*, May 24, 1995.
35. *G & M*, May 24, 1995.
36. *WFP*, May 20, 1995.
37. *WFP*, May 13, 1995.

38. *WFP*, May 13 & 20, 1995.
39. *WFP*, July 13, 1996.
40. *G & M*, Apr. 17, 1995.
41. *WFP*, Aug. 26, 1995.
42. *WFP*, May 15, 1995.
43. CBC, May, 1995.
44. Richard Cloutier, speech, Red River Community College, May 24, 1995.
45. *WS*, May 23, 1995.

7. The Spirit of Manitoba
1. *G & M*, Mar. 20, 1996.
2. *WFP*, June 2 & 5, 1995.
3. *WFP*, June 3, 1995.
4. *WFP*, June 10, 1995.
5. *WFP*, July 6, 1995.
6. *WFP*, July 10, 1995.
7. *WFP*, June 3 & 10, 1995.
8. *WFP*, July 13, 1995.
9. Author's verbatim notes, July 26, 1995.
10. Author's verbatim notes, July 26, 1995.
11. Author's verbatim notes, July 26, 1995.
12. Author's verbatim notes, July 26, 1995.
13. *WS*, July 27 & 28, 1995.
14. *WFP*, Aug. 1, 1995.
15. Author's verbatim notes, August 3, 1995.
16. Author's verbatim notes, August 3, 1995.
17. Author's verbatim notes, August 3, 1995.
18. *WFP*, Aug. 1, 1995.
19. Author's verbatim notes, August 3, 1995.
20. Author's verbatim notes, August 3, 1995.
21. *WS*, Aug. 3, 1995.
22. Winnipeg City Council, *Debates*, Aug. 3, 1995, p. 839.
23. Spirit, July 24, 1995, p. 15.
24. Spirit, July 24, 1995, p. 14.
25. Winnipeg, Aug. 4, 1995, p. 6.
26. Letter from Pash to Sweatman, Aug. 10, 1995.
27. Thin Ice, June, 1995.
28. *WFP*, Mar. 15, 1995.

8. Conclusion
1. *WS*, Apr. 19, 1982.
2. Finkel, 1970; Rea, 1976.
3. Kaniss, 1991, p. 84.
4. Saul, 1995, pp. 15, 22 & 165.
5. Sweatman, personal interview, May 7, 1995.

Bibliography

Artibise, Alan. *Winnipeg: A Social History of Urban Growth, 1874–1914*. Montreal: McGill-Queens University Press, 1975.

———. *Winnipeg: An Illustrated History*. Toronto: James Lorimer & Company, 1977.

———. "Continuity and Change: Elites and Prairie Urban Development, 1914–1950," in Alan Artibise and Gilbert Stetler (eds), *The Usable Urban Past*. Toronto: Macmillan, 1979, pp. 130–154.

Baade, Robert A. "Is There An Economic Rationale For Subsidizing Sports Stadiums," *Heartland Policy Study No. 13*. Chicago: The Heartland Institute, Feb. 23, 1987.

———. *Stadiums, Professional Sports, and Economic Development: Assessing the Reality*. Detroit: The Heartland Institute, March 28, 1994.

——— and Richard F. Dye. "Sports Stadiums and Area Development: A Critical Review," *Economic Development Quarterly*, August 1988, pp. 265–275.

——— . "The Impact of Stadiums and Professional Sports on Metropolitan Area Development," *Growth and Change*, Spring 1990, pp. 1–14.

Beddoes, Richard, Stan Fischler and Ira Gitler. *Hockey: The Story of the World's Fastest Sport*. New York: Macmillan, 1973. 3rd edition.

Black, Errol and Joe Dolecki. *Winnipeg Jets Hockey Club and a New Arena*. A Report Prepared for Thin Ice, October, 1994.

Brooks, Christine. *Sports Marketing: Competitive Business Strategies for Sport*. Englewood Cliffs, New Jersey: Prentice Hall, 1994.

Brunt, Stephen. "One Who Can Fly Ready to Soar in the Skydome," *The Globe and Mail*, January 18, 1996.

Burns, James W. *Implementation Committee Position Paper*. June, 1994.

Burrough, Bryan and John Helyar. *Barbarians at the Gate: The Fall of R.J.R. Nabisco*. New York: Harper and Row, 1990.

Campbell, Neil. "B.C. Company Takes Sports Gamble," *Globe and Mail*, January 6, 1996.

Canadian Broadcasting Corporation Radio. "A Tale of Two Towns," October 28, 1994.

———. "Now the Details," May, 1995.

Cho!ces. *Brief to City Council*. June 30, 1992.

Conway, Russ. *Game Misconduct: Alan Eagleson and the Corruption of Hockey*. Toronto: Macfarlane Walter & Ross, 1995.

Cook, Kevin. "The Heady Rise and Spectacular Fall of Bruce McNall," *GQ*, Volume 65, Number 6, June, 1995, pp. 206–214.

Coopers and Lybrand Consulting Group. *Report on the Aggregate Economic Benefits to Manitoba of the Club's Operations Since 1978*. Submitted to Barry Shenkarow, May 25, 1990.

Cruise, David and Alison Griffiths. *Net Worth: Exploding the Myths of Pro Hockey*. Toronto: Penguin Books, 1991.

Davidson, Gary with Bill Libby. *Breaking the Game Wide Open*. New York:

Atheneum, 1974.

Deacon, James. "Gretzky Inc.," *Maclean's*, December 5, 1994, pp. 50–58.

DeGeorge, Gail. *The Making of a Blockbuster*. New York: John Wiley & Sons, Inc., 1996.

Dowbiggin, Bruce. *The Defense Never Rests*. Toronto: Harper Collins, 1993.

Dryden, Ken and Roy MacGregor. *Home Game: Hockey and Life in Canada*. Toronto: McClelland & Stewart Inc., 1989.

The Economist. "A Survey of the Sports Business," July 25, 1992.

Euchner, Charles. *Playing the Field: Why Sports Teams Move and Cities Fight to Keep Them*. Baltimore: The Johns Hopkins University Press, 1993.

Fennell, Tom and D'Arcy Jenish. "The Riches of Sport," *Maclean's*, April 9, 1990, pp. 42–45.

Fenson, Ken. *Winnipeg Jets: Tenth Anniversary Limited Edition*. Winnipeg: Winnipeg Jets Hockey Club, 1982.

Finkel, Alvin. "The Beautiful People of Winnipeg," *Canadian Dimension*, Vol. 7, Numbers 1 and 2, 1970.

Fischler, Stan. *Cracked Ice: An Insider's Look at the NHL in Turmoil*. Toronto: McGraw-Hill Ryerson, 1995.

Gammons, Peter. "A Matter of Dollars and Sense," *Sports Illustrated*, November 29, 1976.

Gorman, Jerry and Kirk Calhoun. *The Name of the Game: The Business of Sports*. New York: John Wiley & Sons, Inc., 1994.

Gruneau, Richard and David Whitson. *Hockey Night in Canada: Sport, Identities and Cultural Politics*. Toronto: Garamond Press, 1993.

Guterson, David. "Moneyball! On the Relentless Promotion of Pro Sports," *Harper's Magazine*, September 1994, pp. 37–46.

Heinzl, John. "Playoff Pressure," *Report on Business Magazine*, April, 1995, pp. 90–97.

Helyar, John. *Lords of the Realm: The REAL History of Baseball*. New York: Ballantine Books, 1994.

Houston, William. *Inside Maple Leaf Gardens: The Rise and Fall of the Toronto Maple Leafs*. Toronto: McGraw-Hill Ryerson, 1989.

―――― and David Shoalts. *Eagleson: The Fall of a Hockey Czar*. Toronto: McGraw-Hill Ryerson, 1993.

Jennings, Kenneth M. *Balls and Strikes: The Money Game in Professional Baseball*. New York: Praeger Publishers, 1990.

Jhally, Sut. "The Spectacle of Accumulation: Material and Cultural Factors in the Evolution of the Sports/Media Complex," *Insurgent Sociologist*, 12, 3, 1984, pp. 41–57.

Johnson, William Oscar. "The Day the Money Ran Out," *Sports Illustrated*, December 1, 1975.

Kaniss, Phyllis. *Making Local News*. Chicago: The University of Chicago Press, 1991.

Katz, Donald. *Just Do It: The Nike Spirit in the Corporate World*. Holbrook, Mass: Adams Publishing, 1994.

Klatell, David A. and Norman Marcus. *Sports For Sale: Television, Money and the Fans*. New York: Oxford University Press, 1988.

Lavalin, Inc. *Review of Professional Sporting and Public Assembly Facilities*.

November, 1990.

Logan, John R. and Harvey L. Molotch. *Urban Fortunes: The Political Economy of Place*. Berkeley: University of California Press, 1987.

MacGregor, Roy. *Road Games: A Year in the Life of the NHL*. Toronto: MacFarlane Walter & Ross, 1993.

Maguire, Joseph. "Globalization, Sport Development, and the Media/Sport Production Complex," *Sport Science Review*, 2, 1, 1993, pp. 29–47.

Manitoba Entertainment Complex, Inc. "News Release," August 24, 1994.

_____. "Comparing the Two Downtown Sites For a Winnipeg Entertainment Complex," October 8, 1994.

_____. "Project Update: Manitoba Entertainment Complex at the Portage East Site," April, 1995.

Manitoba Securities Commission. *Minutes*. June 28, 1995.

Mauro, Arthur. *Report on the Preservation of NHL Hockey in Winnipeg*. 1993.

McGrath, Charles. "Rocking The Pond," *The New Yorker*, Jan. 24, 1994, pp. 44–51.

McKay, Jim and Toby Miller. "From Old Boys to Men and Women of the Corporation: The Americanization and Commodification of Australian Sport," *Sociology of Sport Journal*, 8, 1991, pp. 86–94.

Mills, David. "The Blue and the Bottom Line: Entrepreneurs and the Business of Hockey in Canada, 1927–1990," in Paul D. Staudohar and James A. Mangau (eds), *The Business of Professional Sports*. Urbana: University of Illinois Press, 1991, pp. 175–201.

Morton, W.L. *Manitoba: A History*, 2nd ed. Toronto: University of Toronto Press, 1967.

Mott, Morris. "You Couldn't Run a Game on Saturday Night: The Winnipeg Warriors, Television, and the Business of Pro Hockey, 1955–1961," *Manitoba History*, Spring 1994, pp. 9–14.

Nagler, Barney. *James Norris and the Decline of Boxing*. Indianapolis: The Bobbs-Merrill Company, Inc. 1964.

National Hockey League. "Analysis of Spirit of Manitoba Inc. Proposal Dated July 25, 1995," by Joseph DeSousa, August 7, 1995.

Newman, Peter. *The Canadian Establishment*. Toronto: McClelland and Stewart, 1975.

Ogden Entertainment Services. *Revised Final Draft*, April 7, 1994.

————. *Report to the Interim Steering Committee, Inc., Updated Final Draft*. April 20, 1994.

Papanek, John and Bill Brubaker. "The Man Who Rules Hockey," *Sports Illustrated*, July 2, 1984, pp. 60–74.

Price Waterhouse. *City of Winnipeg: Economic Development Strategy*. January, 1990.

Provincial Auditor of Manitoba and the City Auditor, City of Winnipeg. *Summary of the Province of Manitoba and the City of Winnipeg Direct Expenditures and Share of Expenditures Incurred by the Interim Steering Committee, Inc., Jets Private Sector Inc., MEC Inc., Spirit of Manitoba Inc., and Jets Hockey Ventures for Periods from July 1, 1991 to September 30, 1995*. December 22, 1995.

Quirk, James and Rodney Fort. *Pay Dirt: The Business of Professional Team Sports*. Princeton University Press, 1992.

Rea, J.E. "The Politics of Class: Winnipeg City Council, 1914–1945, in Carl Berger